S0-AVA-737

OBJECTIVE-C PROGRAMMING
THE BIG NERD RANCH GUIDE

AARON HILLEGASS

BiG
nerD
ranch

Objective-C Programming: The Big Nerd Ranch Guide
by Aaron Hillegass

Copyright © 2011 Big Nerd Ranch, Inc.

All rights reserved. Printed in the United States of America. This publication is protected by copyright, and permission must be obtained from the publisher prior to any prohibited reproduction, storage in a retrieval system, or transmission in any form or by any means, electronic, mechanical, photocopying, recording, or likewise. For information regarding permissions, contact

Big Nerd Ranch, Inc.
154 Krog Street
Suite 100
Atlanta, GA 30307
(404) 478-9005
http://www.bignerdranch.com/
book-comments@bignerdranch.com

The 10-gallon hat with propeller logo is a trademark of Big Nerd Ranch, Inc.

Exclusive worldwide distribution of the English edition of this book by

Pearson Technology Group
800 East 96th Street
Indianapolis, IN 46240 USA
http://www.informit.com

The authors and publisher have taken care in writing and printing this book but make no expressed or implied warranty of any kind and assume no responsibility for errors or omissions. No liability is assumed for incidental or consequential damages in connection with or arising out of the use of the information or programs contained herein.

App Store, Apple, Cocoa, Cocoa Touch, Instruments, Interface Builder, iOS, iPad, iPhone, iTunes, iTunes Store, Mac, Mac OS, Objective-C, and Xcode are trademarks of Apple, Inc., registered in the U.S. and other countries.

Many of the designations used by manufacturers and sellers to distinguish their products are claimed as trademarks. Where those designations appear in this book, and the publisher was aware of a trademark claim, the designations have been printed with initial capital letters or in all capitals.

ISBN-10 0321706285
ISBN-13 978-0321706287

Library of Congress Control Number: 2011931707

First printing, November 2011

Acknowledgments

It is a great honor that I get to work with such amazing people. Several of them put a lot of time and energy into making this book great. I'd like to take this moment to thank them.

- Mikey Ward wrote several chapters of this book including *Your First iOS Application*, *Your First Cocoa Program*, and *Blocks*. If I were a nicer boss, I would have put his name on the cover.

- The other instructors who teach the Objective-C materials fed us with a never-ending stream of suggestions and corrections. They are Scott Ritchie, Mark Fenoglio, Brian Hardy, Christian Keur, and Alex Silverman.

- My tireless editor, Susan Loper, took my stream-of-consciousness monologue that stumbled across everything a programmer needs to know and honed it into an approachable primer.

- Several technical reviewers helped me find and fix flaws. They are James Majors, Mark Dalrymple, Scott Steinman, Bart Hoffman, Bolot Kerimbaev, and Nate Chandler.

- Ellie Volckhausen designed the cover.

- Chris Loper at IntelligentEnglish.com designed and produced the EPUB and Kindle versions.

- The amazing team at Pearson Technology Group patiently guided us through the business end of book publishing.

Table of Contents

Part I
Getting Started

1

You and This Book

Let's talk about you for a minute. You want to write applications for iOS or Mac OS X, but you haven't done much (or any) programming in the past. Your friends have raved about my other books (*iOS Programming: The Big Nerd Ranch Guide* and *Cocoa Programming for Mac OS X*), but they are written for experienced programmers. What should you do? Read this book.

There are similar books, but this one is the one you should read. Why? I've been teaching people how to write applications for iOS and the Mac for a long time now, and I've identified what you need to know at this point in your journey. I've worked hard to capture that knowledge and dispose of everything else. There is a lot of wisdom and very little fluff in this book.

My approach is a little unusual. Instead of simply trying to get you to understand the syntax of Objective-C, I'll show you how programming works and how experienced programmers think about it.

Because of this approach, I'm going to cover some heavy ideas early in the book. You should not expect this to be an easy read. In addition, nearly every idea comes with a programming experiment. This combination of learning concepts and immediately putting them into action is the best way to learn programming.

C and Objective-C

When you run a program, a file is copied from the file system into memory (RAM), and the instructions in that file are executed by your computer. Those instructions are inscrutable to humans. So, humans write computer programs in a programming language. The very lowest-level programming language is called *assembly code*. In assembly code, you describe every step that the CPU (the computer's brain) must take. This code is then transformed into *machine code* (the computer's native tongue) by an *assembler*.

Assembly language is tediously long-winded and CPU-dependent (because the brain of your latest iMac can be quite different from the brain of your well-loved, well-worn PowerBook). In other words, if you want to run the program on a different type of computer, you will need to rewrite the assembly code.

To make code that could be easily moved from one type of computer to another, we developed "high-level languages." With high-level languages, instead of thinking about a particular CPU, you could express the instructions in a general way, and a program (called a *compiler*) would transform that code into highly-optimized, CPU-specific machine code. One of these languages is C. C programmers write code in the C language, and a C compiler then converts the C code into machine code.

The C language was created in the early 1970s at AT&T. The Unix operating system, which is the basis for Mac OS X and Linux, was written in C with a little bit of assembly code for very low-level operations. The Windows operating system is also mostly written in C.

The Objective-C programming language is based on C, but it adds support for object-oriented programming. Objective-C is the programming language that is used to write applications for Apple's iOS and Mac OS X operating systems.

How this book works

In this book, you will learn enough of the C and Objective-C programming languages to learn to develop applications for the Mac or for iOS devices.

Why am I going to teach you C first? Every effective Objective-C programmer needs a pretty deep understanding of C. Also, a lot of the ideas that look complicated in Objective-C have very simple roots in C. I will often introduce an idea using C and then push you toward mastery of the same idea in Objective-C.

This book was designed to be read in front of a Mac. You will read explanations of ideas and carry out hands-on experiments that will illustrate those ideas. These experiments aren't optional. You won't really understand the book unless you do them. The best way to learn programming is to type in code, make typos, fix your typos, and become physically familiar with the patterns of the language. Just reading code and understanding the ideas in theory won't do much for you and your skills.

For even more practice, there are exercises called *Challenges* at the end of each chapter. These exercises provide additional practice and will make you more confident of what you've just learned. I strongly suggest you do as many of the *Challenges* as you can.

You will also see sections called *For the More Curious* at the end of some chapters. These are more in-depth explanations of the topics covered in the chapter. They are not absolutely essential to get you where you're going, but I hope you'll find them interesting and useful.

Big Nerd Ranch hosts a forum where readers discuss this book and the exercises in it. You can find it at `http://forums.bignerdranch.com/`.

You will find this book and programming in general much more pleasant if you know how to touch-type. Touch-typing, besides being much faster, enables you to look at your screen and book instead of at the keyboard. This makes it much easier to catch your errors as they happen. It is a skill that will serve you well for your entire career.

How the life of a programmer works

By starting this book, you've decided to become a programmer. You should know what you've signed up for.

The life of a programmer is mostly a never-ending struggle. Solving problems in an always-changing technical landscape means that programmers are always learning new things. In this case, "learning new things" is a euphemism for "battling against our own ignorance." Even if a programmer is working with a familiar technology, sometimes the software we create is so complex that simply understanding what's going wrong can often take an entire day.

If you write code, you will struggle. Most professional programmers learn to struggle hour after hour, day after day, without getting (too) frustrated. This is another skill that will serve you well. If you are curious about the life of programmers and modern software projects, I highly recommend the book *Dreaming in Code* by Scott Rosenberg.

Now it's time to jump in and write your first program.

2

Your First Program

Now that we know how this book is organized, it's time to see how programming for the Mac and for iPhone and iPad works. To do that, you will

- install Apple's Developer Tools

- create a simple project using those tools

- explore how these tools are used to make sure our project works

At the end of this chapter, you will have successfully written your first program for the Mac.

Installing Apple's developer tools

To write applications for Mac OS X (the Macintosh) or iOS (the iPhone and iPad), you will be using Apple's developer tools. You can download these tools from `http://developer.apple.com/` or purchase them from the Mac App Store.

After you've installed the tools, find the `/Developer` folder at the root level of your hard drive. This folder contains what you need to develop applications for Mac OS X desktops and iOS mobile devices.

Our work in this book is going to be conducted almost entirely with one application – Xcode, which is found in the `/Developer/Applications` folder. (It is a good idea to drag the Xcode icon over to the dock; you'll be using it an awful lot.)

Getting started with Xcode

Xcode is Apple's *Integrated Development Environment*. That means that everything you need to write, build, and run new applications is in Xcode.

A note on terminology: anything that is executable on a computer we call a *program*. Some programs have graphical user interfaces; we will call these *applications*.

Some programs have no graphical user interface and run for days in the background; we call these *daemons*. Daemons sound scary, but they aren't. You probably have about 60 daemons running on your Mac right now. They are waiting around, hoping to be useful. For example, one of the daemons running on your system is called pboard. When you do a copy and paste, the pboard daemon holds onto the data that you are copying.

Some programs have no graphical user interface and run for a short time in the terminal; we call these *command-line tools*. In this book, you will be writing mostly command-line tools to focus on programming essentials without the distraction of creating and managing a user interface.

Now we're going to create a simple command-line tool using Xcode so you can see how it all works.

When you write a program, you create and edit a set of files. Xcode keeps track of those files in a *project*. Launch Xcode. From the File menu, choose New and then New Project....

To help you get started, Xcode suggests a number of possible project templates. You choose a template depending on what sort of program you want to write. In the lefthand column, select Application from the Mac OS X section. Then choose Command Line Tool from the choices that appear to the right.

Figure 2.1   Choosing a template

Press the Next button.

Name your new project AGoodStart. The company identifier won't matter for our exercises in this book, but you have to enter one here to continue. You can use BigNerdRanch or another name. From the Type pop-up menu, choose C because you will write this program in C.

Figure 2.2   Choose options

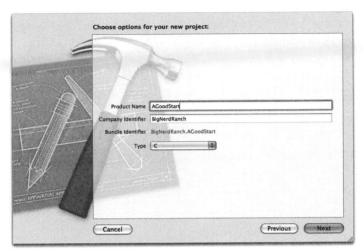

Press the Next button.

Now choose the folder in which your project directory will be created. You won't need a repository for version control, so you can uncheck that box. Finally, click the Create button.

You'll be creating this same type of project for the next several chapters. In the future, I'll just say, "Create a new C Command Line Tool named *program-name-here*" to get you to follow this same sequence.

(Why C? Remember, Objective-C is built on top of the C programming language. You'll need to have an understanding of parts of C before we can get to the particulars of Objective-C.)

Where do I start writing code?

After creating your project, you'll be greeted by a window that shows how AGoodStart will be produced.

Figure 2.3   First view of the AGoodStart project

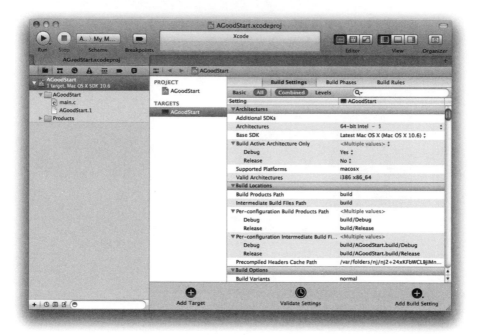

This window includes details like which versions of Mac OS X can run your application, the configurations to use when compiling the code that you write, and any localizations that have been applied to your project. But let's ignore those details for now and find a simple starting point to get to work.

Near the top of the lefthand panel, find a file called main.c and click on it. (If you don't see main.c, click the triangle next to the folder labeled AGoodStart to reveal its contents.)

Figure 2.4 Finding main.c in the AGoodStart group

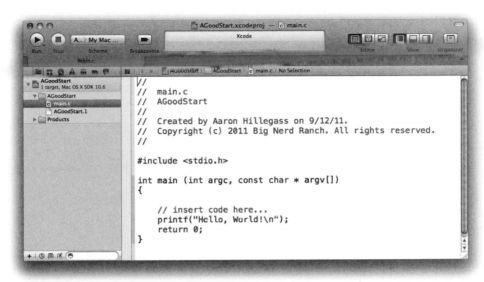

Notice that our original view with the production details changes to show the contents of main.c. The main.c file contains a function called **main**.

A *function* is a list of instructions for the computer to execute, and every function has a name. In a C or Objective-C program, **main** is the function that is called when a program first starts.

```
#include <stdio.h>

int main (int argc, const char * argv[]) {

    // insert code here...
    printf("Hello, World!\n");
    return 0;
}
```

In this function, you'll find the two kinds of information you write in a program: code and comments.

• Code is the set of instructions that tell the computer to do something.

• Comments are ignored by the computer, but we programmers use them to document code we've written. The more difficult the programming problem you are trying to solve, the more comments will help document how you solved the problem. That becomes especially important when you return to your work months later, look at code you forgot to comment, and think, "I'm sure this solution is brilliant, but I have absolutely no memory of how it works."

In C and Objective-C, there are two ways to distinguish comments from code:

- If you put // at the beginning of a line of code, everything from those forward slashes to the end of that line is considered a comment. You can see this used in Apple's "insert code here..." comment.

- If you have more extensive remarks in mind, you can use /* and */ to mark the beginning and end of comments that span more than one line.

These rules for marking comments are part of the *syntax* of C. Syntax is the set of rules that governs how code must be written in a given programming language. These rules are extremely specific, and if you fail to follow them, your program won't work.

While the syntax regarding comments is fairly simple, the syntax of code can vary widely depending on what the code does and how it does it. But there's one feature that remains consistent: every *statement* ends in a semicolon. (We'll see examples of code statements in just a moment.) If you forget a semicolon, you will have made a syntax error, and your program won't work.

Fortunately, Xcode has ways to warn you of these kinds of errors. In fact, one of the first challenges you will face as a programmer is interpreting what Xcode tells you when something goes wrong and then fixing your errors. You'll get to see some of Xcode's responses to common syntax errors as we go through the book.

Let's make some changes to main.c. First, we need to make some space. Find the curly braces ({ and }) that mark the beginning and the end of the **main** function. Then delete everything in between them.

Now update main.c to look like the code below. You'll add a comment, two lines of code, and another comment to the **main** function. For now, don't worry if you don't understand what you are typing. The idea is to get started. You have an entire book ahead to learn what it all means.

```
#include <stdio.h>

int main (int argc, const char * argv[])
{
    // Print the beginning of the novel
    printf("It was the best of times.\n");
    printf("It was the worst of times.\n");
    /* Is that actually any good?
       Maybe it needs a rewrite. */

    return 0;
}
```

(Notice that the new code you need to type in is shown in a bold font. The code that isn't bold is code that is already in place. That's a convention we'll use for the rest of the book.)

As you type, you may notice that Xcode tries to make helpful suggestions. This feature is called *code completion*, and it is very handy. You may want to ignore it right now and focus on typing things in all yourself. But as you continue through the book, start playing with code completion and how it can help you write code more conveniently and more accurately. You can see and set the different options for code completion in Xcode's preferences, which are accessible from the Xcode menu.

In addition, keep an eye on the font color. Xcode uses different font colors to make it easy to identify comments and different parts of your code. (For example, comments are green.) This comes in handy, too: after a while of working with Xcode, you begin to instinctively notice when the colors don't look right. Often, this is a clue that there is a syntax error in what you've written (like a forgotten semicolon). And the sooner you know that you've made a syntax error, the easier it is to find and fix it.

These color differences are just one way in which Xcode lets you know when you (may) have done something wrong.

How do I run my program?

When the contents of your main.c file match what you see above, it's time to run your program and see what it does. This is a two-step process. Xcode *builds* your program and then *runs* it. When building your program, Xcode prepares your code to run. This includes checking for syntax and other kinds of errors.

Look again at the lefthand area of the Xcode window. This area is called the navigator area. At the top of the navigator area is a series of buttons. You are currently viewing the *project navigator*, which shows you the files in your project. The project navigator's icon is ▥.

Now find and click the ▣ button to reveal the *log navigator*. The *log* is Xcode's way of communicating with you when it is building and running your program.

You can also use the log for your own purposes. For instance, the line in your code that reads

```
printf("It was the best of times.\n");
```

is an instruction to display the words "It was the best of times." in the log.

Since you haven't built and run your program yet, there isn't anything in the log navigator. Let's fix that. In the upper lefthand corner of the project window, find the button that looks suspiciously like the Play button in iTunes or on a DVD player. If you leave your cursor over that button, you'll see a tool tip that says Build and then run the current scheme. That is Xcode-speak for "Press this button, and I will build and run your program."

If all goes well, you'll be rewarded with the following:

If not, you'll get this:

What do you do then? Carefully compare your code with the code in the book. Look for typos and missing semicolons. Xcode will highlight the lines it thinks are problematic. After you find the problem, click the Run button again. Repeat until you have a successful build.

(Don't get disheartened when you have failed builds with this code or with any code you write in the future. Making and fixing mistakes helps you understand what you're doing. In fact, it's actually better than lucking out and getting it right the first time.)

Once your build has succeeded, find the item at the top of the log navigator labeled Debug AGoodStart. Click this item to display the log from the most recent run of your program.

The log can be quite verbose. The important part is the Dickens quote at the end. That's your code being executed!

```
GNU gdb 6.3.50-20050815 (Apple version gdb-1705) (Tue Jul  5 07:36:45 UTC 2011)
Copyright 2004 Free Software Foundation, Inc.
GDB is free software, covered by the GNU General Public License, and you are
welcome to change it and/or distribute copies of it under certain conditions.
Type "show copying" to see the conditions.
There is absolutely no warranty for GDB.  Type "show warranty" for details.
This GDB was configured as "x86_64-apple-darwin".tty /dev/ttys001
[Switching to process 2723 thread 0x0]
It was the best of times.
It was the worst of times.
```

(As I'm writing this, Apple is working on a new debugger called LLDB. Eventually it will replace GDB, the current debugger. If you aren't seeing all the GDB information, it means that LLDB is now Xcode's standard debugger. The future must be a terrific place; I envy you.)

So what is a program?

Now that you've built and run your program, let's take a look inside. A program is a collection of functions. A function is a list of operations for the processor to execute. Every function has a name, and the function that you just wrote is named **main**. There was also another function – **printf**. You didn't write this function, but you did use it. (We'll find out where **printf** comes from in Chapter 5.)

To a programmer, writing a function is a lot like writing a recipe: "Stir a quart of water slowly until it boils. Then mix in a cup of flour. Serve while hot."

In the mid-1970's, Betty Crocker started selling a box containing a set of recipe cards. A recipe card is a pretty good metaphor for a function. Like a function, each card has a name and a set of instructions. The difference is that you execute a recipe, and the computer executes a function.

Figure 2.5   A recipe card named Baked Chicken

Betty Crocker's cooking instructions are in English. In the first part of this book, your functions will be written in the C programming language. However, a computer processor expects its instructions in machine code. How do we get there?

When you write a program in C (which is relatively pleasant for you), the *compiler* converts your program's functions into machine code (which is pleasant and efficient for the processor). The compiler is itself a program that is run by Xcode when you press the Run button. Compiling a program is the same as building a program, and we'll use these terms interchangeably.

When you run a program, the compiled functions are copied from the hard drive into memory, and the function called `main` is executed by the processor. The `main` function usually calls other functions. For example, your `main` function called the `printf` function. (We'll see more about how functions interact in Chapter 5.)

Don't stop

At this point, you've probably dealt with several frustrations: installation problems, typos, and lots of new vocabulary. And maybe nothing you've done so far makes any sense. That is completely normal.

As I write this, my son Otto is six. Otto is baffled several times a day. He is constantly trying to absorb knowledge that doesn't fit into his existing mental scaffolding. Bafflement happens so frequently, that it doesn't really bother him. He never stops to wonder, "Why is this so confusing? Should I throw this book away?"

As we get older, we are baffled much less often – not because we know everything, but because we tend to steer away from things that leave us bewildered. For example, reading a book on history is quite pleasant because we get nuggets of knowledge that we can hang from our existing mental scaffolding. This is easy learning.

Learning a new language is an example of difficult learning. You know that there are millions of people who work in that language effortlessly, but it seems incredibly strange and awkward in your mouth. And when people speak it to you, you are often flummoxed.

Learning to program a computer is also difficult learning. You will be baffled from time to time – especially here at the beginning. This is fine. In fact, it's kind of cool. It is a little like being six again.

Stick with this book; I promise that the bewilderment will cease before you get to the final page.

Part II
How Programming Works

In these next chapters, you will create many programs that demonstrate useful concepts. These command-line programs are nothing that you'll show off to your friends, but there should be a small thrill of mastery when you run them. You're moving from computer user to computer programmer.

Your programs in these chapters will be written in C. Note that these chapters are not intended to cover the C language in detail. Quite the opposite: honed from years of teaching, this is the essential subset of what new-to-programming people need to know about programming and programming in C before learning Objective-C programming.

3

Variables and Types

Continuing with the recipe metaphor from the last chapter, sometimes a chef will keep a small blackboard in the kitchen for storing data. For example, when unpacking a turkey, he notices a label that says "14.2 Pounds." Before he throws the wrapper away, he will scribble "weight = 14.2" on the blackboard. Then, just before he puts the turkey in the oven, he will calculate the cooking time (15 minutes + 15 minutes per pound) by referring to the weight on the blackboard.

Figure 3.1 Keeping track of data with a blackboard

During execution, a program often needs places to store data that will be used later. A place where one piece of data can go is known as a *variable*. Each variable has a name (like cookingTime) and a *type* (like a number). In addition, when the program executes, the variable will have a value (like 228.0).

Types

In a program, you create a new variable by *declaring* its type and name. Here's an example of a variable declaration:

```
float weight;
```

The type of this variable is float, and its name is weight. At this point, the variable doesn't have a value.

In C, you must declare the type of each variable for two reasons:

- The type lets the compiler check your work for you and alert you to possible mistakes or problems. For instance, say you have a variable of a type that holds text. If you ask for its logarithm, the compiler will tell you something like "It doesn't make any sense to ask for this variable's logarithm."

- The type tells the compiler how much space in memory (how many bytes) to reserve for that variable.

Here is an overview of the commonly used types. We will return in more detail to each type in later chapters.

short, int, long	These three types are whole numbers; they don't require a decimal point. A short usually has fewer bytes of storage than a long, and int is in between. Thus, you can store a much larger number in a long than in a short.
float, double	A float is a floating point number – a number that can have a decimal point. In memory, a float is stored as a mantissa and an exponent. For example, 346.2 is represented as 3.462×10^2 A double is a double-precision number, which typically has more bits to hold a longer mantissa and larger exponents.
char	A char is a one-byte integer that we usually treat as a character, like the letter 'a'.
pointers	A pointer holds a memory address. It is declared using the asterisk character. For example, a variable declared as int * can hold a memory address where an int is stored. It doesn't hold the actual number's value, but if you know the address of the int then you can easily get to its value. Pointers are very useful, and there will be more on pointers later. Much more.
struct	A struct (or *structure*) is a type made up of other types. You can also create new struct definitions. For example, imagine that you wanted a GeoLocation type that contains two float members: latitude and longitude. In this case, you would define a struct type.

These are the types that a C programmer uses every day. It is quite astonishing what complex ideas can be captured in these five simple ideas.

A program with variables

Back in Xcode, you are going to create another project. First, close the AGoodStart project so that you don't accidentally type new code into the old project.

Now create a new project (File → New → New Project...). This project will be a C Command Line Tool named Turkey.

In the project navigator, find this project's main.c file and open it. Edit main.c so that it matches the following code.

```c
#include <stdio.h>

int main (int argc, const char * argv[])
{
    // Declare the variable called 'weight' of type float
    float weight;

    // Put a number in that variable
    weight = 14.2;

    // Log it to the user
    printf("The turkey weighs %f.\n", weight);

    // Declare another variable of type float
    float cookingTime;

    // Calculate the cooking time and store it in the variable
    // In this case, '*' means 'multiplied by'
    cookingTime = 15.0 + 15.0 * weight;

    // Log that to the user
    printf("Cook it for %f minutes.\n", cookingTime);

    // End this function and indicate success

    return 0;
}
```

Build and run the program. You can either click the Run button at the top left of the Xcode window or use the keyboard shortcut Command-R. Then click the 🗐 button to get to the log navigator. Select the item at the top labeled Debug Turkey to show your output. It should look like this:

```
The turkey weighs 14.200000.
Cook it for 228.000000 minutes.
```

Now click the 🖿 button to return to the project navigator. Then select main.c so that you can see your code again. Let's review what you've done here.

In your line of code that looks like this:

```c
    float weight;
```

we say that you are "declaring the variable weight to be of type float."

In the next line, your variable gets a value:

```c
    weight = 14.2;
```

You are copying data into that variable. We say that you are "assigning a value of 14.2 to that variable."

In modern C, you can declare a variable and assign it an initial value in one line, like this:

```c
    float weight = 14.2;
```

Here is another assignment:

```c
    cookingTime = 15.0 + 15.0 * weight;
```

The stuff on the right-hand side of the = is an *expression*. An expression is something that gets evaluated and results in some value. Actually, every assignment has an expression on the right-hand side of the =.

For example, in this line:

```
weight = 14.2;
```

the expression is just 14.2.

Variables are the building blocks of any program. This is just an introduction to the world of variables. You'll learn more about how variables work and how to use them as we continue.

Challenge

Create a new C Command Line Tool named TwoFloats. In its **main()** function, declare two variables of type float and assign each of them a number with a decimal point, like 3.14 or 42.0. Declare another variable of type double and assign it the sum of the two floats. Print the result using **printf()**. Refer to the code in this chapter if you need to check your syntax.

4

if/else

An important idea in programming is taking different actions depending on circumstances. Have all the billing fields in the order form been filled out? If so, enable the Submit button. Does the player have any lives left? If so, resume the game. If not, show the picture of the grave and play the sad music.

This sort of behavior is implemented using `if` and `else`, the syntax of which is:

```
if (conditional) {
    // execute this code if the conditional evaluates to true
} else {
    // execute this code if the conditional evaluates to false
}
```

You won't create a project in this chapter. Instead, consider the code examples carefully based on what you've learned in the last two chapters.

Here's an example of code using `if` and `else`:

```
float truckWeight = 34563.8;

// Is it under the limit?
if (truckWeight < 40000.0) {
    printf("It is a light truck\n");
} else {
    printf("It is a heavy truck\n");
}
```

If you don't have an `else` clause, you can just leave that part out:

```
float truckWeight = 34563.8;

// Is it under the limit?
if (truckWeight < 40000.0) {
    printf("It is a light truck\n");
}
```

The conditional expression is always either true or false. In C, it was decided that 0 would represent false, and anything that is not zero would be considered true.

In the conditional in the example above, the < operator takes a number on each side. If the number on the left is less than the number on the right, the expression evaluates to 1 (a very common way of expressing trueness). If the number on the left is greater than or equal to the number on the right, the expression evaluates to 0 (the only way to express falseness).

Operators often appear in conditional expressions. Table 4.1 shows the common operators used when comparing numbers (and other types that the computer evaluates as numbers):

Table 4.1   Comparison operators

<	Is the number on the left less than the number on the right?
>	Is the number on the left greater than the number on the right?
<=	Is the number on the left less than or equal to the number on the right?
>=	Is the number on the left greater than or equal to the number on the right?
==	Are they equal?
!=	Are they *not* equal?

The == operator deserves an additional note: In programming, the == operator is what's used to check for equality. We use the single = to *assign* a value. Many, many bugs have come from programmers using = when they meant to use ==. So stop thinking of = as "the equals sign." From now on, it is "the assignment operator."

Some conditional expressions require logical operators. What if you want to know if a number is in a certain range, like greater than zero and less than 40,000? To specify a range, you can use the logical AND operator (&&):

```
if ((truckWeight > 0.0) && (truckWeight < 40000.0)) {
    printf("Truck weight is within legal range.\n");
}
```

Table 4.2 shows the three logical operators:

Table 4.2   Logical operators

&&	Logical AND -- true if and only if both are true
||	Logical OR -- false if and only if both are false
!	Logical NOT -- true becomes false, false becomes true

(If you are coming from another language, note that there is no logical exclusive OR in Objective-C, so we won't discuss it here.)

The logical NOT operator (!) negates the expression contained in parentheses to its right.

```
// Is it not in the legal range?
if (!((truckWeight > 0.0) && (truckWeight < 40000.0))) {
    printf("Truck weight is not within legal range.\n");
}
```

Boolean variables

As you can see, expressions can become quite long and complex. Sometimes it is useful to put the value of the expression into a handy, well-named variable.

```
BOOL isNotLegal = !((truckWeight > 0.0) && (truckWeight <  40000.0));
if (isNotLegal) {
    printf("Truck weight is not within legal range.\n");
}
```

A variable that can be true or false is a *boolean* variable. Historically, C programmers have always used an int to hold a boolean value. Objective-C programmers typically use the type BOOL for boolean variables, so that's what we use here. (BOOL is just an alias for an integer type.)

A syntax note: if the code that follows the conditional expression consists of only one statement, then the curly braces are optional. So the following code is equivalent to the previous example.

```
BOOL isNotLegal = !((truckWeight > 0.0) && (truckWeight <  40000.0));
if (isNotLegal)
    printf("Truck weight is not within legal range.\n");
```

However, the curly braces are necessary if the code consists of more than one statement.

```
BOOL isNotLegal = !((truckWeight > 0.0) && (truckWeight <  40000.0));
if (isNotLegal) {
    printf("Truck weight is not within legal range.\n");
    printf("Impound truck.\n");
}
```

Why? Imagine if you removed the curly braces.

```
BOOL isNotLegal = !((truckWeight > 0.0) && (truckWeight <  40000.0));
if (isNotLegal)
    printf("Truck weight is not within legal range.\n");
    printf("Impound truck.\n");
```

This code would make you very unpopular with truck drivers. In this case, every truck gets impounded regardless of weight. When the compiler doesn't find a curly brace after the conditional, only the next statement is considered part of the if construct. Thus, the second statement is always executed. (What about the indention of the second statement? While indention is very helpful for human readers of code, it means nothing to the compiler.)

else if

What if you have more than two possibilities? You can test for them one-by-one using else if. For example, imagine that a truck belongs to one of three weight categories: floating, light, and heavy.

```
if (truckWeight <= 0) {
    printf("A floating truck\n");
} else if (truckWeight < 40000.0) {
    printf("A light truck\n");
} else {
    printf("A heavy truck\n");
}
```

You can have as many else if clauses as you wish. They will each be tested in the order in which they appear until one evaluates as true. The "in the order in which they appear" part is important. Be sure to order your conditions so that you don't get a false positive. For instance, if you swapped the first two tests in the above example, you would never find a floating truck because floating trucks are also light trucks. The final else clause is optional, but it's useful when you want to catch everything that did not meet the earlier conditions.

For the More Curious: Conditional (ternary) operator

It is not uncommon that you will use if and else to set the value of an instance variable. For example, you might have the following code:

```
int minutesPerPound;
if (isBoneless)
    minutesPerPound = 15;
else
    minutesPerPound = 20;
```

Whenever you have a scenario where a value is assigned to a variable based on a conditional, you have a candidate for the *conditional operator*, which is ?. (You will sometimes see it called the *ternary operator*).

```
int minutesPerPound = isBoneless ? 15 : 20;
```

This one line is equivalent to the previous example. Instead of writing if and else, you write an assignment. The part before the ? is the conditional. The values after the ? are the alternatives for whether the conditional is found to be true or false.

If this notation strikes you as odd, there is nothing wrong with continuing to use if and else instead. I suspect over time you will embrace the ternary operator as a concise way to do conditional value assignment. More importantly, you will see it used by other programmers, and it will be nice to understand what you see!

Challenge

Consider the following code snippet:

```
int i = 20;
int j = 25;

int k = ( i > j ) ? 10 : 5;

if ( 5 < j - k ) { // first expression
    printf("The first expression is true.");
} else if ( j > i ) { // second expression
    printf("The second expression is true.");
} else {
    printf("Neither expression is true.");
}
```

What will be printed to the console?

5

Functions

Back in Chapter 3, I introduced the idea of a variable: a name associated with a chunk of data. A function is a name associated with a chunk of code. You can pass information to a function. You can make the function execute code. You can make a function return information to you.

Functions are fundamental to programming, so there's a lot in this chapter – three new projects, a new tool, and many new ideas. Let's get started with an exercise that demonstrates what functions are good for.

When should I use a function?

Suppose you are writing a program to congratulate students for completing a Big Nerd Ranch course. Before worrying about retrieving the student list from a database or about printing certificates on spiffy Big Nerd Ranch paper, you want to experiment with the message that will be printed on the certificates.

To do that experiment, create a new project: a C Command Line Tool named ClassCertificates.

Your first thought in writing this program might be:

```
int main (int argc, const char * argv[])
{
    printf("Mark has done as much Cocoa Programming as I could fit into 5 days\n");
    printf("Bo has done as much Objective-C Programming as I could fit into 2 days\n");
    printf("Mike has done as much Python Programming as I could fit into 5 days\n");
    printf("Ted has done as much iOS Programming as I could fit into 5 days\n");

    return 0;
}
```

Does the thought of typing all this in bother you? Does it seem annoyingly repetitive? If so, you have the makings of an excellent programmer. When you find yourself repeating work that is very similar in nature (in this case, the words in the **printf** statement), you want to start thinking about a function as a better way of accomplishing the same task.

How do I write and use a function?

Now that you've realized that you need a function, you need to write one. Open main.c in your ClassCertificates project and add a new function before the **main** function. Name this function **congratulateStudent**.

```
#include <stdio.h>

void congratulateStudent(char *student, char *course, int numDays)
{
    printf("%s has done as much %s Programming as I could fit into %d days.\n",
        student, course, numDays);
}
```

(Wondering what the %s and %d mean? Hold on for now; we'll talk about those in the next chapter.)

Now edit **main** to use your new function:

```
int main (int argc, const char * argv[])
{
    congratulateStudent("Mark", "Cocoa", 5);
    congratulateStudent("Bo", "Objective-C", 2);
    congratulateStudent("Mike", "Python", 5);
    congratulateStudent("Ted", "iOS", 5);

    return 0;
}
```

Build and run the program. You will probably get a *warning* marked by an exclamation point inside a small yellow triangle. A warning in Xcode will not prevent your program from running; it just draws your attention to a possible problem. The text of the warning is to the right of the code. This warning says something like No previous prototype for function 'congratulateStudent'. Ignore this warning for now, and we'll come back to it at the end of this section.

Find your output in the log navigator. It should be identical to what you would have seen if you had typed in everything yourself.

```
Mark has done as much Cocoa Programming as I could fit into 5 days.
Bo has done as much Objective-C Programming as I could fit into 2 days.
Mike has done as much Python Programming as I could fit into 5 days.
Ted has done as much iOS Programming as I could fit into 5 days.
```

Think about what you have done here. You noticed a repetitive pattern. You took all the shared characteristics of the problem (the repetitive text) and moved them into a separate function. That left the differences (student name, course name, number of days). You handled those differences by adding three *parameters* to the function. Let's look again at the line where you name the function.

```
void congratulateStudent(char *student, char *course, int numDays)
```

Each parameter has two parts: the type of data the argument represents and the name of the parameter. Parameters are separated by commas and placed in parentheses to the right of the name of the function.

What about the void to the left of our function name? That is the type of information returned from the function. When you do not have any information to return, you use the keyword void. We'll talk more about returning later in this chapter.

You also used, or *called*, your new function in **main**. When you called **congratulateStudent**, you passed it values. Values passed to a function are known as *arguments*. The argument's value is then assigned to the corresponding parameter name. That parameter name can be used inside the function as a variable that contains the passed-in value.

Let's get specific. In the first call to **congratulateStudent**, you pass three arguments: "Mark", "Cocoa", 5.

```
congratulateStudent("Mark", "Cocoa", 5);
```

For now, we'll focus on the third argument. When 5 is passed to **congratulateStudent**, it is assigned to the third parameter, numDays. Arguments and parameters are matched up in the order in which they appear. They must also be the same (or very close to the same) type. Here, 5 is an integer value, and the type of numDays is int. Good.

Now, when **congratulateStudent** uses, or *references*, the numDays variable within the function, its value will be 5. You can see numDays is referenced just before the semi-colon. Finally, you can prove that all of this worked by looking at the first line of the output, which correctly displays the number of days.

Look back to our first proposed version of ClassCertificates with all the repetitive typing. What's the point of using a function instead? To save on the typing? Well, yes, but that's definitely not all. It's also about error-checking. The less you type and the more the computer crunches, the fewer chances for typos. Also if you do mistype a function name, Xcode will alert you, but Xcode has no idea if you've mistyped text.

Another benefit to writing functions is reusability. Now that you've written this handy function, you could use it in another program. Making changes is simpler, too. You only need to adjust the wording of the congratulatory phrase in one place for it to take effect everywhere.

The final benefit of functions is if there is a "bug," you can fix that one function and suddenly everything that calls it will start working properly. Partitioning your code into functions makes it easier to understand and maintain.

Now back to that warning in your code. It is pretty common to *declare* a function in one place and *define* it in another. Declaring a function just warns the compiler that a function with a particular name is coming. Defining the function is where you describe the steps that should be executed. In this exercise, you actually declared and defined your function in the same place. Because this is uncommon, Xcode issues a warning if your function was not declared in advance.

It is OK to ignore this warning in any of the projects you build in this book. Or you can take the time to disable it. To do so, select the ClassCertificates target, which is the item at the top of the project navigator. In the editor pane, select All under the Build Settings tab. Scroll through the different build settings and find the Missing Function Prototypes setting. Change this setting to No.

Figure 5.1   Disabling Missing Function Prototypes warning

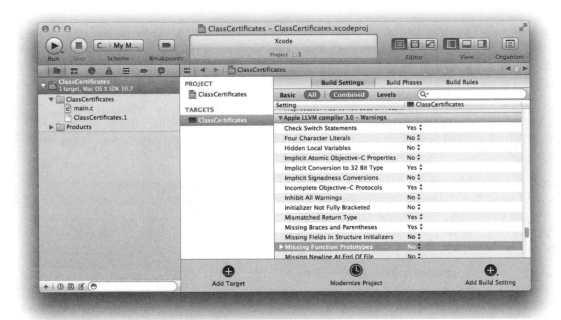

How functions work together

A *program* is a collection of functions. When you run a program, those functions are copied from the hard drive into memory, and the processor finds the function called "main" and executes it.

Remember that a function is like a recipe card. If I began to execute the "Baked Chicken" card, I would discover that the second instruction is "Make Seasoned Bread Crumbs," which is explained on another card. A programmer would say "the Baked Chicken function *calls* the Seasoned Bread Crumbs function."

Figure 5.2 Recipe cards

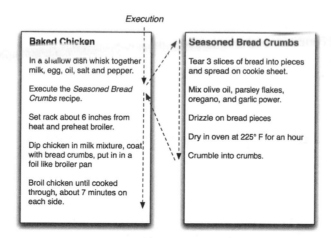

Similarly, the **main** function can call other functions. For example, your **main** function in ClassCertificates called the **congratulateStudent** function, which in turn called **printf**.

While you are preparing the seasoned bread crumbs, you stop executing the "Baked Chicken" card. When the bread crumbs are ready, you resume working through the "Baked Chicken" card.

Similarly, the **main** function stops executing and "blocks" until the function it calls is done executing. To see this happen, we're going to call a **sleep** function that does nothing but wait a number of seconds. In your **main** function, add a call to **sleep**.

```
int main (int argc, const char * argv[])
{
    congratulateStudent("Mark", "Cocoa", 5);
    sleep(2);
    congratulateStudent("Bo", "Objective-C", 2);
    sleep(2);
    congratulateStudent("Mike", "PHP and PostgreSQL", 5);
    sleep(2);
    congratulateStudent("Ted", "iOS", 5);

    return 0;
}
```

Build and run the program. (Ignore the warning about an implicit declaration for now.) You should see a 2-second pause between each message of congratulations. That's because the **main** function stops running until the **sleep** function is done sleeping.

Notice that when you call a function, you use its name and a pair of parentheses for its arguments. Thus, when we talk about functions, we usually include a pair of empty parentheses. From now on, we will say **main()** when we talk about the **main** function.

Your computer came with many functions built-in. Actually, that is a little misleading – here is the truth: Before Mac OS X was installed on your computer, it was nothing but an expensive space heater. Among the things that were installed as part of Mac OS X were files containing a collection of precompiled functions. These collections are called *the standard libraries*. **sleep()** and **printf()** are included in these standard libraries.

At the top of main.c, you included the file stdio.h. This file contains a declaration of the function **printf()** and lets the compiler check to make sure that you are using it correctly. The function **sleep()** is declared in stdlib.h. Include that file, too, so that the compiler will stop complaining that **sleep()** is implicitly declared:

```
#include <stdio.h>
#include <stdlib.h>

void congratulateStudent(char *student, char *course, int numDays)
{
    ...
```

The standard libraries serve two functions:

- They represent big chunks of code that you don't need to write and maintain. Thus, they empower you to build much bigger, better programs than you would be able to do otherwise.

- They ensure that most programs look and feel similar.

Programmers spend a lot of time studying the standard libraries for the operating systems that they work on. Every company that creates an operating system also has documentation for the standard libraries that come with it. You'll learn how to browse the documentation for iOS and Mac OS X in Chapter 16.

Local variables, frames, and the stack

Every function can have *local variables*. Local variables are variables declared inside a function. They exist only during the execution of that function and can only be accessed from within that function. For example, imagine that you were writing a function that computed how long to cook a turkey. It might look like this:

```
void showCookTimeForTurkey(int pounds)
{
    int necessaryMinutes = 15 + 15 * pounds;
    printf("Cook for %d minutes.\n", necessaryMinutes);
}
```

necessaryMinutes is a local variable. It came into existence when **showCookTimeForTurkey()** started to execute and will cease to exist once that function completes execution. The parameter of the function, pounds, is also a local variable. A parameter is a local variable that has been initialized to the value of the corresponding argument.

A function can have many local variables, and all of them are stored in the *frame* for that function. Think of the frame as a blackboard that you can scribble on while the function is running. When the function is done executing, the blackboard is discarded.

Imagine for a moment that you are working on the Baked Chicken recipe. In your kitchen, all recipes get their own blackboards, so you have a blackboard for the Baked Chicken recipe ready. Now, when you call the Seasoned Bread Crumbs recipe, you need a new blackboard. Where are you going to put it? Right on top of the blackboard for Baked Chicken. After all, you've suspended execution of Baked Chicken to make Seasoned Bread Crumbs. You won't need the Baked Chicken frame until the Seasoned Bread Crumbs recipe is complete and its frame is discarded. What you have now is a stack of frames.

Figure 5.3 Two blackboards in a stack

Programmers say, "When a function is called, its frame is created on top of *the stack*. When the function finishes executing, its frame is popped off the stack and destroyed."

Let's look more closely at how the stack works by putting **showCookTimeForTurkey()** into a hypothetical program:

```
void showCookTimeForTurkey(int pounds)
{
    int necessaryMinutes = 15 + 15 * pounds;
    printf("Cook for %d minutes.\n", necessaryMinutes);
}

int main(int argc, const char * argv[])
{
    int totalWeight = 10;
    int gibletsWeight = 1;
    int turkeyWeight = totalWeight - gibletsWeight;
    showCookTimeForTurkey(turkeyWeight);
    return 0;
}
```

Recall that **main()** is always executed first. **main()** calls **showCookTimeForTurkey()**, which begins executing. What, then, does this program's stack look like just after pounds is multiplied by 15?

Figure 5.4   Two frames on the stack

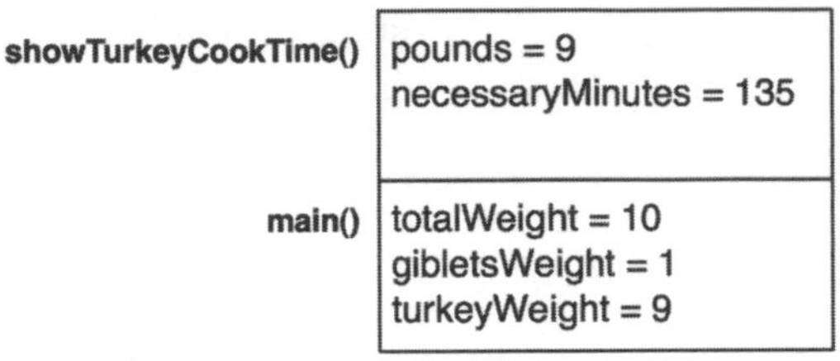

showTurkeyCookTime()	pounds = 9 necessaryMinutes = 135
main()	totalWeight = 10 gibletsWeight = 1 turkeyWeight = 9

The stack is always last-in, first-out. That is, the **showCookTimeForTurkey()** will pop its frame off the stack before **main()** pops its frame off the stack.

Notice that pounds, the single parameter of **showCookTimeForTurkey()**, is part of the frame. Recall that a parameter is a local variable that has been assigned the value of the corresponding argument. For this example, the variable turkeyWeight with a value of 9 is passed as an argument to **showCookTimeForTurkey()**. Then that value is assigned to the parameter pounds and copied to the function's frame.

Recursion

Can a function call itself? You bet! We call that *recursion*. There is a notoriously dull song called "99 Bottles of Beer." Create a new C Command Line Tool named BeerSong. Open main.c and add a function to write out the words to this song and then kick it off in **main()**:

```
#include <stdio.h>

void singTheSong(int numberOfBottles)
{
    if (numberOfBottles == 0) {
        printf("There are simply no more bottles of beer on the wall.\n");
    } else {
        printf("%d bottles of beer on the wall. %d bottles of beer.\n",
                numberOfBottles, numberOfBottles);
        int oneFewer = numberOfBottles - 1;
        printf("Take one down, pass it around, %d bottles of beer on the wall.\n",
                oneFewer);
        singTheSong(oneFewer); // This function calls itself!
        printf("Put a bottle in the recycling, %d empty bottles in the bin.\n",
                numberOfBottles);
    }
}


int main(int argc, const char * argv[])
{
    singTheSong(99);
    return 0;
}
```

Build and run the program. The output looks like this:

```
99 bottles of beer on the wall. 99 bottles of beer.
Take one down, pass it around, 98 bottles of beer on the wall.
98 bottles of beer on the wall. 98 bottles of beer.
Take one down, pass it around, 97 bottles of beer on the wall.
97 bottles of beer on the wall. 97 bottles of beer.
...
1 bottles of beer on the wall. 1 bottles of beer.
Take one down, pass it around, 0 bottles of beer on the wall.
There are simply no more bottles of beer on the wall.
Put a bottle in the recycling, 1 empty bottles in the bin.
Put a bottle in the recycling, 2 empty bottles in the bin.
...
Put a bottle in the recycling, 98 empty bottles in the bin.
Put a bottle in the recycling, 99 empty bottles in the bin.
```

What does the stack look like when the last bottle is taken off the wall?

Figure 5.5   Frames on the stack for a recursive function

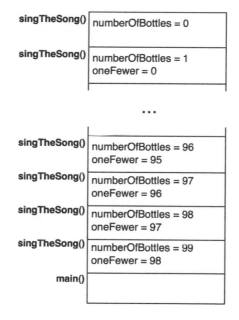

Discussing the frames and the stack is usually not covered in a beginning programming course, but I've found the ideas to be exceedingly useful to new programmers. First, it gives you a more concrete understanding of the answers to questions like "What happens to my local variables when the function finishes executing?" Second, it helps you understand the *debugger*. The debugger is a program that helps you understand what your program is actually doing, which, in turn, helps you find and fix "bugs" (problems in your code). When you build and run a program in Xcode, the debugger is *attached* to the program so that you can use it.

Looking at the frames in the debugger

You can use the debugger to browse the frames on the stack. To do this, however, you have to stop your program in mid-execution. Otherwise, `main()` will finish executing, and there won't be any frames left to look at. To see as many frames as possible in our BeerSong program, we want to halt execution on the line that prints "There are simply no more bottles of beer on the wall."

How do we do this? In main.c, find the line

```
printf("There are simply no more bottles of beer on the wall.\n");
```

There are two shaded columns to the left of your code. Click on the wider, lefthand column next to this line of code.

Figure 5.6   Setting a breakpoint

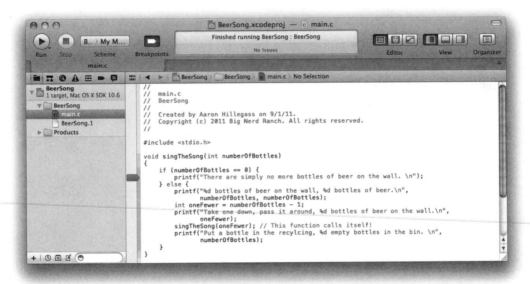

The blue indicator shows that you've set a *breakpoint*. A breakpoint is a location in code where you want the debugger to pause the execution of your program. Run the program again. It will start and then stop right before it executes the line where you set the breakpoint.

Now your program is temporarily frozen in time, and you can examine it more closely. In the navigator area, click the ☰ icon to open the *debug navigator*. This navigator shows all the frames currently on the stack, also called a *stack trace*.

In the stack trace, frames are identified by the name of their function. Given your program consists almost entirely of a recursive function, these frames have the same name and you must distinguish them by the value of oneFewer that gets passed to them. At the bottom of the stack, you will, of course, find the frame for **main()**.

You can select a frame to see the variables in that frame and the source code for the line of code that is currently being executed. Select the frame for the first time **singTheSong** is called.

Figure 5.7　Frames on the stack for a recursive function

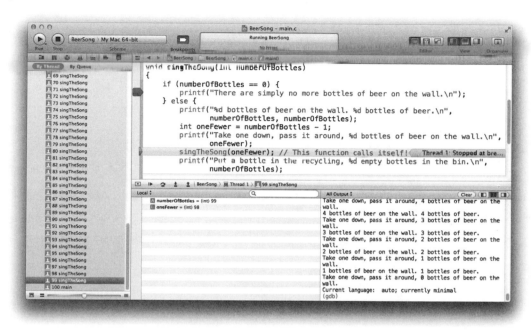

You can see this frame's variables and their values on the bottom left of the window. To the right, you can also see the output in an area called the *console*. (If you don't see the console, find the ▭▭▭ buttons at the right of the screen towards the bottom half. Click the middle button to reveal the console.) In the console, you can see the effect of your breakpoint: the program stopped before reaching the line that ends the song.

Now we need to remove the breakpoint so that the program will run normally. You can simply drag the blue indicator off the gutter. Or click the ➡ icon at the top of the navigator area to reveal the *breakpoint navigator* and see all the breakpoints in a project. From there, you can select your breakpoint and delete it.

To resume execution of your program, click the ▶ button on the debugger bar between the editor and the variables view.

We just took a quick look at the debugger here to demonstrate how frames work. However, using the debugger to set breakpoints and browse the frames in a program's stack will be helpful when your program is not doing what you expect and you need to look at what is really happening.

return

Many functions return a value when they complete execution. You know what type of data a function will return by the type that precedes the function name. (If a function doesn't return anything, its return type is void.)

Create a new C Command Line Tool named Degrees. In main.c, add a function before **main()** that converts a temperature from Celsius to Fahrenheit. Then update **main()** to call the new function.

```
#include <stdio.h>

float fahrenheitFromCelsius(float cel)
{
    float fahr = cel * 1.8 + 32.0;
    printf("%f Celsius is %f Fahrenheit\n", cel, fahr);
    return fahr;
}

int main(int argc, const char * argv[])
{
    float freezeInC = 0;
    float freezeInF = fahrenheitFromCelsius(freezeInC);
    printf("Water freezes at %f degrees Fahrenheit\n", freezeInF);
    return 0;
}
```

See how we took the return value of **fahrenheitFromCelsius()** and assigned it to the freezeInF variable of type float? Pretty slick, huh?

The execution of a function stops when it returns. For example, imagine that you had this function:

```
float average(float a, float b)
{
    return (a + b)/2.0;
    printf("The mean justifies the end\n");
}
```

If you called this function, the **printf()** call would never get executed.

A natural question, then, is "Why do we always return 0 from **main()**?" When you return 0 to the system, you are saying "Everything went OK." If you are terminating the program because something has gone wrong, you'll return 1.

This may seem contradictory to how 0 and 1 work in if statements; because 1 is true and 0 is false, it's natural to think of 1 as success and 0 as failure. So think of **main()** as returning an error report. In that case, 0 is good news! Success is a lack of errors.

To make this clearer, some programmers use the constants EXIT_SUCCESS and EXIT_FAILURE, which are just aliases for 0 and 1 respectively. These constants are defined in the header file stdlib.h:

```
#include <stdio.h>
#include <stdlib.h>

float fahrenheitFromCelsius(float cel)
{
    float fahr = cel * 1.8 + 32.0;
    printf("%f Celsius is %f Fahrenheit\n", cel, fahr);
    return fahr;
}

int main(int argc, const char * argv[])
{
    float freezeInC = 0;
    float freezeInF = fahrenheitFromCelsius(freezeInC);
    printf("Water freezes at %f degrees Fahrenheit\n", freezeInF);
    return EXIT_SUCCESS;
}
```

In this book, we will generally use 0 instead of EXIT_SUCCESS.

Global and static variables

In this chapter, we talked about local variables that only exist while a function is running. There are also variables that can be accessed from any function at any time. We call these *global variables*. To make a variable global, you declare it outside of a particular function. For example, you could add a lastTemperature variable that holds the temperature that was converted from Celsius. Add a global variable to the program:

```
#include <stdio.h>
#include <stdlib.h>

// Declare a global variable
float lastTemperature;

float fahrenheitFromCelsius(float cel)
{
    lastTemperature = cel;
    float fahr = cel * 1.8 + 32.0;
    printf("%f Celsius is %f Fahrenheit\n", cel, fahr);
    return fahr;
}
int main(int argc, const char * argv[])
{
    float freezeInC = 0;
    float freezeInF = fahrenheitFromCelsius(freezeInC);
    printf("Water freezes at %f degrees Fahrenheit\n", freezeInF);
    printf("The last temperature converted was %f\n", lastTemperature);
    return EXIT_SUCCESS;
}
```

Any complex program will involve dozens of files containing different functions. Global variables are available to the code in every one of those files. Sometimes sharing a variable between different files is what you want. But, as you can imagine, having a variable that can be accessed by multiple functions can also lead to great confusion. To deal with this, we have *static variables*. A static variable is like a global variable in that it is declared outside of any function. However, a static variable is only accessible from the code in the file where it was declared. So you get the non-local, "exists outside of any function" benefit while avoiding the "you touched my variable!" issue.

You can change your global variable to a static variable, but because you have only one file, main.c, it will have no effect whatsoever.

```
// Declare a static variable
static float lastTemperature;
```

Both static and global variables can be given an initial value when they are created:

```
// Initialize lastTemperature to 50 degrees
static float lastTemperature = 50.0;
```

If you don't give them an initial value, they are automatically initialized to zero.

In this chapter, you have learned about functions. When we get to Objective-C in Part III, you will hear the word *method* – a method is very, very similar to a function.

Challenge

The interior angles of a triangle must add up to 180 degrees. Create a new C Command Line Tool named Triangle. In main.c, write a function that takes the first two angles and returns the third. Here's what it will look like when you call it:

```
#include <stdio.h>

// Add your new function here

int main(int argc, const char * argv[])
{
    float angleA = 30.0;
    float angleB = 60.0;
    float angleC = remainingAngle(angleA, angleB);
    printf("The third angle is %.2f\n", angleC);
    return 0;
}
```

The output should be:

```
The third angle is 90.00
```

6

Numbers

We've used numbers to measure and display temperature, weight, and how long to cook a turkey. Now let's take a closer look at how numbers work in C programming. On a computer, numbers come in two flavors: integers and floating-point numbers. You have already used both. This chapter is an attempt to codify what a C programmer needs to know about these numbers.

printf()

But before we get to numbers, let's take a closer look at the **printf()** function you've been using. **printf()** prints a *string* to the log. A string is a string of characters. Basically, it's text.

Reopen your ClassCertificates project. In main.c, find **congratulateStudent()**.

```
void congratulateStudent(char *student, char *course, int numDays)
{
    printf("%s has done as much %s Programming as I could fit into %d days.\n",
        student, course, numDays);
}
```

What does this call to **printf()** do? Well, you've seen the output; you know what it does. Now let's figure out how.

printf() is a function that accepts a string as an argument. You can make a *literal string* (as opposed to a string that's stored in a variable) by surrounding text in double quotes.

The string that **printf()** takes as an argument is known as the *format string*, and the format string can have *tokens*. The three tokens in this string are %s, %s, and %d. When the program is run, the tokens are replaced with the values of the variables that follow the string. In this case, those variables are student, course, and numDays. Notice that they are replaced in order in the output. If you swapped student and course in the list of variables, you would see

```
Cocoa has done as much Mark Programming as I could fit into 5 days.
```

However, tokens and variables are not completely interchangeable. The %s token expects a string. The %d expects an integer. (Try swapping them and see what happens.)

Notice that student and course are declared as type char *. For now, just read char * as a type that is a string. We'll come back to strings in Objective-C in Chapter 14 and back to char * in Chapter 34.

Finally, what's with the \n? In **printf()** statements, you have to include an explicit new-line character or all the log output will run together on one line. \n represents the new-line character.

Now let's get back to numbers.

Integers

An integer is a number without a decimal point – a whole number. Integers are good for problems like counting. Some problems, like counting every person on the planet, require really large numbers. Other problems, like counting the number of children in a classroom, require numbers that aren't as large.

To address these different problems, integer variables come in different sizes. An integer variable has a certain number of bits in which it can encode a number, and the more bits the variable has, the larger the number it can hold. Typical sizes are: 8-bit, 16-bit, 32-bit, and 64-bit.

Similarly, some problems require negative numbers, while others do not. So, integer types come in signed and unsigned varieties.

An unsigned 8-bit number can hold any integer from 0 to 255. How did I get that? $2^8 = 256$ possible numbers. And we choose to start at 0.

A signed 64-bit number can hold any integer from -9,223,372,036,854,775,807 to 9,223,372,036,854,775,807. $2^{63} = 9,223,372,036,854,775,808$ minus one bit for the sign (+ or -).

When you declare an integer, you can be very specific:

```
UInt32 x; // An unsigned 32-bit integer
SInt16 y; // An signed 16-bit integer
```

However, it is more common for programmers just to use the descriptive types that you learned in Chapter 3.

```
char a;      // 8 bits
short b;     // Usually 16 bits (depending on the platform)
int c;       // Usually 32 bits (depending on the platform)
long d;      // 32 or 64 bits   (depending on the platform)
long long e; // 64 bits
```

Why is char a number? Any character can be described as an 8-bit number, and computers prefer to think in numbers. What about sign? char, short, int, long, and long long are signed by default, but you can prefix them with unsigned to create the unsigned equivalent.

Also, the sizes of integers depend on the platform. (A *platform* is a combination of an operating system and a particular computer or mobile device.) Some platforms are 32-bit and others are 64-bit. The difference is in the size of the memory address, and we'll talk more about that in Chapter 8.

Apple has created two integer types that are 32-bit on 32-bit platforms and 64-bit on 64-bit platforms:

```
NSInteger g;
NSUInteger h;
```

In much of Apple's code, you will see these types used. They are, for all intents and purposes, the same as long and unsigned long.

Tokens for displaying integers

Create a new project: a C Command Line Tool called Numbers. In main.c, create an integer and print it out in base-10 (as a decimal number) using **printf()**:

```
#include <stdio.h>

int main (int argc, const char * argv[])
{
    int x = 255;
    printf("x is %d.\n", x);
    return 0;
}
```

You should see something like

```
x is 255.
```

As we've seen, %d prints an integer as a decimal number. What other tokens work? You can print the integer in base-8 (octal) or base-16 (hexadecimal). Add a couple of lines to the program:

```
#include <stdio.h>

int main (int argc, const char * argv[])
{
    int x = 255;
    printf("x is %d.\n", x);
    printf("In octal, x is %o.\n", x);
    printf("In hexadecimal, x is %x.\n", x);

    return 0;
}
```

When you run it, you should see something like:

```
x is 255.
In octal, x is 377.
In hexadecimal, x is ff.
```

(We'll return to hexadecimal numbers in Chapter 33.)

What if the integer has lots of bits? You slip an l (for long) or an ll (for long long) between the % and the format character. Change your program to use a long instead of an int:

```
#include <stdio.h>

int main (int argc, const char * argv[])
{
    long x = 255;
    printf("x is %ld.\n", x);
    printf("In octal, x is %lo.\n", x);
    printf("In hexadecimal, x is %lx.\n", x);

    return 0;
}
```

If you are printing an unsigned decimal number, you should use %u:

```
#include <stdio.h>

int main (int argc, const char * argv[])
{
    unsigned long x = 255;
    printf("x is %lu.\n", x);

    // Octal and hex already assumed the number was unsigned
    printf("In octal, x is %lo.\n", x);
    printf("In hexadecimal, x is %lx.\n", x);

    return 0;
}
```

Integer operations

The arithmetic operators +, -, and * work as you would expect. They also have the precedence rules that you would expect: * is evaluated before + or -. In main.c, replace the previous code with a calculation:

```
#include <stdio.h>

int main (int argc, const char * argv[])
{

    printf("3 * 3 + 5 * 2 = %d\n", 3 * 3 + 5 * 2);

    return 0;
}
```

You should see

```
3 * 3 + 5 * 2 = 19
```

Integer division

Most beginning C programmers are surprised by how integer division works. Try it:

```
#include <stdio.h>

int main (int argc, const char * argv[])
{
    printf("3 * 3 + 5 * 2 = %d\n", 3 * 3 + 5 * 2);
    printf("11 / 3 = %d\n", 11 / 3);

    return 0;
}
```

You'll get 11 / 3 = 3.666667, right? Nope. You get 11 / 3 is 3. When you divide one integer by another, you always get a third integer. The system rounds off toward zero. (So, -11 / 3 is -3)

This actually makes sense if you think "11 divided by 3 is 3 with a remainder of 2." And it turns out that the remainder is often quite valuable. The modulus operator (%) is like /, but it returns the remainder instead of the quotient:

```
#include <stdio.h>

int main (int argc, const char * argv[])
{
    printf("3 * 3 + 5 * 2 = %d\n", 3 * 3 + 5 * 2);
    printf("11 / 3 = %d remainder of %d \n", 11 / 3, 11 % 3);

    return 0;
}
```

What if you *want* to get 3.666667? You convert the int to a float using the *cast operator*. The cast operator is the type that you want placed in parentheses to the left of the variable you want converted. Cast your denominator as a float before you do the division:

```
int main (int argc, const char * argv[])
{
    printf("3 * 3 + 5 * 2 = %d\n", 3 * 3 + 5 * 2);
    printf("11 / 3 = %d remainder of %d \n", 11 / 3, 11 % 3);
    printf("11 / 3.0 = %f\n", 11 / (float)3);

    return 0;
}
```

Now, floating point division will be done instead of integer division, and you'll get 3.666667. Here's the rule for integer vs. floating-point division: / is integer division only if both the numerator and denominator are integer types. If either is a floating-point number, floating-point division is done instead.

Operator shorthand

All the operators that you've seen so far yield a new result. So, for example, to increase x by 1, you would use the + operator and then assign the result back into x:

```
int x = 5;
x = x + 1; // x is now 6
```

C programmers do these sorts of operations so often that operators were created that change the value of the variable without an assignment. For example, you can increase the value held in x by 1 with the *increment operator* (++):

```
int x = 5;
x++; // x is now 6
```

There is also a *decrement operator* (--) that decreases the value by 1:

```
int x = 5;
x--; // x is now 4
```

What if you want to increase x by 5 instead of just 1? You could use addition and assignment:

```
int x = 5;
x = x + 5; // x is 10
```

But there is a shorthand for this, too:

```
int x = 5;
x += 5; // x is 10
```

You can think of the second line as "assign x the value of x + 5." In addition to +=, there is also -=, *=, /=, and %=.

To get the absolute value of an int, you use a function instead of an operator. The function is **abs()**. If you want the absolute value of a long, use **labs()**. Both functions are declared in stdlib.h:

```
#include <stdio.h>
#include <stdlib.h>

int main (int argc, const char * argv[])
{
    printf("3 * 3 + 5 * 2 = %d\n", 3 * 3 + 5 * 2);
    printf("11 / 3 = %d remainder of %d \n", 11 / 3, 11 % 3);
    printf("11 / 3.0 = %f\n", 11 / (float)3);
    printf("The absolute value of -5 is %d\n", abs(-5));

    return 0;
}
```

Floating-point numbers

If you need a number with a decimal point, like 3.2, you use a floating-point number. Most programmers think of a floating-point number as a mantissa multiplied by 10 to an integer exponent. For example, 345.32 is thought of as 3.4532×10^2. And this is essentially how they are stored: a 32-bit floating number has 8 bits dedicated to holding the exponent (a signed integer) and 23 bits dedicated to holding the mantissa with the remaining 1 bit used to hold the sign.

Like integers, floating-point numbers come in several sizes. Unlike integers, floating-point numbers are *always* signed:

```
float g;       // 32-bits
double h;      // 64-bits
long double i; // 128-bits
```

Tokens for displaying floating-point numbers

printf() can also display floating point numbers, most commonly using the tokens %f and %e. In main.c, replace the integer-related code:

```
int main (int argc, const char * argv[])
{
    double y = 12345.6789;
    printf("y is %f\n", y);
    printf("y is %e\n", y);

    return 0;
}
```

When you build and run it, you should see:

```
y is 12345.678900
y is 1.234568e+04
```

So %f uses normal decimal notation, and %e uses scientific notation.

Notice that %f is currently showing 6 digits after the decimal point. This is often a bit much. Limit it to two digits by modifying the token:

```
int main (int argc, const char * argv[])
{
    double y = 12345.6789;
    printf("y is %.2f\n", y);
    printf("y is %.2e\n", y);
    return 0;
}
```

When you run it, you should see:

```
y is 12345.68
y is 1.23e+04
```

Functions for floating-point numbers

The operators +, -, *, and / do exactly what you would expect. If you will be doing a lot of math, you will need the math library. To see what's in the math library, open the Terminal application on your Mac and type man math. You will get a great summary of everything in the math library: trigonometry, rounding, exponentiation, square and cube root, etc.

If you use any of these math functions in your code, be sure to include the math library header at the top that file:

```
#include <math.h>
```

One warning: all of the trig-related functions are done in radians, not degrees!

Challenge

Use the math library! Add code to main.c that displays the sine of 1 radian. Show the number rounded to three decimal points.

7

Loops

In Xcode, create yet another new project: a C Command Line Tool named Coolness.

The first program I ever wrote printed the words, "Aaron is Cool". (I was 10 at the time.) Write that program now:

```
#include <stdio.h>

int main(int argc, const char * argv[])
{
    printf("Aaron is Cool\n");
    return 0;
}
```

Build and run the program.

Let's suppose for a moment that you could make my 10-year-old self feel more confident if the program printed the affirmation a dozen times. How would you do that?

Here's the dumb way:

```
#include <stdio.h>

int main(int argc, const char * argv[])
{
    printf("Aaron is Cool\n");
    printf("Aaron is Cool\n");
    printf("Aaron is Cool\n");
    printf("Aaron is Cool\n");
    printf("Aaron is Cool\n");
    printf("Aaron is Cool\n");
    printf("Aaron is Cool\n");
    printf("Aaron is Cool\n");
    printf("Aaron is Cool\n");
    printf("Aaron is Cool\n");
    printf("Aaron is Cool\n");
    printf("Aaron is Cool\n");
    return 0;
}
```

The smart way is to create a loop.

The while loop

The first loop we'll use is a while loop. The while construct works something like the if construct we discussed in Chapter 4. You give it an expression and a block of code contained by curly braces. In the if construct, if the expression is true, the block of code is run once. In the while construct, the block is run again and again until the expression becomes false.

Rewrite the **main()** function to look like this:

```
#include <stdio.h>

int main(int argc, const char * argv[])
{
    int i = 0;
    while (i < 12) {
        printf("%d. Aaron is Cool\n", i);
        i++;
    }
    return 0;
}
```

Build and run the program.

The conditional (i < 12) is being checked before each execution of the block. The first time it evaluates to false, execution leaps to the code after the block.

Notice that the second line of the block increments i. This is important. If i wasn't incremented, then this loop, as written, would continue forever because the expression would always be true. Here's a flow-chart of this while loop:

Figure 7.1   while loop

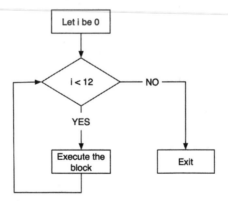

The for loop

The while loop is a general looping structure, but C programmers use the same basic pattern a lot:

```
some initialization
while (some check) {
    some code
    some last step
}
```

So, the C language has a shortcut: the for loop. In the for loop, the pattern shown above becomes:

```
for (some initialization; some check; some last step) {
    some code;
}
```

Change the program to use a for loop:

```
#include <stdio.h>

int main(int argc, const char * argv[])
{
    for (int i = 0; i < 12; i++) {
        printf("%d. Aaron is Cool\n", i);
    }
    return 0;
}
```

Figure 7.2   for loop

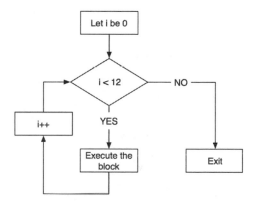

Note that in this simple loop example, you used the loop to dictate the number of times something happens. More commonly, however, loops are used to *iterate* through a collection of items, such as a list of names. For instance, I could modify this program to use a loop in conjunction with a list of friends' names. Each time through the loop, a different friend would get to be cool. We'll see more of collections and loops starting in Chapter 15.

break

Sometimes it is necessary to stop the loop's execution from the inside the loop. For example, let's say you want to step through the positive integers looking for the number x, where $x + 90 = x^2$. Your plan is to step through the integers 0 through 11 and pop out of the loop when you find the solution. Change the code:

```
#include <stdio.h>

int main(int argc, const char * argv[])
{
    int i;
    for (i = 0; i < 12; i++) {
        printf("Checking i = %d\n", i);
```

```
        if (i + 90 == i * i) {
            break;
        }
    }
    printf("The answer is %d.\n", i);
    return 0;
}
```

Build and run the program. You should see

```
Checking i = 0
Checking i = 1
Checking i = 2
Checking i = 3
Checking i = 4
Checking i = 5
Checking i = 6
Checking i = 7
Checking i = 8
Checking i = 9
Checking i = 10
The answer is 10.
```

Notice that when break is called execution skips directly to the end of the code block.

Figure 7.3   Breaking out of a loop

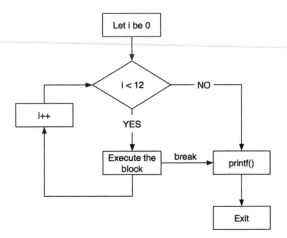

continue

Sometimes you will find yourself in the middle of the code block, and you need to say, "Forget the rest of this run through the code block and start the next run through the code block." This is done with the continue command. For example, what if you were pretty sure that no multiples of 3 satisfied the equation? How would you avoid wasting precious time checking those?

```
#include <stdio.h>

int main(int argc, const char * argv[])
{
    int i;
    for (i = 0; i < 12; i++) {
        if (i % 3 == 0) {
            continue;
        }
        printf("Checking i = %d\n", i);
        if (i + 90 == i * i) {
            break;
        }
    }
    printf("The answer is %d.\n", i);
    return 0;
}
```

Build and run it:

```
Checking i = 1
Checking i = 2
Checking i = 4
Checking i = 5
Checking i = 7
Checking i = 8
Checking i = 10
The answer is 10.
```

Figure 7.4 continue

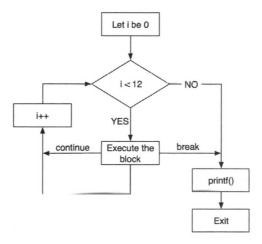

The do-while loop

None of the cool kids use the do-while loop, but for completeness, here it is. The do-while loop doesn't check the expression until it has executed the block. Thus, it ensures that the block is always executed at least once. If you rewrote the original exercise to use a do-while loop, it would look like this:

```
int main(int argc, const char * argv[])
{
    int i = 0;
    do {
        printf("%d. Aaron is Cool\n", i);
        i++;
    } while (i < 13);
    return 0;
}
```

Notice the trailing semicolon. That's because unlike the other loops, a do-while loop is actually one long statement:

```
do { something } while ( something else stays true );
```

Here's a flow-chart of this do-while loop:

Figure 7.5   do-while loop

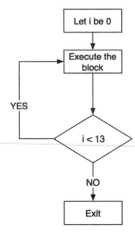

Challenge

Write a program that counts backward from 99 through 0 by 3, printing each number. However, if the number is divisible by 5, it should also print the words "Found one!". Thus, the output should look something like this:

```
99
96
93
90
Found one!
87
...
0
Found one!
```

8

Addresses and Pointers

Your computer is, at its core, a processor (the Central Processing Unit or CPU) and a vast meadow of switches (the Random-Access memory or RAM) that can be turned on or off by the processor. We say that a switch holds one *bit* of information. You'll often see 1 used to represent "on" and 0 used to represent "off."

Eight of these switches make a *byte* of information. The processor can fetch the state of these switches, do operations on the bits, and store the result in another set of switches. For example, the processor might fetch a byte from here and another byte from there, add them together, and store the result in a byte way over someplace else.

Figure 8.1 Memory and the CPU

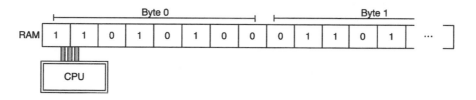

The memory is numbered, and we typically talk about the *address* of a particular byte of data. When people talk about a 32-bit CPU or a 64-bit CPU, they are usually talking about how big the address is. A 64-bit CPU can deal with much, much more memory than a 32-bit CPU.

Getting addresses

In Xcode, create a new project: a C Command Line Tool named Addresses.

The address of a variable is the location in memory where the value for that variable is stored. To get the variable's address, you use the & operator:

```
#include <stdio.h>

int main(int argc, const char * argv[])
{
    int i = 17;
    printf("i stores its value at %p\n", &i);
```

```
        return 0;
}
```

Notice the %p token. That's the token you can replace with a memory address. Build and run the program. You'll see something like:

```
i stores its value at 0xbffff738
```

although your computer may put i at a completely different address. Memory addresses are nearly always printed in hexadecimal format.

In a computer, everything is stored in memory, and thus everything has an address. For example, a function starts at some particular address. To get that address, you just use the function's name:

```
int main(int argc, const char * argv[])
{
    int i = 17;
    printf("i stores its value at %p\n", &i);
    printf("this function starts at %p\n", main);
    return 0;
}
```

Build and run the program.

Storing addresses in pointers

What if you wanted to store an address in a variable? You could stuff it into an unsigned integer that was the right size, but the compiler will help you catch your mistakes if you are more specific when you give that variable its type. For example, if you wanted a variable named ptr that holds the address where a float can be found, you would declare it like this:

```
    float *ptr;
```

We say that ptr is a variable that is a *pointer* to a float. It doesn't store the value of a float; it points to an address where a float may be stored.

Declare a new variable named addressOfI that is a pointer to an int. Assign it the address of i.

```
int main(int argc, const char * argv[])
{
    int i = 17;
    int *addressOfI = &i;
    printf("i stores its value at %p\n", addressOfI);
    printf("this function starts at %p\n", main);
    return 0;
}
```

Build and run the program. You should see no change in its behavior.

We're using integers right now to be simple. But if you're wondering what the point of pointers is, I hear you. It would be just as easy to pass the integer value assigned to this variable as it is to pass its address. Soon, however, your data will be much larger and much more complex than single integers. That's why we pass addresses. It's not always possible to pass a copy of data you want to work with, but you can always pass the *address* of where that data begins. And it's easy to access data once you have its address.

Getting the data at an address

If you have an address, you can get the data stored there using the * operator. Have the log display the value of the integer stored at addressofI.

```
int main(int argc, const char * argv[])
{
    int i = 17;
    int *addressOfI = &i;
    printf("i stores its value at %p\n", addressOfI);
    printf("this function starts at %p\n", main);
    printf("the int stored at addressOfI is %d\n", *addressOfI);
    return 0;
}
```

Notice that the asterisk is used two different ways The first is in the declaration where you declare the variable addressOfI to be an int *. That is, it is a pointer to a place where an int can be stored.

The second is where you read the int value that is stored at the address stored in addressOfI. (Pointers are also called references. Thus, using the pointer to read data at the address is sometimes called *dereferencing* the pointer.)

You can also use the * operator on the left-hand side of an assignment to store data at a particular address:

```
int main(int argc, const char * argv[])
{
    int i = 17;
    int *addressOfI = &i;
    printf("i stores its value at %p\n", addressOfI);
    *addressOfI = 89;
    printf("Now i is %d\n", i);
    return 0;
}
```

Build and run your program.

Don't worry if you don't have pointers squared away in your mind just yet. We'll spend a lot of time working with pointers in this book, so you'll get plenty of practice.

Now let's make a common programming mistake. Remove the * from the fourth line of **main()** so that it reads

```
    addressOfI = 89;
```

Notice Xcode pops up a warning that says Incompatible integer to pointer conversion assigning to 'int *' to 'int'. Fix the problem.

How many bytes?

Given that everything lives in memory and that you now know how to find the address where data starts, the next question is "How many bytes does this data type consume?"

Using **sizeof()** you can find the size of a data type. For example,

```
int main(int argc, const char * argv[])
{
    int i = 17;
    int *addressOfI = &i;
    printf("i stores its value at %p\n", addressOfI);
    *addressOfI = 89;
    printf("Now i is %d\n", i);
    printf("An int is %zu bytes\n", sizeof(int));
    printf("A pointer is %zu bytes\n", sizeof(int *));
    return 0;
}
```

We see yet another new token in the calls to **printf()**: %zu. The **sizeof()** function returns a value of type size_t, for which %zu is the correct placeholder token. This one's not very common in the wild.

Build and run the program. If your pointer is 4 bytes long, your program is running in 32-bit mode. If your pointer is 8 bytes long, your program is running in 64-bit mode.

sizeof() will also take a variable as an argument, so you could have written the previous program like this:

```
int main(int argc, const char * argv[])
{
    int i = 17;
    int *addressOfI = &i;
    printf("i stores its value at %p\n", addressOfI);
    *addressOfI = 89;
    printf("Now i is %d\n", i);
    printf("An int is %zu bytes\n", sizeof(i));
    printf("A pointer is %zu bytes\n", sizeof(addressOfI));
    return 0;
}
```

NULL

Sometimes you need a pointer to nothing. That is, you have a variable that can hold an address, and you want to store something in it that makes it explicit that the variable is not set to anything. We use NULL for this:

```
float *myPointer;
// Set myPointer to NULL for now, I'll store a pointer there
// later in the program
myPointer = NULL;
```

What is NULL? Remember that an address is just a number. NULL is zero. This is very handy in if statements:

```
float *myPointer;
...
// Has myPointer been set?
if (myPointer) {
    // myPointer is not NULL
    ...do something with the data at myPointer...
} else {
    // myPointer is NULL
}
```

Later, when we discuss pointers to objects, we will use nil instead of NULL. They are equivalent, but Objective-C programmers use nil to mean the address where no object lives.

Stylish pointer declarations

When you declare a pointer to `float`, it looks like this:

```
float *powerPtr;
```

Because the type is a pointer to a float, you may be tempted to write it like this:

```
float* powerPtr;
```

This is fine, and the compiler will let you do it. However, stylish programmers don't.

Why? You can declare multiple variables in a single line. For example, if I wanted to declare variables x, y, and z, I could do it like this:

```
float x, y, z;
```

Each one is a float.

What do you think these are?

```
float* b, c;
```

Surprise! b is a pointer to a `float`, but c is just a `float`. If you want them both to be pointers, you must put a * in front of each one:

```
float *b, *c;
```

Putting the * directly next to the variable name makes this clearer.

Challenges

Write a program that shows you how much memory a `float` consumes.

On your Mac, a `short` is a 2-byte integer, and one bit is used to hold the sign (positive or negative). What is the smallest number it can store? What is the largest? An `unsigned short` only holds non-negative numbers. What is the largest number it can store?

9

Pass By Reference

There is a standard C function called **modf()**. You give **modf()** a double, and it calculates the integer part and the fraction part of the number. For example, if you give it 3.14, 3 is the integer part and 0.14 is the fractional part.

You, as the caller of **modf()** want both parts. However, a C function can only return one value. How can **modf()** give you both pieces of information?

When you call **modf()**, you will supply an address where it can stash one of the numbers. In particular, it will return the fractional part and copy the integer part to the address you supply. Create a new project: a C Command Line Tool named PBR.

Edit main.c:

```
#include <stdio.h>
#include <math.h>

int main(int argc, const char * argv[])
{
    double pi = 3.14;
    double integerPart;
    double fractionPart;

    // Pass the address of integerPart as an argument
    fractionPart = modf(pi, &integerPart);

    // Find the value stored in integerPart
    printf("integerPart = %.0f, fractionPart = %.2f\n", integerPart, fractionPart);

    return 0;
}
```

This is known as *pass-by-reference*. That is, you supply an address (also known as "a reference"), and the function puts the data there.

Figure 9.1   The stack as modf() returns

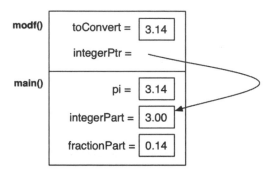

Here's another way to think about pass-by-reference. Imagine that you give out assignments to spies. You might tell one, "I need photos of the finance minister with his girlfriend. I've left a short length of steel pipe at the foot of the angel statue in the park. When you get the photos, roll them up and leave them in the pipe. I'll pick them up Tuesday after lunch." In the spy biz, this is known as a *dead drop*.

modf() works just like a dead drop. You are asking it to execute and telling it a location where the result can be placed so you can find it later. The only difference is that instead of a steel pipe, you are giving it a location in memory where the result can be placed.

Writing pass-by-reference functions

There are two popular ways to describe the location of a point in 2-dimensional space: Cartesian coordinates and polar coordinates. In Cartesian coordinates, (x, y) indicates that you should go to the right x and then up y. In polar coordinates, (theta, radius) indicates that you should turn to the left by theta radians and go forward radius.

Figure 9.2   Polar and Cartesian coordinates

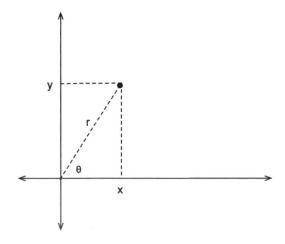

What if you wanted to write a function that converted a point in Cartesian coordinates to polar coordinates? It would need to read two floating point numbers and return two floating point numbers. The declaration of the function would look like this:

```
void cartesianToPolar(float x, float y, float *rPtr, float *thetaPtr)
```

That is, when the function is called, it will be passed values for x and y. It will also be supplied with locations where the values for radius and theta can be stored.

Now write the function near the top of your main.c file and call it from **main()**:

```
#include <stdio.h>
#include <math.h>

void cartesianToPolar(float x, float y, double *rPtr, double *thetaPtr)
{
    // Store the radius in the supplied address
    *rPtr = sqrt(x * x + y * y);

    // Calculate theta
    float theta;
    if (x == 0.0) {
        if (y == 0.0) {
            theta = 0.0;      // technically considered undefined
        } else if (y > 0) {
            theta = M_PI_2;
        } else {
            theta = - M_PI_2;
        }
    } else {
        theta = atan(y/x);
    }
    // Store theta in the supplied address
    *thetaPtr = theta;
}

int main(int argc, const char * argv[])
{
    double pi = 3.14;
    double integerPart;
    double fractionPart;

    // Pass the address of integerPart as an argument
    fractionPart = modf(pi, &integerPart);

    // Find the value stored in integerPart
    printf("integerPart - %.0f, fractionPart - %.2f\n", integerPart, fractionPart);

    double x = 3.0;
    double y = 4.0;
    double radius;
    double angle;

    cartesianToPolar(x, y, &angle, &radius);
    printf("(%.2f, %.2f) becomes (%.2f radians, %.2f)\n", x, y, radius, angle);

    return 0;
}
```

Build and run the program.

Figure 9.3   The stack as cartesianToPolar() returns

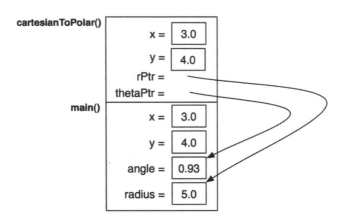

Avoid dereferencing NULL

Sometimes a function can supply many values by reference, but you may only care about some of them. How do you avoid declaring these variables and passing their addresses when you're not going to use them anyway? Typically, you pass NULL as an address to tell the function "I don't need this particular value."

This means that you should always check to make sure the pointers are non-NULL before you dereference them. Add these checks in **cartesianToPolar()**:

```
void cartesianToPolar(float x, float y,  double *rPtr, double *thetaPtr)
{
    // Is rPtr non-NULL?
    if (rPtr) {
        // Store the radius in the supplied address
        *rPtr = sqrt(x * x + y * y);
    }

    // Is thetaPtr NULL?
    if (!thetaPtr) {
        // Skip the rest of the function
        return;
    }

    // Calculate theta
    float theta;
    if (x == 0.0) {
        if (y == 0.0) {
            theta = 0.0;     // technically considered undefined
        } else if (y > 0) {
            theta = M_PI_2;
        } else {
            theta = - M_PI_2;
        }
    } else {
        ...
```

10

Structs

Sometimes you need a variable to hold several related chunks of data. For example, imagine that you were writing a program that computed a person's Body Mass Index. (What is your BMI? It is your weight in kilograms divided by the square of your height in meters. A BMI under 20 suggests that you may be underweight. A BMI over 30 suggests that you may be obese. It is a very imprecise tool for measuring a person's fitness, but it makes a fine programming example.) A person, for your purposes, consists of a float that represents height in meters and an int that represents weight in kilograms.

Now you're going to create your own Person type. A variable of type Person will be a structure and will have two members: a float called heightInMeters and an int called weightInKilos.

Create a new project: a C Command Line Tool called BMICalc. Edit main.c to create a structure that contains the data you need for a person:

```
#include <stdio.h>

// Here is the declaration of the struct Person
struct Person {
    float heightInMeters;
    int weightInKilos;
};

int main(int argc, const char * argv[])
{
    struct Person person;
    person.weightInKilos = 96;
    person.heightInMeters = 1.8;
    printf("person weighs %i kilograms\n", person.weightInKilos);
    printf("person is %.2f meters tall\n", person.heightInMeters);
    return 0;
}
```

Notice that you access the members of a struct using a period.

Here's the frame for **main()** after the struct's members have been assigned values.

Figure 10.1 Frame after member assignments

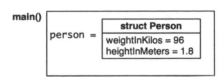

Most of the time, you use a structure declaration over and over again. So it's common to create a typedef for the structure type. A typedef defines an alias for a type declaration and allows us to use it more like the usual data types. Change main.c to create and use a typedef for struct Person:

```
#include <stdio.h>

// Here is the declaration of the type Person
typedef struct {
    float heightInMeters;
    int weightInKilos;
} Person;

int main(int argc, const char * argv[])
{
    Person person;
    person.weightInKilos = 96;
    person.heightInMeters = 1.8;
    printf("person weighs %i kilograms\n", person.weightInKilos);
    printf("person is %.2f meters tall\n", person.heightInMeters);
    return 0;
}
```

Now that you've created a typedef, you can pass a Person structure to another function. Add a function named **bodyMassIndex()** that accepts a Person as a parameter and calculates BMI. Then update **main()** to call it:

```
#include <stdio.h>

typedef struct _Person {
    float heightInMeters;
    int weightInKilos;
} Person;

float bodyMassIndex(Person p)
{
   return p.weightInKilos / (p.heightInMeters * p.heightInMeters);
}

int main(int argc, const char * argv[])
{
    Person person;
    person.weightInKilos = 96;
    person.heightInMeters = 1.8;
    float bmi = bodyMassIndex(person);
    printf("person has a BMI of %.2f\n", bmi);
    return 0;
}
```

Challenge

The first structure I had to deal with as a programmer was struct tm, which the standard C library uses to hold time broken down into its components. The struct is defined:

```
struct tm {
    int    tm_sec;      /* seconds after the minute [0-60] */
    int    tm_min;      /* minutes after the hour [0-59] */
    int    tm_hour;     /* hours since midnight [0-23] */
    int    tm_mday;     /* day of the month [1-31] */
```

```
int     tm_mon;     /* months since January [0-11] */
int     tm_year;    /* years since 1900 */
int     tm_wday;    /* days since Sunday [0-6] */
int     tm_yday;    /* days since January 1 [0-365] */
int     tm_isdst;   /* Daylight Savings Time flag */
long    tm_gmtoff;  /* offset from CUT in seconds */
char    *tm_zone;   /* timezone abbreviation */
};
```

The function **time()** returns the number of seconds since the first moment of 1970 in Greenwich, England. **localtime_r()** can read that duration and pack a struct tm with the appropriate values. (It actually takes the *address* of the number of seconds since 1970 and the *address* of an struct tm.) Thus, getting the current time as a struct tm looks like this:

```
long secondsSince1970 = time(NULL);
printf("It has been %ld seconds since 1970\n", secondsSince1970);

struct tm now;
localtime_r(&secondsSince1970, &now);
printf("The time is %d:%d:%d\n", now.tm_hour, now.tm_min, now.tm_sec);
```

The challenge is to write a program that will tell you what the date (4-30-2015 format is fine) will be in 4 million seconds.

(One hint: tm_mon = 0 means January, so be sure to add 1. Also, include the <time.h> header at the start of your program.)

11
The Heap

So far, your programs have only used memory that has been in frames on the stack. This memory is automatically allocated when the function starts and automatically destroyed when the function ends. (In fact, local variables are often called *automatic variables* because of this convenient behavior.)

Sometimes, however, you need to explicitly claim a long line of bytes of memory and use it in many functions. For example, you might read a file of text into memory and then call a function that would count all the vowels in that memory. Typically, once you were finished with the text, you would let the program know you were all done so the program could reuse that memory for something else.

Programmers often use the word *buffer* to mean a long line of bytes of memory. (This explains the term "buffering" to describe the wait for YouTube to send you enough bytes for that cat video to get started.)

You claim a buffer of memory using the function **malloc()**. The buffer comes from a region of memory known as the *heap*, which is separate from the stack. When you're done using the buffer, you call the function **free()** to release your claim on that memory and return it to the heap. Let's say, for example, I needed a chunk of memory big enough to hold 1,000 floats.

```
#include <stdio.h>
#include <stdlib.h> // malloc and free are in stdlib

int main(int argc, const char * argv[])
{
    // Declare a pointer
    float *startOfBuffer;

    // Ask to use some bytes from the heap
    startOfBuffer = malloc(1000 * sizeof(float));

    // ...use the buffer here...

    // Relinquish your claim on the memory so it can be reused
    free(startOfBuffer);

    // Forget where that memory is
    startOfBuffer = NULL;

    return 0;
}
```

startOfBuffer would be a pointer to the first floating point number in the buffer.

Figure 11.1 A pointer on the stack to a buffer on the heap

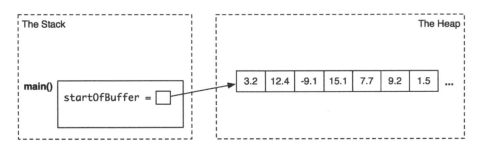

At this point, most C books would spend a lot of time talking about how to read and write data in assorted locations in that buffer of floating pointer numbers. This book, however, is trying to get you to objects as quickly as possible. So, we will put off C arrays and pointer arithmetic until later.

You can also use **malloc()** to claim space for a struct on the heap. For example, if you wanted to allocate a Person struct on the heap, you might have a program like this:

```c
#include <stdio.h>
#include <stdlib.h>

typedef struct {
    float heightInMeters;
    int weightInKilos;
} Person;

float bodyMassIndex(Person *p)
{
  return p->weightInKilos / (p->heightInMeters * p->heightInMeters);
}

int main(int argc, const char * argv[])
{
    // Allocate memory for one Person structure
    Person *x = (Person *)malloc(sizeof(Person));

    // Fill in two members of the structure
    x->weightInKilos = 81;
    x->heightInMeters = 2.0;

    // Print out the BMI of the original Person
    float xBMI = bodyMassIndex(x);
    printf("x has a BMI of = %f\n", xBMI);

    // Let the memory be recycled
    free(x);

    // Forget where it was
    x = NULL;

    return 0;
}
```

Notice the operator ->. p->weightInKilos says, "Dereference the pointer p to the structure and get me the member called weightInKilos."

This idea of structures on the heap is a very powerful one. It forms the basis for Objective-C objects, which we turn to next.

Part III
Objective-C and Foundation

Now that you have an understanding of the basics of programs, functions, variables, and data types, you are ready to learn Objective-C. We'll stick with command-line programs for now to keep the focus on programming essentials.

All Objective-C programming is done with the Foundation framework. A *framework* is library of classes that you use to write programs. What's a class? That's what we'll talk about first…

12
Objects

Many computer languages have the idea of *objects*. An object is like a structure in that it holds data. However, unlike a structure, an object also contains a set of functions that act upon that data. To trigger one of these functions, you send a *message* to the object. To use the correct word, a function that is triggered by a message is known as a *method*.

In the early 1980's, Brad Cox and Tom Love decided to add object-oriented ideas to the C language. For objects, they built upon the idea of structs allocated on the heap and added a message-sending syntax. The result was the language Objective-C.

Objects are very chatty by nature. They do work and send and receive messages about the work they are doing. A complex Objective-C program can have hundreds of objects in memory all at once, doing work and sending messages to each other.

A *class* describes a particular type of object. This description includes methods and *instance variables* where an object of this type stores its data. You ask a class to create an object of its type for you on the heap. We say that the resulting object is an *instance* of that class.

For example, an iPhone ships with many classes, one of which is `CLLocation`. You can ask the `CLLocation` class to create an *instance* of `CLLocation`. Inside this `CLLocation` object are several instance variables that hold location data, like longitude, latitude, and altitude. The object also has several methods. For example, you can ask one instance of `CLLocation` how far it is from another `CLLocation` object.

Creating and using your first object

Now you're going to create your first Objective-C program. Create a new project: a Command Line Tool, but instead of C, make its type Foundation. Name it TimeAfterTime.

Figure 12.1   Creating a Foundation command-line tool

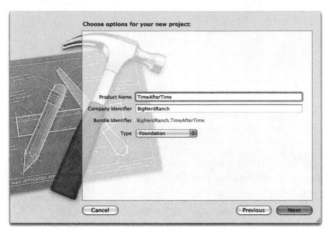

Files containing Objective-C code are typically given the suffix .m. Find and open main.m and type in these two lines of code:

```
#import <Foundation/Foundation.h>

int main (int argc, const char * argv[])
{
    @autoreleasepool {

        NSDate *now = [NSDate date];
        NSLog(@"The new date lives at %p", now);

    }
    return 0;
}
```

Voilà! Your first message send. You sent the message **date** to the **NSDate** class. The **date** method asks the **NSDate** class to create an instance of **NSDate**, initialize it to the current date/time, and return the address where the new object starts. You then stored the returned address in the variable now. This variable is a pointer to an **NSDate** object.

NSLog() is an Objective-C function not unlike **printf()**; it takes a format string, replaces % tokens with actual values, and writes the result to the console. However, its format string always begins with an @, and it does not require a \n at the end.

Build and run the program. You should see something like:

```
2011-08-05 11:53:54.366 TimeAfterTime[4862:707] The new date lives at 0x100114dc0
```

Unlike **printf()**, **NSLog()** prefaces its output with the date, time, program name, and process ID. From now on when I show output from **NSLog()**, I'll skip this data – the page is just too narrow.

In **NSLog()**, %p printed out the location of the object. To print out something more date-like, you can use %@, which asks the object to describe itself as a string:

```
#import <Foundation/Foundation.h>

int main (int argc, const char * argv[])
{
    @autoreleasepool {

        NSDate *now = [NSDate date];
        NSLog(@"The date is %@", now);

    }
    return 0;
}
```

Now you should see something like:

```
The date is 2011-08-05 16:09:14 +0000
```

Message anatomy

A message send is always surrounded by square brackets, and it always has at least two parts:

- a pointer to the object that is receiving the message

- the name of the method to be triggered

A message send (like a function call) can also have arguments. Let's look at an example.

NSDate objects represent a particular date and time. An instance of **NSDate** can tell you the difference (in seconds) between the date/time it represents and 12:00AM (GMT) on Jan 1, 1970. Ask yours this question by sending the message **timeIntervalSince1970** to the **NSDate** object pointed to by now.

```
#import <Foundation/Foundation.h>

int main (int argc, const char * argv[])
{
    @autoreleasepool {

        NSDate *now = [NSDate date];
        NSLog(@"The date is %@", now);
        double seconds = [now timeIntervalSince1970];
        NSLog(@"It has been %f seconds since the start of 1970.", seconds);

    }
    return 0;
}
```

Now say you want a new date object – one that is 100,000 seconds later from the one you already have.

The **NSDate** class has a method called **dateByAddingTimeInterval:**. You can send this message to the original date object to get the new date object. This method takes an argument: the number of seconds to add. Use it to create a new date object in your **main()** function:

```
#import <Foundation/Foundation.h>

int main (int argc, const char * argv[])
{
    @autoreleasepool {

        NSDate *now = [NSDate date];
        NSLog(@"The date is %@", now);

        double seconds = [now timeIntervalSince1970];
        NSLog(@"It has been %f seconds since the start of 1970.", seconds);

        NSDate *later = [now dateByAddingTimeInterval:100000];
        NSLog(@"In 100,000 seconds it will be %@", later);

    }
    return 0;
}
```

In the message send [now dateByAddingTimeInterval:100000],

- now is a pointer to the object that is receiving the message (also known as "the receiver")

- **dateByAddingTimeInterval:** is the method name (also known as "the selector")

- 100000 is the only argument

Figure 12.2   A message send

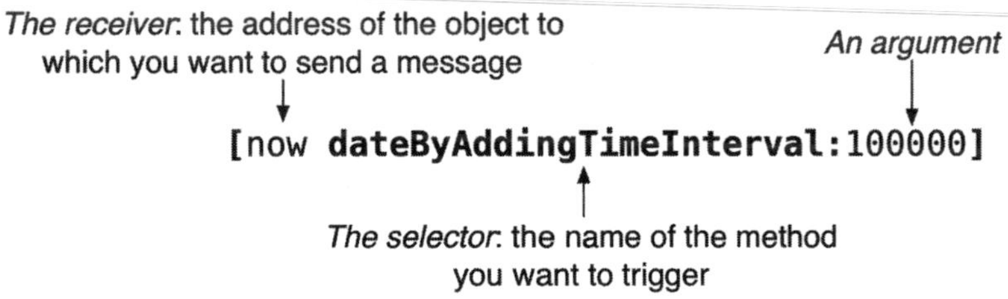

Objects in memory

Figure 12.3 is an *object diagram*. This diagram shows two **NSDate** instances on the heap. The two variables now and later are part of the frame for the function **main()**. They point to the **NSDate** objects, as shown by the arrows

Figure 12.3 Object diagram for TimeAfterTime

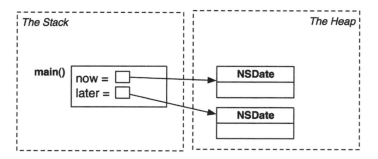

You've only seen one class thus far: **NSDate**. There are, in fact, hundreds of classes that come with iOS and Mac OS X. We'll work with some of the more common ones in the coming chapters.

id

When declaring a pointer to hold on to an object, most of the time you specify the class of the object that the pointer will refer to:

```
NSDate *expiration;
```

However, often you need a way to create a pointer without knowing exactly what kind of object the pointer will refer to. For this case, we use the type id to mean "a pointer to some kind of Objective-C object" Here is what it looks like when you use it:

```
id delegate;
```

Notice that there is no asterisk in this declaration. id implies the asterisk.

The ideas of classes, objects, messages, and methods can be difficult to get your head around at the beginning. Don't worry if you're feeling a little uncertain about objects. This is just the beginning. You'll be using these patterns over and over again, and they will make more sense each time you do.

Challenge

Use two instances of **NSDate** to figure out how many seconds you have been alive. Hint: here is how you create a new date object from the year, month, etc.:

```
NSDateComponents *comps = [[NSDateComponents alloc] init];
[comps setYear:1969];
[comps setMonth:4];
[comps setDay:30];
[comps setHour:13];
[comps setMinute:10];
[comps setSecond:0];

NSCalendar *g = [[NSCalendar alloc] initWithCalendarIdentifier:NSGregorianCalendar];
NSDate *dateOfBirth = [g dateFromComponents:comps];
```

To get the number of seconds between two instances of **NSDate**, use the method **timeIntervalSinceDate:**.

```
double d = [laterDate timeIntervalSinceDate:earlierDate];
```

13

More Messages

In the last chapter, you sent a few messages. Let's look again at the lines where you sent those messages and triggered the corresponding methods:

```
NSDate *now = [NSDate date];
```

We say that the **date** method is a *class method*. That is, you cause the method to execute by sending a message to the **NSDate** *class*. The **date** method returns a pointer to an instance of **NSDate**.

```
double seconds = [now timeIntervalSince1970];
```

We say that **timeIntervalSince1970** is an *instance method*. You cause the method to execute by sending a message to an *instance* of the class. The **timeIntervalSince1970** method returns a double.

```
NSDate *later = [now dateByAddingTimeInterval:100000];
```

dateByAddingTimeInterval: is another instance method. This method takes one argument. You can determine this by the colon in the method name. This method also returns a pointer to an instance of **NSDate**.

Nesting message sends

There is a class method **alloc** that returns a pointer to a new object that needs to be initialized. That pointer is then used to send the new object the message **init**. Using **alloc** and **init** is the most common way to create objects in Objective-C. It is good practice (and the only Apple-approved way) to send both of these messages in one line of code by *nesting* the message sends:

```
[[NSDate alloc] init];
```

The system will execute the messages on the inside first and then the messages that contain them. So, **alloc** is sent to the **NSDate** class, and the result of that (a pointer to the newly-created instance) is then sent **init**.

init returns a pointer to the new object (which is nearly always the pointer that came out of the **alloc** method), so we can use what's returned from **init** for the assignment. Try out these nested messages in your code by changing the line:

```
NSDate *now = [NSDate date];
```

to

```
NSDate *now = [[NSDate alloc] init];
```

Multiple arguments

Some methods take several arguments. For example, an **NSDate** object doesn't know what day of the month it is. If you needed this information, you would use an **NSCalendar** object. The **NSCalendar** method that can tell you the day of the month takes three arguments. Create an **NSCalendar** object and use it in main.m:

```
#import <Foundation/Foundation.h>

int main (int argc, const char * argv[])
{
    @autoreleasepool {

        NSDate *now = [[NSDate alloc] init];
        NSLog(@"The date is %@", now);

        double seconds = [now timeIntervalSince1970];
        NSLog(@"It has been %f seconds since the start of 1970.", seconds);

        NSDate *later = [now dateByAddingTimeInterval:100000];
        NSLog(@"In 100,000 seconds it will be %@", later);

        NSCalendar *cal = [NSCalendar currentCalendar];
        NSUInteger day = [cal ordinalityOfUnit:NSDayCalendarUnit
                                         inUnit:NSMonthCalendarUnit
                                        forDate:now];
        NSLog(@"This is day %lu of the month", day);

    }
    return 0;
}
```

The method's name is **ordinalityOfUnit:inUnit:forDate:**, and it takes three arguments. You can tell because the method name includes three colons. Notice that I split that message send into three lines. This is fine; the compiler does not mind the extra whitespace. Objective-C programmers typically line up the colons so that it is easy to tell the parts of the method name from the arguments. (Xcode should do this for you: every time you start a new line, the previous line should indent properly. If that isn't happening, check your Xcode preferences for indention.)

The first and second arguments of this method are the constants NSDayCalendarUnit and NSMonthCalendarUnit. These constants are defined in the **NSCalendar** class. They tell the method that you want to know what day it is within the month. The third argument is the date you want to know about.

If you wanted to know the hour of the year instead of the day of the month, you'd use these constants:

```
        NSUInteger hour = [cal ordinalityOfUnit:NSHourCalendarUnit
                                          inUnit:NSYearCalendarUnit
                                         forDate:now];
```

Sending messages to nil

Nearly all object-oriented languages have the idea of nil, the pointer to no object. In Objective-C, nil is the zero pointer (same as NULL, which was discussed in Chapter 8).

In most object-oriented languages, sending a message to nil is not allowed. As a result, you have to check for non-nil-ness before accessing an object. So you see this sort of thing a lot:

```
if (fido != nil) {
    [fido goGetTheNewspaper];
}
```

When Objective-C was designed, it was decided that sending a message to `nil` would be OK; it just wouldn't do anything at all. Thus, this code is completely legal:

```
Dog *fido = nil;
[fido goGetTheNewspaper];
```

Important thing #1: If you are sending messages and nothing is happening, make sure you aren't sending messages to a pointer that has been set to `nil`.

Important thing #2: If you send a message to `nil`, the return value doesn't mean anything.

```
Dog *fido = nil;
Newspaper *daily = [fido goGetTheNewspaper];
```

In this case, `daily` will be zero. (In general, if you expect a number or a pointer as a result, sending a message to `nil` will return zero. However, for other types like structs, you will get strange and unexpected return values.)

Challenge

On your Mac, there is a class **NSTimeZone**. Among its many methods are the class method **systemTimeZone**, which returns the time zone of your computer (as an instance of **NSTimeZone**), and the instance method **isDaylightSavingTime**, which returns YES if the time zone is currently in daylight savings time.

Write a Foundation Command Line Tool that tells you if it is currently daylight savings time.

14

NSString

NSString is another class like **NSDate**. Instances of **NSString** hold character strings. In code, you can create a literal instance of **NSString** like this;

```
NSString *lament = @"Why me!?";
```

In your TimeAfterTime project, you typed in this code:

```
NSLog(@"The date is %@", now);
```

NSLog() is an Objective-C function (not a method!) that works a lot like **printf()**. In **NSLog()**, however, the format string is actually an instance of **NSString**.

Instances of **NSString** can also be created programmatically using the **stringWithFormat:** class method:

```
NSString *x = [NSString stringWithFormat:@"The best number is %d", 5];
```

To get the number of characters in a string, you use the **length** method:

```
NSUInteger charCount = [x length];
```

And you check to see if two strings are equal using the **isEqual:** method:

```
if ([lament isEqual:x])
    NSLog(@"%@ and %@ are equal", lament, x);
```

The C language also has a character string construct. Here's what the preceding string examples would look like in C:

```
char *lament = "Why me!?",
char *x;
asprintf(&x, "The best number is %d", 5);
size_t charCount = strlen(x);
if (strcmp(lament, x) == 0)
    printf("%s and %s are equal\n", lament, x);
free(x);
```

We will discuss C strings in Chapter 34. But whenever you have a choice, use **NSString** objects instead of C strings. The **NSString** class has many methods designed to make your life easier. Plus, **NSString** (which is based on the UNICODE standard) is exceedingly good at holding text from any language on the planet. Strange characters? No problem. Text that reads from right to left? No worries.

Challenge

There is a class called **NSHost** which has information about your computer. To get an instance of **NSHost**, you can use the **NSHost** class method **currentHost**. This method returns a pointer to an **NSHost** object:

```
+ (NSHost *)currentHost
```

To get the localized name of your computer, you can use the **NSHost** instance method **localizedName** that returns a pointer to an **NSString** object:

```
- (NSString *)localizedName
```

Write a Foundation Command Line Tool that prints out the name of your computer. (This sometimes takes a surprisingly long time to run.)

15
NSArray

Like **NSString**, **NSArray** is another class that Objective-C programmers use a lot. An instance of **NSArray** holds a list of pointers to other objects. For example, let's say you want to make a list of three **NSDate** objects and then go through the list and print each date.

Create a new project : a Foundation Command Line Tool called DateList. Open main.m and change the **main()** function:

```
#import <Foundation/Foundation.h>

int main(int argc, const char * argv[])
{
    @autoreleasepool {

        // Create three NSDate objects
        NSDate *now = [NSDate date];
        NSDate *tomorrow = [now dateByAddingTimeInterval:24.0 * 60.0 * 60.0];
        NSDate *yesterday = [now dateByAddingTimeInterval:-24.0 * 60.0 * 60.0];

        // Create an array containing all three (nil terminates the list)
        NSArray *dateList = [NSArray arrayWithObjects:now, tomorrow, yesterday, nil];

        // How many dates are there?
        NSLog(@"There are %lu dates", [dateList count]);

        // Print a couple
        NSLog(@"The first date is %@", [dateList objectAtIndex:0]);
        NSLog(@"The third date is %@", [dateList objectAtIndex:2]);

    }
    return 0;
}
```

NSArray has two methods, shown in this example, that you will use all the time:

- **count** returns the number of items in an array

- **objectAtIndex:** returns the pointer that the array has stored at the index specified by the argument.

Arrays are ordered, and you access an item in the array by its *index*. Arrays are zero-based: the first item is stored at index 0, the second item is stored at index 1, and so on. Thus, if the **count** method says there are 100 items in the array, you can use **objectAtIndex:** to ask for the objects at indices 0 to 99.

Figure 15.1 is an object diagram of your program. Notice that the instance of **NSArray** has pointers to the **NSDate** objects.

Figure 15.1   Object diagram for DateList

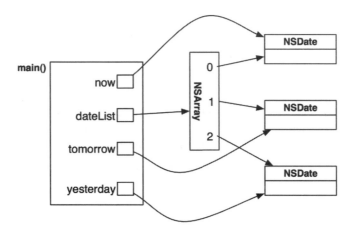

Thus, if you want to loop and process each item in the array (or "iterate over the array"), you can create a for-loop. Edit main.m:

```
#import <Foundation/Foundation.h>

int main(int argc, const char * argv[])
{
    @autoreleasepool {

        // Create three NSDate objects
        NSDate *now = [NSDate date];
        NSDate *tomorrow = [now dateByAddingTimeInterval:24.0 * 60.0 * 60.0];
        NSDate *yesterday = [now dateByAddingTimeInterval:-24.0 * 60.0 * 60.0];

        // Create an array containing all three (nil terminates the list)
        NSArray *dateList = [NSArray arrayWithObjects:now, tomorrow, yesterday, nil];

        NSUInteger dateCount = [dateList count];
        for (int i = 0; i < dateCount; i++) {
            NSDate *d = [dateList objectAtIndex:i];
            NSLog(@"Here is a date: %@", d);
        }

    }
    return 0;
}
```

Programmers do this so often that they made a special addition to the for-loop for iterating over arrays. Edit the code to use this mechanism:

```
#import <Foundation/Foundation.h>

int main(int argc, const char * argv[])
{
    @autoreleasepool {

        // Create three NSDate objects
        NSDate *now = [NSDate date];
        NSDate *tomorrow = [now dateByAddingTimeInterval:24.0 * 60.0 * 60.0];
        NSDate *yesterday = [now dateByAddingTimeInterval:-24.0 * 60.0 * 60.0];

        // Create an array containing all three (nil terminates the list)
        NSArray *dateList = [NSArray arrayWithObjects:now, tomorrow, yesterday, nil];

        for (NSDate *d in dateList) {
            NSLog(@"Here is a date: %@", d);
        }

    }
    return 0;
}
```

This type of loop is known as *fast enumeration*, and it is an extremely efficient way to walk through the items in an array. There is one restriction: you may not add to or remove from the array while enumerating over it.

NSMutableArray

Arrays come in two flavors:

- An instance of **NSArray** is created with a list of pointers. You can never add or remove a pointer from that array.

- An instance of **NSMutableArray** is similar to an instance of **NSArray**, but you can add and remove pointers. (**NSMutableArray** is a *subclass* of **NSArray**. More about subclasses in Chapter 18.)

Change your example to use an **NSMutableArray** instance and methods from the **NSMutableArray** class:

```
#import <Foundation/Foundation.h>

int main(int argc, const char * argv[])
{
    @autoreleasepool {

        // Create three NSDate objects
        NSDate *now = [NSDate date];
        NSDate *tomorrow = [now dateByAddingTimeInterval:24.0 * 60.0 * 60.0];
        NSDate *yesterday = [now dateByAddingTimeInterval:-24.0 * 60.0 * 60.0];

        // Create an empty array
        NSMutableArray *dateList = [NSMutableArray array];

        // Add the dates to the array
        [dateList addObject:now];
        [dateList addObject:tomorrow];
```

```
        // Put yesterday at the beginning of the list
        [dateList insertObject:yesterday atIndex:0];

        for (NSDate *d in dateList) {
            NSLog(@"Here is a date: %@", d);
        }

        // Remove yesterday
        [dateList removeObjectAtIndex:0];
        NSLog(@"Now the first date is %@", [dateList objectAtIndex:0]);

    }
    return 0;
}
```

Challenges

Create a new Foundation Command Line Tool named Groceries. Start by creating an empty **NSMutableArray** object. Then add several grocery-like items to the array. (You'll have to create those, too.) Finally, use fast enumeration to print out your grocery list.

This next challenge is, well, more challenging. Read through the following program, which finds common proper names that contain two adjacent A's.

```
#import <Foundation/Foundation.h>

int main (int argc, const char * argv[])
{
    @autoreleasepool {

        // Read in a file as a huge string (ignoring the possibility of an error)
        NSString *nameString
                = [NSString stringWithContentsOfFile:@"/usr/share/dict/propernames"
                                        encoding:NSUTF8StringEncoding
                                           error:NULL];

        // Break it into an array of strings
        NSArray *names = [nameString componentsSeparatedByString:@"\n"];

        // Go through the array one string at a time
        for (NSString *n in names) {

            // Look for the string "aa" in a case-insensitive manner
            NSRange r = [n rangeOfString:@"AA" options:NSCaseInsensitiveSearch];

            // Was it found?
            if (r.location != NSNotFound) {
                NSLog(@"%@", n);
            }
        }

    }
    return 0;
}
```

The file /usr/share/dict/propernames contains common proper names. The file/usr/share/dict/
words contains regular words (not proper names). Now write a program based on the one above that

finds common proper names that are also regular words. For example, "Glen" is a guy's name, and "glen" is a narrow valley.

When a computer orders strings, it typically considers uppercase letters as coming before lowercase letters. To do a comparison that ignores the case, use the method **caseInsensitiveCompare:**.

```
NSString *a = @"ABC";
NSString *b = @"abc";
if ([a caseInsensitiveCompare:b] == NSOrderedSame) {
    NSLog(@"a and b are equal");
}

if ([a caseInsensitiveCompare:b] == NSOrderedAscending) {
    NSLog(@"a comes before b");
}

if ([a caseInsensitiveCompare:b] == NSOrderedDescending) {
    NSLog(@"b comes before a");
}
```

In this challenge, use **caseInsensitiveCompare:** to see that "Glen" and "glen" are equivalent.

16

Developer Documentation

In the last chapter, I gave you some useful tidbits about the class **NSArray**. When you begin programming without my guidance (including taking on Challenges in this book), you will need to find such tidbits yourself. This is where Apple's documentation comes in.

To see the documentation in Xcode, bring up the Organizer (click the 🔲 button at the top right of the Xcode window) and choose the Documentation tab.

Figure 16.1   Docs in the Organizer

There are essentially five types of documentation that Apple provides:

- *References*: Every Objective-C class and every C function is tersely documented in these pages.

- *Guides and Getting Starteds*: Guides are less terse and group ideas conceptually. For example, there is an *Error Handling Programming Guide* that describes the myriad of ways that Mac and iOS developers can be informed that something has gone wrong.

- *Sample Code*: These are small, complete projects that demonstrate how Apple expects its technology to be used. For example, there is a WeatherMap project that shows how to make custom annotations on iOS map views.

- *Release Notes*: Every time a new version of Mac OS or iOS comes out, it is accompanied by a set of release notes. The release notes tell developers what has changed since the last version.

- *Technical notes, Articles, Coding How-to's,* and *Technical Q&As,*: These are bite-sized documents that address specific issues.

You can browse the documentation, but there is a lot of it. More commonly, you will access the documentation via search.

Reference pages

At the top of the lefthand pane in Organizer, click the ● button to bring up the search panel. Type NSArray into the search field, and the search results will appear below the search field. In the Reference section, click on NSArray to see the *reference page* for **NSArray**.

Figure 16.2   NSArray reference page

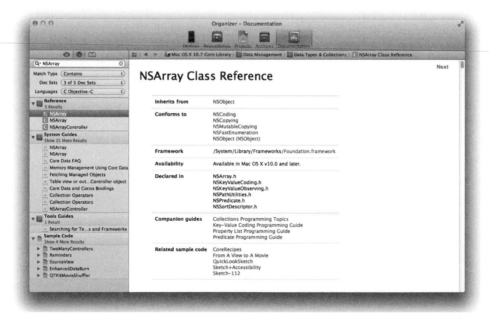

It would be difficult to overstate how important these reference pages will be to you and how important they are for programmers of all levels. Apple has worked really hard to create huge libraries of code for your convenience. You will learn about these libraries primarily through reference pages. As you go through this book, take a moment to look up the reference pages for new classes as you use them and see what else they can do. You can also search for methods, functions, constants, and properties by name. (You'll learn about properties in Chapter 17.) The more comfortable you get using these pages, the faster your development will go.

At the top of the class reference for **NSArray**, you can learn several things about the class. It inherits from **NSObject**. (More about this soon in Chapter 18.) It conforms to several protocols (which we'll discuss in Chapter 25). It is part of the Foundation framework and has shipped with every version of Mac OS X and every version of iOS.

At the end of the header, there is a list of guides that discuss **NSArray** and sample code that shows off the capabilities of **NSArray**. Click on *Collections Programming Topics* to open that guide.

Figure 16.3   Collections Programming Topics

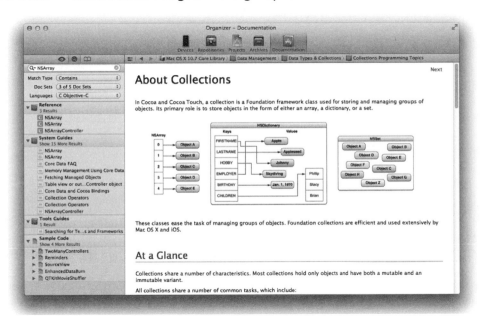

This particular guide discusses the collection classes (including **NSArray** and **NSMutableArray**). Unlike the class reference, a guide is a pleasant read, in which ideas are introduced in a sensical order.

Now use the back button at the top of the document pane to go back to the **NSArray** reference page. Curious about what other messages you can send to an **NSArray**? Scroll down the reference page and find the list of methods that **NSArray** implements. Say you're looking for a way to check if an array contains a particular item. In that case, you'd run across the **containsObject:** method and read its description:

Figure 16.4   Reference for containsObject:

---

containsObject:

Returns a Boolean value that indicates whether a given object is present in the array.

```
- (BOOL)containsObject:(id)anObject
```

Parameters
anObject
   An object.

Return Value
YES if *anObject* is present in the array, otherwise NO.

Discussion
This method determines whether *anObject* is present in the array by sending an isEqual: message to each of the array's objects (and passing *anObject* as the parameter to each isEqual: message).

Availability
Available in Mac OS X v10.0 and later.

See Also
   — indexOfObject:
   — indexOfObjectIdenticalTo:

Related Sample Code
Sketch+Accessibility
TimelineToTC

Declared In
NSArray.h

Now you know everything you need to know to send this message in your code.

Quick Help

But there's an easier way to get from the editor where you're writing code to the wellspring of knowledge in the documentation. Close the Organizer and return to your DateList project.

In main.m, find the line that includes [dateList addObject:now]. Hold down the Option key and click on **addObject:**. The Quick Help window will appear with the information about that method:

Figure 16.5   Quick Help window

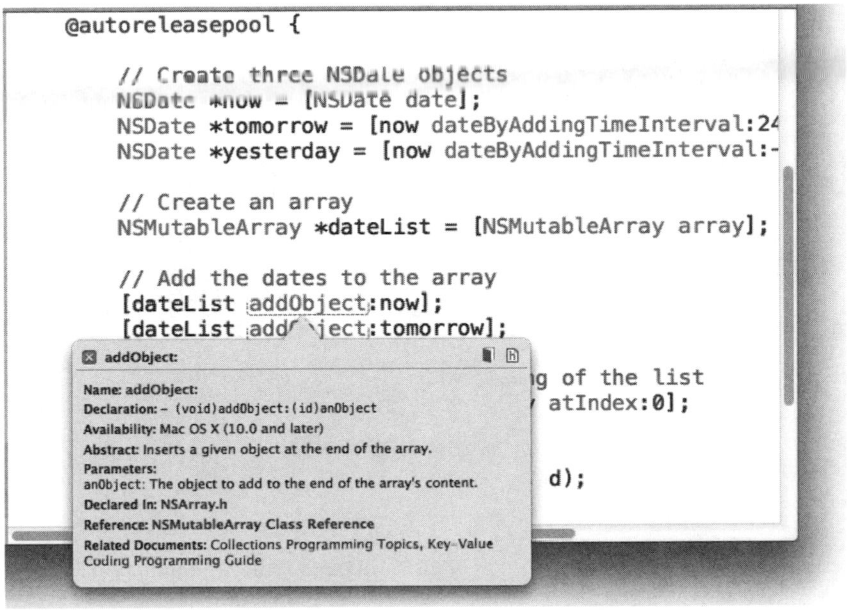

Notice that there are links in the Quick Help window. If you click a link, it will open the appropriate documentation in the Organizer. Handy, right?

If you want to see that Quick Help all the time, you can open it as a pane in Xcode.

In the upper-right corner of the Xcode window, find a segmented control called View that looks like ▢▢▢ and indicates Xcode's lefthand, bottom, and righthand panes. Selecting and de-selecting these buttons will hide and show the respective panes.

The lefthand pane, which you've used plenty by now, is called the navigator. The bottom pane, which you've also seen, includes the console and is called the debug area. The righthand pane is called Utilities. Click the righthand View button to reveal Utilities. At the top of Utilities, click the ⦦ button to reveal the Quick Help pane.

This pane will show help for the text selected in the editor. Try it: just select the word "NSMutableArray" in the editor:

Figure 16.6   Quick Help pane

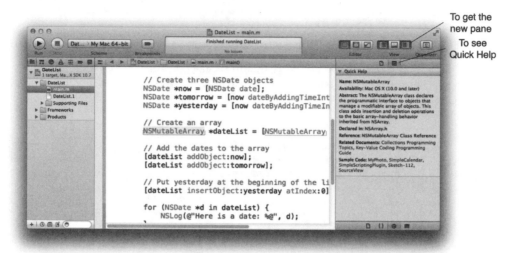

Note that when you select something else, the Quick Help pane will immediately update to show the documentation for the new selection.

Other options and resources

If you Option-double-click on any text, the Organizer will search for that string.

If you Command-click on any class, function, or method, Xcode will show you the file where it is declared. (Try Command-clicking the word "NSMutableArray".)

Figure 16.7   The declaration of NSMutableArray

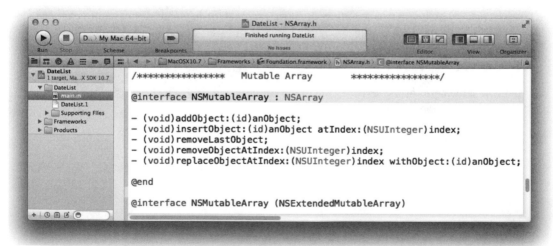

If there are several declarations that match, you'll get a pop-up when you Command-click. Try Command-clicking **addObject:**.

From time to time, Xcode will call back to the mothership to see if there is any updated documentation. It will download the updates and re-index them for easy searching. You can trigger an immediate check for updates in the preferences panel for Xcode.

Apple hosts a collection of discussion mailing lists at `http://lists.apple.com/`, and several of them are devoted to developer topics. If you can't find an answer in the docs, try searching the archives of the lists. (As a courtesy to the thousands of people on each list, please search the archives carefully before posting a question.)

There is one more resource that you should know about: `stackoverflow.com`. This website is a very popular place where programmers ask and answer questions. If you can think up a few keywords that describe the sort of problem you are having, you can probably find an answer there.

17

Your First Class

So far, you have only used classes created by Apple. Now you get to write your own class. Remember that a class describes objects in two ways:

- methods (both instance methods and class methods) implemented by the class

- instance variables within each instance of the class

You're going to write a **Person** class, similar to the struct Person you wrote in Chapter 10. Your class will be defined in two files: Person.h and Person.m. Person.h, known as the *header* or *interface file*, will contain the declarations of instance variables and methods. Person.m is known as the *implementation file*. This is where you write out the steps for, or *implement*, each method.

Create a new project: a Foundation Command Line Tool named BMITime.

To create a new class, select File → New → New File.... From the Mac OS X section on the left, select Cocoa and choose the Objective-C class template. Name your class Person and make it a subclass of NSObject. Finally, make sure the BMITime target is checked and click Save.

Notice that the new class files, Person.h and Person.m, now appear in the project navigator. Open Person.h. Declare two instance variables and three instance methods:

```
#import <Foundation/Foundation.h>

// The class Person inherits all the instance variables
// and methods defined by the class NSObject
@interface Person : NSObject
{
    // It has two instance variables
    float heightInMeters;
    int weightInKilos;
}

// You will be able to set those instance variables using these methods
- (void)setHeightInMeters:(float)h;
- (void)setWeightInKilos:(int)w;

// This method calculates the Body Mass Index
- (float)bodyMassIndex;
@end
```

Notice that you declared the instance variables inside of curly braces and you declared the methods after the variables and outside of the curly braces.

To the compiler, this code says "I am defining a new class called **Person** that has all the methods and instance variables of the class **NSObject**. Furthermore, I'm adding in two new instance variables: a float called heightInMeters and an int called weightInKilos. Also, I'm going to add three instance methods, which will be implemented in Person.m."

Notice that **setHeightInMeters:** expects a float argument and does not return a value, **setWeightInKilos:** expects an int argument and does not return a value, and **bodyMassIndex** takes no arguments and returns a float.

Now open Person.m. Delete any existing methods and implement the methods you declared:

```objc
#import "Person.h"

@implementation Person

- (void)setHeightInMeters:(float)h
{
    heightInMeters = h;
}
- (void)setWeightInKilos:(int)w
{
    weightInKilos = w;
}
- (float)bodyMassIndex
{
    return weightInKilos / (heightInMeters * heightInMeters);
}

@end
```

Note that Xcode imported Person.h for you. Also note that the names of the methods you implement must exactly match the ones you declared in the header file. In Xcode, this is easy; as you start typing a method in the implementation file, Xcode will suggest names of methods you've already declared.

Now that you've implemented all the methods you declared in Person.h, your class is complete. Edit main.m to exercise it a bit:

```objc
#import <Foundation/Foundation.h>
#import "Person.h"

int main(int argc, const char * argv[])
{
    @autoreleasepool {

        // Create an instance of Person
        Person *person = [[Person alloc] init];

        // Give the instance variables interesting values
        [person setWeightInKilos:96];
        [person setHeightInMeters:1.8];

        // Call the bodyMassIndex method
        float bmi = [person bodyMassIndex];
        NSLog(@"person has a BMI of %f", bmi);

    }
    return 0;
}
```

Build and run the program. Notice that you imported `Person.h` so that the compiler will know how your methods are declared before they are used in **main()**.

Figure 17.1   Object diagram for BMITime

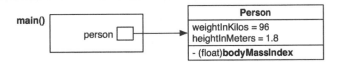

Accessor methods

Note that when we did this same exercise with structs instead of objects, we accessed the data members of the structure directly in **main()**:

```
person.weightInKilos = 96;
person.heightInMeters = 1.8;
```

In object-oriented thinking, we do our best to keep the instance variables of an object private; that is, they are known and accessed only by the object itself. However, because we want to give methods and functions outside of **Person** the ability to set a person's weight and height, we created the methods **setWeightInKilos:** and **setHeightInMeters:**. We call these *setter methods*.

A setter method allows other methods to set the value of an instance variable. A *getter method* allows other methods to read the value of an instance variable. Setter and getter methods are also known as *accessor methods*, or just *accessors*.

Add declarations for the getter methods to `Person.h`:

```
#import <Foundation/Foundation.h>

@interface Person : NSObject
{
    float heightInMeters;
    int weightInKilos;
}

// You will be able to set those instance variables
- (float)heightInMeters;
- (void)setHeightInMeters:(float)h;
- (int)weightInKilos;
- (void)setWeightInKilos:(int)w;

- (float)bodyMassIndex;

@end
```

You might wonder why the names of the getter methods don't include **get** to match the setter method names. This is an Objective-C naming convention. The name of the method for reading an instance variable is simply the name of that instance variable.

Now return to `Person.m` and implement your getter methods:

```
@implementation Person

- (float)heightInMeters
{
    return heightInMeters;
}

- (void)setHeightInMeters:(float)h
{
    heightInMeters = h;
}

- (int)weightInKilos
{
    return weightInKilos;
}

- (void)setWeightInKilos:(int)w
{
    weightInKilos = w;
}
- (float)bodyMassIndex
{
    return weightInKilos / (heightInMeters * heightInMeters);
}

@end
```

Finally, in main.m, use those methods:

```
#import "Person.h"

int main(int argc, const char * argv[])
{
    @autoreleasepool {

        // Create an instance of Person
        Person *person = [[Person alloc] init];

        // Give the instance variables interesting values
        [person setWeightInKilos:96];
        [person setHeightInMeters:1.8];

        // Call the bodyMassIndex method
        float bmi = [person bodyMassIndex];
        NSLog(@"person (%d, %f) has a BMI of %f",
            [person weightInKilos], [person heightInMeters], bmi);

    }
    return 0;
}
```

Build and run the program.

Dot notation

Objective-C programmers call accessor methods a lot. Apple decided to create a shortcut for calling an accessor. This shortcut makes these two lines of code exactly the same:

```
p = [x fido];
p = x.fido;
```

It also makes these two lines of code exactly the same:

```
[x setFido:3];
x.fido = 3;
```

The form that uses the period instead of the square brackets is known as *dot notation*.

I avoid using dot notation. I feel it obscures the fact that a message is being sent, and it isn't consistent with the way we do every other message send in the system. You are welcome to use dot notation, but it will not appear anywhere else in this book.

Properties

Notice that most of our code in the **Person** class is devoted to accessor methods. Apple has created a handy way to simplify writing accessor methods called *properties*. With a property, you can declare both the setter and getter methods in one line.

In Person.h, replace the declaration of the setter and getter methods with the @property construct:

```
#import <Foundation/Foundation.h>

@interface Person : NSObject
{
    float heightInMeters;
    int weightInKilos;
}
@property float heightInMeters;
@property int weightInKilos;

- (float)bodyMassIndex;
@end
```

You have not changed this class at all with this edit. You are just using a terser syntax.

Now, take a look at the Person.m file. It is chock-full of simple and predictable accessor methods. In the case where your accessors do nothing special, you can just tell the compiler to *synthesize* default accessor methods based on each @property declaration. Delete the accessors and replace them with a call to @synthesize:

```
#import "Person.h"

@implementation Person

@synthesize heightInMeters, weightInKilos;

- (float)bodyMassIndex
{
    return weightInKilos / (heightInMeters * heightInMeters);
}

@end
```

Build and run the program. Everything should work the same as before with code that is far simpler and easier to maintain.

self

Inside any method, you have access to the implicit local variable self. self is a pointer to the object that is running the method. It is used when an object wants to send a message to itself. For example, many Objective-C programmers are quite religious about accessor methods; they never read or write to an instance variable except using its accessor methods. Update your **bodyMassIndex** method to please the purists:

```
- (float)bodyMassIndex
{
    float h = [self heightInMeters];
    return [self weightInKilos] / (h * h);
}
```

Here an instance of **Person** sends itself two messages, **heightInMeters** and **weightInKilos**, to get the values of its instance variables.

You can also pass self as an argument to let other objects know where the current object is. For example, your **Person** class might have a method **addYourselfToArray:** that would look like this:

```
- (void)addYourselfToArray:(NSMutableArray *)theArray
{
    [theArray addObject:self];
}
```

Here you use self to tell the array where the instance of **Person** lives. It is literally its address.

Multiple files

Notice that your project now has executable code in two files: main.m and Person.m. (Person.h is a declaration of a class, but there is no executable code in it.) When you build the project, these files are compiled separately and then linked together. It is not uncommon that a real-world project will consist of hundreds of files of C and Objective-C code.

You can also link in libraries of code. For example, you might find a great library for parsing data from digital telescopes on the Internet. If your program needed this capability, you would compile that library and add it to your project. When Xcode built your program, it would link in all the functions and classes defined in that library.

Challenge

Create new Foundation Command Line Tool called Stocks. Then create a class called **StockHolding** to represent a stock that you have purchased. It will be a subclass of **NSObject**. For instance variables, it will have two floats named purchaseSharePrice and currentSharePrice and one int named numberOfShares. Create accessor methods for the instance variables. Create two other instance methods:

```
- (float)costInDollars;  // purchaseSharePrice * numberOfShares
- (float)valueInDollars; // currentSharePrice * numberOfShares
```

In **main()**, fill an array with three instances of **StockHolding**. Then iterate through the array printing out the value of each.

Figure 17.2　An array of StockHolding objects

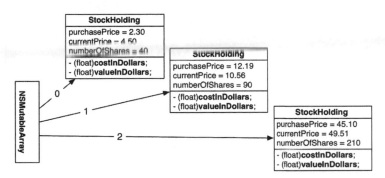

18

Inheritance

When you created the **Person** class, you declared it to be a subclass of **NSObject**. This means that every instance of **Person** will have the instance variables and methods defined in **NSObject** as well as the instance variables and methods defined in **Person**. We say that **Person** *inherits* the instance variables and methods from **NSObject**. In this section, we are going to delve a bit into inheritance.

Open up the BMITime project and create a new file: an Objective-C class. Name it Employee and create it as a subclass of **NSObject**. Soon, we will change the **Employee** class to be a subclass of **Person**. Makes sense, right? Employees are people. They have heights and weights. However, not all people are employees. We'll also add an employee-specific instance variable to our class – an employee ID.

Figure 18.1   Inheritance diagram of some classes you know

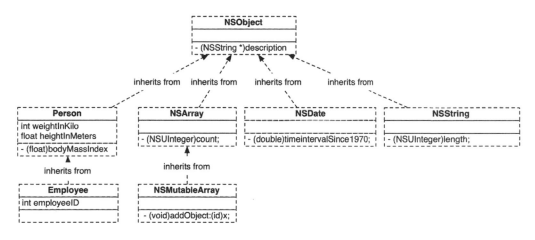

Open Employee.h. Import Person.h, change the superclass to **Person**, and add an instance variable to hold the employee's ID number:

```
#import "Person.h"

@interface Employee : Person
{
    int employeeID;
}
@property int employeeID;
@end
```

Open `Employee.m` and synthesize the accessors:

```
#import "Employee.h"
@implementation Employee

@synthesize employeeID;

@end
```

Now you have a new **Employee** class with all the instance variables of **Person** and a new instance variable called `employeeID`. Instances of **Employee** will respond to all the same messages that an instance of **Person** will. Instances of **Employee** will also respond to the messages **setEmployeeID:** and **employeeID**.

And, because **Person** inherits from **NSObject**, **Employee** also inherits all the instance variables and methods from **NSObject**. All objects inherit (either directly or indirectly) from **NSObject**.

NSObject has many methods, but only one instance variable: the `isa` pointer. Every object's `isa` pointer points back to the class that created it.

Figure 18.2   Object diagram for BMITime

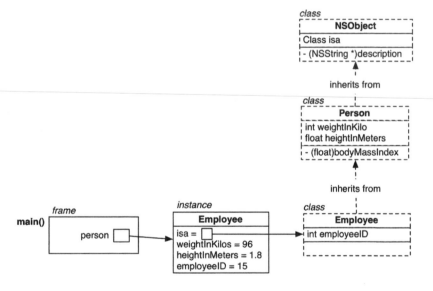

Let's say that you send the message **fido** to an object. In order to respond to this message, the object uses the `isa` pointer to find its class and ask, "Do you have an instance method named **fido**?" If the class has a method named **fido**, it gets executed. If the class doesn't have a **fido** method, it asks its superclass, "Do you have an instance method called **fido**?" And up, up the chain it goes on the hunt for a method named **fido**. The hunt stops when the method is found or when the top of the chain is reached. At the top of the chain, **NSObject** says, "Nope, no **fido** method." Then you get an error message that says something like "This instance of **Employee** does not respond to the **fido** selector."

Try it. Open up main.m and send the instance of **Person** a message it won't understand:

```
int main(int argc, const char * argv[])
{
    @autoreleasepool {

        // Create an instance of Person
        id person = [[Person alloc] init];

        // Give the instance variables interesting values
        [person setWeightInKilos:96];
        [person setHeightInMeters:1.8];

        // Call the bodyMassIndex method
        float bmi = [person bodyMassIndex];
        NSLog(@"person (%d, %f) has a BMI of %f",
              [person weightInKilos], [person heightInMeters], bmi);

        [person count];

    }
    return 0;
}
```

Build and run the program. (Ignore the warning from the compiler because you're doing this on purpose. In most cases, you'll want to pay attention to this warning if you see it!) You should see a runtime exception logged to the console:

```
*** Terminating app due to uncaught exception 'NSInvalidArgumentException',
    reason: '-[Person count]: unrecognized selector sent to instance 0x100108de0'
```

After examining the exception, delete the problematic line before continuing.

You've created this new **Employee** class, but you haven't used it yet. Change main.m to use **Employee**:

```
#import <Foundation/Foundation.h>
#import "Employee.h"

int main(int argc, const char * argv[])
{
    @autoreleasepool {

        // Create an instance of Person
        Person * person = [[Employee alloc] init];

        // Give the instance variables interesting values
        [person setWeightInKilos:96];
        [person setHeightInMeters:1.8];

        // Call the bodyMassIndex method
        float bmi = [person bodyMassIndex];
        NSLog(@"person (%d, %f) has a BMI of %f",
              [person weightInKilos], [person heightInMeters], bmi);

    }
    return 0;
}
```

Notice that your person variable is still declared as a pointer to a **Person**. Think this will cause a problem? Build and run the program, and you'll see that your program still works fine. This is because an employee is a kind of person – it can do anything a person can. That is, we can use an instance of **Employee** anywhere that the program expects an instance of **Person**.

Now, however, you're going to use a method that is unique to **Employee**, so you must change the type of the pointer variable:

```
#import <Foundation/Foundation.h>
#import "Employee.h"

int main(int argc, const char * argv[])
{
    @autoreleasepool {

        // Create an instance of Person
        Employee *person = [[Employee alloc] init];

        // Give the instance variables interesting values
        [person setWeightInKilos:96];
        [person setHeightInMeters:1.8];
        [person setEmployeeID:15];

        // Call the bodyMassIndex method
        float bmi = [person bodyMassIndex];
        NSLog(@"Employee %d has a BMI of %f", [person employeeID], bmi);

    }
    return 0;
}
```

Overriding methods

To review, when a message is sent, the search for the method of that name starts at the object's class and goes up the inheritance hierarchy. The first implementation that is found is the one that gets executed. Thus, you can *override* inherited methods with a custom implementation. Let's say, for example, that you decided that employees always have a Body Mass Index of 19. In this case, you might override the **bodyMassIndex** method in **Employee**. Open Employee.m and do so:

```
#import "Employee.h"
@implementation Employee

@synthesize employeeID;

- (float)bodyMassIndex
{
    return 19.0;
}
@end
```

Build and run the program and note that your new implementation of **bodyMassIndex** is the one that gets executed – not the implementation from **Person**.

Notice that you implemented **bodyMassIndex** in Employee.m, but you didn't declare it in Employee.h. Declaring a method in the header file advertises the method so that instances of other classes can call it. However, because **Employee** inherits from **Person**, everyone already knows that instances of **Employee** have a **bodyMassIndex** method. There is no need to advertise it again.

super

What if you decided that all employees get an automatic 10% off their BMI as calculated in the **Person**'s implementation? You could, of course, retype the code in the **Employee** implementation, but it would be so much more convenient to call **Person**'s version of **bodyMassIndex** and multiply the result by 0.9 before returning it. To do this, you use the super directive. Try it in **Employee.m**:

```
#import "Employee.h"
@implementation Employee

@synthesize employeeID;

- (float)bodyMassIndex
{
    float normalBMI = [super bodyMassIndex];
    return normalBMI * 0.9;
}

@end
```

Build and run the program.

To be precise, the super directive says "Run this method, but start the search for its implementation at my superclass."

Challenge

This challenge builds on the challenge from the previous chapter.

Create a subclass of **StockHolding** called **ForeignStockHolding**. Give **ForeignStockHolding** an additional instance variable: conversionRate, which will be a float. (The conversion rate is what you need to multiply the local price by to get a price in US dollars. Assume the purchasePrice and currentPrice are in the local currency.) Override **costInDollars** and **valueInDollars** to do the right thing.

In **main()**, add a few instances of **ForeignStockHolding** to your array.

Figure 18.3   StockHolding and ForeignStockHolding objects

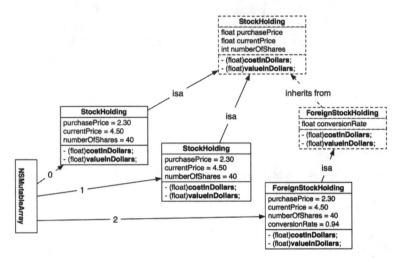

19

Object Instance Variables

Thus far, the instance variables declared in your classes have been simple C types like int or float. It's far more common for instance variables to be pointers to other objects. An object instance variable points to another object and describes a relationship between the two objects. Usually, object instance variables fall into one of three categories:

- *Object-type attributes*: a pointer to a simple, value-like object like an **NSString** or an **NSNumber**. For example, an employee's last name would be stored in an **NSString**. Thus, an instance of **Employee** would have an instance variable that would be a pointer to an instance of **NSString**.

- *To-one relationships*: a pointer to a single complex object. For example, an employee might have a spouse. Thus, an instance of **Employee** would have an instance variable that would be a pointer to an instance of **Person**.

- *To-many relationships*: a pointer to an instance of a collection class, such as an **NSMutableArray**. (We'll see other examples of collections in Chapter 21.) For example, an employee might have children. In this case, the instance of **Employee** would have an instance variable that would be a pointer to an instance of **NSMutableArray**. The **NSMutableArray** would hold a list of pointers to one or more **Person** objects.

(Notice that, in the above list, I refer to "an **NSString**." **NSString** is the class, but "an **NSString**" is shorthand for an **NSString** *instance*. This usage is a little confusing but very common, so it's good to get comfortable with it.)

Figure 19.1   An Employee with object instance variables

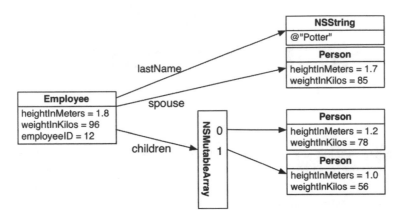

Notice that, as in other diagrams, pointers are represented by arrows. In addition, those pointers are named. So an **Employee** would have three new instance variables: lastName, spouse, and children. The declaration of **Employee**'s instance variables would look like this:

```
@interface Employee : Person
{
    int employeeID;
    NSString *lastName;
    Person *spouse;
    NSMutableArray *children;
}
```

With the exception of employeeID, these variables are all pointers. Object instance variables are always pointers. For example, the variable spouse is a pointer to another object that lives on the heap. The *pointer* spouse is inside the **Employee** object, but the **Person** *object* it points to is not. Objects don't live inside other objects. The employee object contains its employee ID (the variable and the value itself), but it only knows where its spouse lives in memory.

There are two important side-effects to objects pointing to rather than containing other objects:

- One object can take on several roles. For example, it is likely that the employee's spouse is also listed as the emergency contact for the children:

Figure 19.2   One object, multiple roles

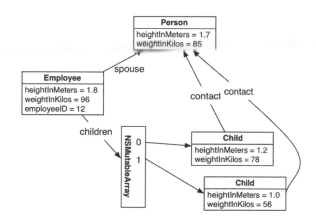

- You end up with a lot of distinct objects using up your program's memory. You need the objects being used to stay around, but you want the unnecessary ones to be deallocated (have their memory returned to the heap) so that their memory can be reused. Reusing memory keeps your program's memory footprint as small as possible, which will make your entire computer feel more responsive. On a mobile device (like an iPhone), the operating system will kill your program if its memory footprint gets too big.

Object ownership and ARC

To manage these issues, we have the idea of *object ownership*. When an object has an object instance variable, the object with the pointer is said to *own* the object that is being pointed to.

From the other end of things, an object knows how many *owners* it currently has. For instance, in the diagram above, the instance of **Person** has three owners: the **Employee** object and the two **Child** objects. When an object has zero owners, it figures no one needs it around anymore and deallocates itself.

The owner count of each object is handled by Automatic Reference Counting. ARC is a recent development in Objective-C. Before Xcode 4.2, we managed ownership manually and spent a lot of time and effort doing so. (There's more about manual reference counting and how it worked in the final section of Chapter 20. All the code in this book, however, assumes that you are using ARC.)

Let's expand the BMITime project to see how ownership works in practice. It is not uncommon for a company to keep track of what assets have been issued to which employee. We are going to create an **Asset** class, and each **Employee** will have an array containing his or her assets.

Figure 19.3   Employees and assets

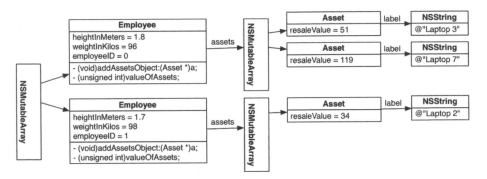

This is often called a "parent-child" relationship: The parent (an instance of **Employee**) has a collection of children (an **NSMutableArray** of **Asset** objects).

Creating the Asset class

Create a new file: an Objective-C subclass of **NSObject**. Name it Asset. Open Asset.h and declare two instance variables and two properties:

```
#import <Foundation/Foundation.h>

@interface Asset : NSObject
{
    NSString *label;
    unsigned int resaleValue;
}
@property (strong) NSString *label;
@property unsigned int resaleValue;
@end
```

Notice the strong modifier on the @property declaration for label. That says, "This is a pointer to an object upon which I claim ownership." (We'll talk about other options for this property attribute in Chapter 20.)

Remember that when an object doesn't have any owners, it is deallocated. When an object is being deallocated, it is sent the message **dealloc**. (Every object inherits the **dealloc** method from **NSObject**.) You are going to override **dealloc** so that you can see when instances of **Asset** are being deallocated.

To make it clear which particular instance of **Asset** is being deallocated, you'll also implement another **NSObject** method, **description**. This method returns a string that is a useful description of an instance of the class. For **Asset**, you're going to have **description** return a string that includes the instance's label and resaleValue.

Open Asset.m. Synthesize the accessors for your instance variables and then override **description** and **dealloc**.

```
#import "Asset.h"

@implementation Asset

@synthesize label, resaleValue;

- (NSString *)description
{
    return [NSString stringWithFormat:@"<%@: $%d >",
                [self label], [self resaleValue]];
}

- (void)dealloc
{
    NSLog(@"deallocating %@", self);
}

@end
```

Notice the %@ token in the format strings in the code above. This token is replaced with the result of sending the **description** message to the corresponding variable (which must be a pointer to an object so that it can receive this message).

Try building what you have so far to see if you made any errors typing it in. You can build your program without running it by using the keyboard shortcut Command-B. This is useful for testing your code without taking the time to run the program or when you know the program isn't ready to run yet. Plus, it's always a good idea to build after making changes so that if you've introduced a syntax error, you can find and fix it right away. If you wait, you won't be as sure what changes are responsible for your "new" bug.

Adding a to-many relationship to Employee

Now you are going to add a to-many relationship to the **Employee** class. Recall that a to-many relationship includes a collection object (like an array) and the objects contained in the collection. There are two other important things to know about collections and ownership:

- When an object is added to the collection, the collection establishes a pointer to the object, and the object gains an owner.

- When an object is removed from a collection, the collection gets rid of its pointer to the object, and the object loses an owner.

To set up the to-many relationship in **Employee**, you'll need a new instance variable to hold a pointer to the mutable array of assets. You'll also need a couple of methods. Open Employee.h and add them:

```
#import "Person.h"
@class Asset;

@interface Employee : Person
{
    int employeeID;
    NSMutableArray *assets;
}
@property int employeeID;
- (void)addAssetsObject:(Asset *)a;
- (unsigned int)valueOfAssets;

@end
```

Notice the line that says @class Asset;. As the compiler is reading this file, it will come across the class name **Asset**. If it doesn't know about the class, it will throw an error. The @class Asset; line tells the compiler "There is a class called **Asset**. Don't panic when you see it in this file. That's all you need to know for now."

Using @class instead of #import gives the compiler less information, but makes the processing of this particular file faster. You can use @class with Employee.h and other header files because the compiler doesn't need to know a lot to process a file of declarations.

Now turn your attention to Employee.m. With a to-many relationship, you need to create the collection object (an array, in our case) before you put anything in it. You can do this when the original object (an employee) is first created, or you can be lazy and wait until the collection is needed. Let's be lazy.

```
#import "Employee.h"
#import "Asset.h"

@implementation Employee

@synthesize employeeID;

- (void)addAssetsObject:(Asset *)a
{
    // Is assets nil?
    if (!assets) {

        // Create the array
        assets = [[NSMutableArray alloc] init];
    }
    [assets addObject:a];
}

- (unsigned int)valueOfAssets
{
    // Sum up the resale value of the assets
    unsigned int sum = 0;
    for (Asset *a in assets) {
        sum += [a resaleValue];
    }
    return sum;
}
```

```
- (float)bodyMassIndex
{
    float normalBMI = [super bodyMassIndex];
    return normalBMI * 0.9;
}

- (NSString *)description
{
    return [NSString stringWithFormat:@"<Employee %d: $%d in assets>",
            [self employeeID], [self valueOfAssets]];
}

- (void)dealloc
{
    NSLog(@"deallocating %@", self);
}

@end
```

To process the Employee.m file, the compiler needs to know a lot about the **Asset** class. Thus, you imported Asset.h instead of using @class.

Also notice that you overrode **description** and **dealloc** to track the deallocation of **Employee** instances.

Build the project to see if you've made any mistakes.

Now you need to create some assets and assign them to employees. Edit main.m:

```
#import <Foundation/Foundation.h>
#import "Employee.h"
#import "Asset.h"

int main(int argc, const char * argv[])
{
    @autoreleasepool {

        // Create an array of Employee objects
        NSMutableArray *employees = [[NSMutableArray alloc] init];

        for (int i = 0; i < 10; i++) {

            // Create an instance of Employee
            Employee *person = [[Employee alloc] init];

            // Give the instance variables interesting values
            [person setWeightInKilos:90 + i];
            [person setHeightInMeters:1.8 - i/10.0];
            [person setEmployeeID:i];

            // Put the employee in the employees array
            [employees addObject:person];
        }

        // Create 10 assets
        for (int i = 0; i < 10; i++) {

            // Create an asset
            Asset *asset = [[Asset alloc] init];
```

```
                    // Give it an interesting label
                    NSString *currentLabel = [NSString stringWithFormat:@"Laptop %d", i];
                    [asset setLabel:currentLabel];
                    [asset setResaleValue:i * 17];

                    // Get a random number between 0 and 9 inclusive
                    NSUInteger randomIndex = random() % [employees count];

                    // Find that employee
                    Employee *randomEmployee = [employees objectAtIndex:randomIndex];

                    // Assign the asset to the employee
                    [randomEmployee addAssetsObject:asset];
                }


            NSLog(@"Employees: %@", employees);

            NSLog(@"Giving up ownership of one employee");

            [employees removeObjectAtIndex:5];

            NSLog(@"Giving up ownership of array");

            employees = nil;

        }
        return 0;
    }
```

Build and run the program. You should see something like this:

```
Employees: (
    "<Employee 0: $0 in assets>",
    "<Employee 1: $153 in assets>",
    "<Employee 2: $119 in assets>",
    "<Employee 3: $68 in assets>",
    "<Employee 4: $0 in assets>",
    "<Employee 5: $136 in assets>",
    "<Employee 6: $119 in assets>",
    "<Employee 7: $34 in assets>",
    "<Employee 8: $0 in assets>",
    "<Employee 9: $136 in assets>"
)
Giving up ownership of one employee
deallocating <Employee 5: $136 in assets>
deallocating <Laptop 3: $51 >
deallocating <Laptop 5: $85  >
Giving up ownership of array
deallocating <Employee 0: $0 in assets>
deallocating <Employee 1: $153 in assets>
deallocating <Laptop 9: $153 >
…
deallocating <Employee 9: $136 in assets>
deallocing <Laptop 8: $136 >
```

When employee #5 is removed from the array, it is deallocated because it has no owner. Then its assets are deallocated because they have no owner. (And you'll have to trust me on this: the labels (instances of **NSString**) of the deallocated assets are also deallocated once they have no owner.)

When `employees` is set to `nil`, the array no longer has an owner. So it is deallocated, which sets up an even larger chain reaction of memory clean-up and deallocation when, suddenly, none of the employees has an owner.

Tidy, right? As the objects become unnecessary, they are being deallocated. This is good. When unnecessary objects don't get deallocated, you are said to have a *memory leak*. Typically a memory leak causes more and more objects to linger unnecessarily over time. The memory footprint of your application just gets bigger and bigger. On iOS, the operating system will eventually kill your application. On Mac OS X, the performance of the entire system will suffer as the machine spends more and more time swapping data out of memory and onto disk.

Challenge

Using the **StockHolding** class from a previous challenge, make a tool that creates an instance of a **Portfolio** class and fills it with stock holdings. A portfolio can tell you what its current value is.

20

Preventing Memory Leaks

It is pretty common to have relationships that go in two directions. For example, maybe an asset should know which employee is currently holding it. Let's add that relationship. The new object diagram would look like this:

Figure 20.1   Adding holder relationship

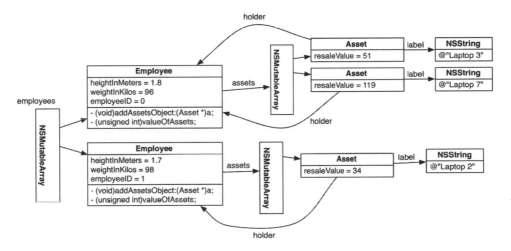

From a design standpoint, you would say that we are adding a pointer from the child (an instance of **Asset**) back to its parent (the instance of **Employee** that is holding it).

In Asset.h, add a pointer instance variable to hold on to the holding employee:

```
#import <Foundation/Foundation.h>
@class Employee;

@interface Asset : NSObject
{
    NSString *label;
    Employee *holder;
    unsigned int resaleValue;
}
@property (strong) NSString *label;
@property (strong) Employee *holder;
```

```
@property unsigned int resaleValue;
@end
```

In `Asset.m`, synthesize the accessors and extend the **description** method to display the holder:

```
#import "Asset.h"
#import "Employee.h"

@implementation Asset

@synthesize label, resaleValue, holder;


- (NSString *)description
{
    // Is holder non-nil?
    if ([self holder]) {
        return [NSString stringWithFormat:@"<%@: $%d, assigned to %@>",
                [self label], [self resaleValue], [self holder]];
    } else {
        return [NSString stringWithFormat:@"<%@: $%d unassigned>",
                [self label], [self resaleValue]];
    }
}

- (void)dealloc
{
    NSLog(@"deallocing %@", self);
}

@end
```

This brings us to a style question: When people use the **Asset** class and **Employee** class together, how do we make sure that the two relationships are consistent? That is, an asset should appear in an employee's assets array if and only if the employee is the asset's holder. There are three options:

• Set both relationships explicitly:

```
[vicePresident addAssetsObject:townCar];
[townCar setHolder:vicePresident];
```

• In the method that sets the child's pointer, add the child to the parent's collection.

```
- (void)setHolder:(Employee *)e
{
    holder = e;
    [e addAssetsObject:self];
}
```

This approach is not at all common.

• In the method that adds the child to the parent's collection, set the child's pointer.

In this exercise, you will take this last option. In `Employee.m`, extend the **addAssetsObject:** method to also set `holder`:

```
- (void)addAssetsObject:(Asset *)a
{
    // Is assets nil?
    if (!assets) {
        // Create the array
        assets = [[NSMutableArray alloc] init];
    }
    [assets addObject:a];
    [a setHolder:self];
}
```

(One of my favorite bugs: have both accessors automatically call the other. This creates an infinite loop: **addAssetsObject:** calls **setHolder:** which calls **addAssetsObject:** which calls **setHolder:** which....)

Build and run the program. You should see something like this:

```
Employees: (
    "<Employee 0: $0 in assets>",
    "<Employee 1: $153 in assets>",
    "<Employee 2: $119 in assets>",
    "<Employee 3: $68 in assets>",
    "<Employee 4: $0 in assets>",
    "<Employee 5: $136 in assets>",
    "<Employee 6: $119 in assets>",
    "<Employee 7: $34 in assets>",
    "<Employee 8: $0 in assets>",
    "<Employee 9: $136 in assets>"
)
Giving up ownership of one employee
Giving up ownership of array
deallocating <Employee 0: $0 in assets>
deallocating <Employee 4: $0 in assets>
deallocating <Employee 8: $0 in assets>
```

Notice that now none of the employees with assets are getting deallocated properly. Also, none of the assets are being deallocated, either. Why?

Retain cycles

The asset owns the employee and the employee owns the assets array, and the assets array owns the asset. It is an island of garbage created by this circle of ownership. These objects should be getting deallocated to free up memory, but they aren't. This is known as a *retain cycle*. Retain cycles are a very common source of memory leaks.

To find retain cycles in your program, you can use Apple's profiling tool, Instruments. When you *profile* a program, you monitor it while it runs to see what's happening behind the scenes with your code and the system. However, your program runs and exits very, very quickly. To give you time to profile, put in a hundred seconds of **sleep()** at the end of your **main()** function:

```
    ...
    }
    sleep(100);
    return 0;
}
```

In Xcode, choose Product → Profile in the menu. Instruments will launch. When the list of possible profiling instruments appears, choose Leaks:

Figure 20.2   Picking a profiler

As your program runs, you can browse the state of things. You have two instruments to choose from on the lefthand side of the window (Figure 20.3). Clicking on the Allocations instrument will let you see a bar graph of everything that has been allocated in your heap:

Figure 20.3   Allocations instrument

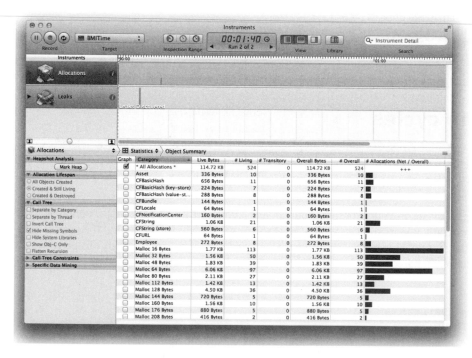

You can see, for example, that 10 instances of **Asset** are still living on your heap.

To look for retain cycles, change to the Leaks instrument and choose the Cycles view from the menu bar above the table. Select a particular cycle to see an object graph of it:

Figure 20.4   Leaks instrument

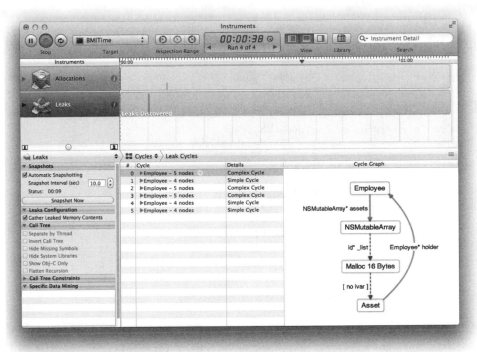

Weak references

How do you fix a retain cycle? Use a weak reference. A *weak reference* is a pointer that *does not* imply ownership. To fix our retain cycle, an asset should not own its holder. Edit Asset.h to make holder a weak reference:

```
#import <Foundation/Foundation.h>
@class Employee;

@interface Asset : NSObject
{
    NSString *label;
    __weak Employee *holder;
    unsigned int resaleValue;
}
@property (strong) NSString *label;
@property (weak) Employee *holder;
@property unsigned int resaleValue;
@end
```

Build and run the program. Note that all the objects are now being deallocated correctly.

In a parent-child relationship, the general rule for preventing this type of retain cycle is the parent owns the child, but the child should not own the parent.

Zeroing of weak references

To see weak references in action, let's add another array to the mix. What if we wanted an array of all assets – even ones that have not been assigned to a particular employee? We could add the assets to an array as they are created. Add a few lines of code to main.m:

```
#import <Foundation/Foundation.h>
#import "Employee.h"
#import "Asset.h"

int main(int argc, const char * argv[])
{
    @autoreleasepool {

        // Create an array of Employee objects
        NSMutableArray *employees = [[NSMutableArray alloc] init];

        for (int i = 0; i < 10; i++) {

            // Create an instance of Employee
            Employee *person = [[Employee alloc] init];

            // Give the instance variables interesting values
            [person setWeightInKilos:90 + i];
            [person setHeightInMeters:1.8 - i/10.0];
            [person setEmployeeID:i];

            // Put the employee in the employees array
            [employees addObject:person];
        }

        NSMutableArray *allAssets = [[NSMutableArray alloc] init];

        // Create 10 assets
        for (int i = 0; i < 10; i++) {

            // Create an asset
            Asset *asset = [[Asset alloc] init];

            // Give it an interesting label
            NSString *currentLabel = [NSString stringWithFormat:@"Laptop %d", i];
            [asset setLabel:currentLabel];
            [asset setResaleValue:i * 17];

            // Get a random number between 0 and 9 inclusive
            NSUInteger randomIndex = random() % [employees count];

            // Find that employee
            Employee *randomEmployee = [employees objectAtIndex:randomIndex];

            // Assign the asset to the employee
            [randomEmployee addAssetsObject:asset];

            [allAssets addObject:asset];
        }

        NSLog(@"Employees: %@", employees);

        NSLog(@"Giving up ownership of one employee");
```

```
        [employees removeObjectAtIndex:5];

        NSLog(@"allAssets: %@", allAssets);

        NSLog(@"Giving up ownership of arrays");

        allAssets = nil;
        employees = nil;
    }
    sleep(100);
    return 0;
}
```

Before you build and run your program, think about what you expect your output to look like. You'll see the contents of the allAssets array – after Employee #5 has been deallocated. What will the status of Employee #5's assets be at this point? These assets lose one owner (Employee #5), but they are still owned by allAssets, so they won't be deallocated.

What about holder for the assets previously owned by Employee #5? When the object that a weak reference points to is deallocated, the pointer variable is *zeroed*, or set to nil. So Employee #5's assets will not be deallocated, and their holder variables will be automatically set to nil.

Now build and run the program and check your output:

```
Employees: (
    "<Employee 0: $0 in assets>",
...
    "<Employee 9: $136 in assets>"
)
Giving up ownership of one employee
deallocating <Employee 5: $136 in assets>
allAssets: (
    "<Laptop 0: $0, assigned to <Employee 3: $68 in assets>>",
    "<Laptop 1: $17, assigned to <Employee 6: $119 in assets>>",
    "<Laptop 2: $34, assigned to <Employee 7: $34 in assets>>",
    "<Laptop 3: $51 unassigned>",
    "<Laptop 4: $68, assigned to <Employee 3: $68 in assets>>",
    "<Laptop 5: $85 unassigned>",
    "<Laptop 6: $102, assigned to <Employee 6: $119 in assets>>",
    "<Laptop 7: $119, assigned to <Employee 2: $119 in assets>>",
    "<Laptop 8: $136, assigned to <Employee 9: $136 in assets>>",
    "<Laptop 9: $153, assigned to <Employee 1: $153 in assets>>"
)
Giving up ownership of arrays
deallocing <Laptop 3: $51 unassigned>
...
deallocing <Laptop 8: $136 unassigned>
```

For the More Curious: Manual reference counting and ARC History

As mentioned at the beginning of Chapter 19, before automatic reference counting (ARC) was added to Objective-C, we had *manual reference counting*, which used *retain counts*. With manual reference counting, ownership changes only happened when you sent an explicit message to an object that decremented or incremented the retain count.

```
[anObject release]; // anObject loses an owner
[anObject retain]; // anObject gains an owner
```

You would see these sorts of calls primarily in accessor methods (where the new value was retained and the old value was released) and in **dealloc** methods (where all the previously retained objects were released). The **setHolder:** method for **Asset** would have looked like this:

```
- (void)setHolder:(Employee *)newEmp
{
    [newEmp retain];
    [holder release];
    holder = newEmp;
}
```

The **dealloc** method would have looked like this:

```
- (void)dealloc
{
    [label release];
    [holder release];
    [super dealloc];
}
```

What about the **description** method? It creates and returns a string. Should **Asset** claim ownership of it? That wouldn't make sense; the asset is giving away the string it created. When you **autorelease** an object, you are marking it to be sent **release** in the future. Before ARC, the **description** method for **Asset** would look like this:

```
- (NSString *)description
{
    NSString *result = [[NSString alloc] initWithFormat:@"<%@: $%d >",
                                         [self label], [self resaleValue]];
    [result autorelease];
    return result;
}
```

When would it be sent **release**? When the current autorelease pool was drained:

```
// Create the autorelease pool
NSAutoreleasePool *arp = [[NSAutoreleasePool alloc] init];
Asset *asset = [[Asset alloc] init];

NSString *d = [asset description];
// The string that d points to is in the autorelease pool

[arp drain]; // The string is sent the message release
```

ARC *uses* the autorelease pool automatically, but you must create and drain the pool. When ARC was created, we also got a new syntax for creating an autorelease pool. The code above now looks like this:

```
// Create the autorelease pool
@autoreleasepool {
    Asset *asset = [[Asset alloc] init];

    NSString *d = [asset description];
    // The string that d points to is in the autorelease pool

} // The pool is drained
```

Retain count rules

There are a set of memory management conventions that all Objective-C programmers follow. If you are using ARC, it is following these conventions behind the scenes for you.

In these rules, I use the word "you" to mean "an instance of whatever class you are currently working on." It is a useful form of empathy; you imagine that you are the object you are writing. So, for example, "If you retain the string, it will not be deallocated." really means "If an instance of the class that you are currently working on retains the string, it will not be deallocated."

Here, then, are the rules. (Implementation details are in parentheses.)

- If you create an object using a method whose name starts with **alloc** or **new** or contains **copy**, then you have taken ownership of it. (That is, assume that the new object has a retain count of 1 and is *not* in the autorelease pool.) You have a responsibility to release the object when you no longer need it. Here are some of the common methods that convey ownership: **alloc** (which is always followed by an **init** method), **copy**, and **mutableCopy**.

- An object created through *any* other means is *not* owned by you. (That is, assume it has a retain count of one and is already in the autorelease pool, and thus doomed unless it is retained before the autorelease pool is drained.)

- If you don't own an object and you want to ensure its continued existence, take ownership by sending it the message **retain**. (This increments the retain count.)

- When you own an object and no longer need it, send it the message **release** or **autorelease**. (**release** decrements the retain count immediately. **autorelease** causes the message **release** to be sent when the autorelease pool is drained.)

- As long as an object has at least one owner, it will continue to exist. (When its retain count goes to zero, it is sent the message **dealloc**.)

One of the tricks to understanding memory management is to think locally. The **Asset** class does not need to know anything about other objects that also care about its `label`. As long as an **Asset** instance retains objects it wants to keep, you won't have any problems. Programmers new to the language sometimes make the mistake of trying to keep tabs on objects throughout an application. Don't do this. If you follow these rules and always think local to a class, you never have to worry what the rest of an application is doing with an object.

Following the idea of ownership, now it becomes clear why you need to autorelease the string in your **description** method: The employee object created the string, but it doesn't want to own it. It wants to give it away.

21

Collection Classes

You have already used two collection classes: **NSArray** and its subclass **NSMutableArray**. As you know, an array holds a collection of pointers to other objects. The pointers are ordered, so you use an index (an integer) to access the objects in the collection. In this chapter, we will delve deeper into arrays and look at some other collection classes: **NSSet/NSMutableSet** and **NSDictionary/NSMutableDictionary**.

NSArray/NSMutableArray

When you add an object to an array, the array claims ownership of it. When you remove the object from the array, the array gives up ownership. Open BMITime, and take a look at how you are using the employees array. If we ignore all the other stuff, you see something like this:

```
// Create an array of Employee objects
NSMutableArray *employees = [[NSMutableArray alloc] init];

for (int i = 0; i < 10; i++) {

    // Create an instance of Employee
    Employee *person = [[Employee alloc] init];

    // Put the employee in the employees array
    [employees addObject:person];
}

[employees removeObjectAtIndex:5];
employees = nil;
```

You typically create an empty mutable array using **alloc/init** or the class method **array**. For example, you could have created the mutable array like this:

```
NSMutableArray *employees = [NSMutableArray array];
```

Note that the **addObject:** method adds the object to the end of the list. As objects are added, an array will grow as big as necessary to hold them.

Immutable objects

When you create an instance of **NSArray**, you assign all its objects to it when it is created. This typically looks like this:

```
NSArray *colors = [NSArray arrayWithObjects:@"Orange", @"Yellow", @"Green", nil];
```

The nil at the end is how you tell the method to stop. Thus, this colors array would only have three strings. (If you forget the nil, it will probably crash your program.)

Most beginning programmers are surprised by the existence of **NSArray**. Why would anyone want a list that can't be changed? There are two reasons:

- You don't trust the people you work with. That is, you want to let them look at an array, but you don't want them to be able change it. A gentler approach is to give them an **NSMutableArray**, but *tell* them it is an **NSArray**. For example, imagine the following method:

```
// Returns an array of 30 odd numbers
- (NSArray *)odds
{
    static NSMutableArray *odds = [[NSMutableArray alloc] init];
    int i = 1;
    while ([odds count] < 30) {
        [odds addObject:[NSNumber numberWithInt:i]];
        i += 2;
    }
    return odds;
}
```

Anyone calling this method assumes it is returning an immutable **NSArray**. If the caller tries to add or remove items from the returned object, the compiler will issue a stern warning – even though, it is, in fact, an instance of **NSMutableArray**.

- The other reason is performance: an immutable object never needs to be copied. With a mutable object, you might make a private copy so that you know that no other code in the system can change it from underneath you. This is unnecessary for immutable objects. In fact, while the **copy** method of **NSMutableArray** makes a new copy of itself and returns a pointer to the new array, the **copy** method of **NSArray** does nothing – it just returns a pointer to itself.

As a result, immutable objects are fairly common in Objective-C programming. In Foundation, there are many classes that create immutable instances: **NSArray**, **NSString**, **NSAttributedString**, **NSData**, **NSCharacterSet**, **NSDictionary**, **NSSet**, **NSIndexSet**, and **NSURLRequest**. All of these have mutable subclasses: **NSMutableArray**, **NSMutableString**, **NSMutableAttributedString**, etc. **NSDate** and **NSNumber**, on the other hand, are immutable but don't have mutable subclasses.

Sorting

There are several ways to sort an array, but the most common way is to use an array of *sort descriptors*. **NSMutableArray** has the following method:

```
- (void)sortUsingDescriptors:(NSArray *)sortDescriptors;
```

The argument is an array of **NSSortDescriptor** objects. A sort descriptor has the name of a property of the objects contained in the array and whether that property should be sorted in ascending or descending order. Why do we pass an array of sort descriptors? Imagine you said, "Sort this list of doctors by last name in ascending order." What if two doctors have the same last name? You can specify "Sort by last name ascending, and if the last names are the same, sort by first name ascending, and if the first and last names are the same, sort by zip code."

Figure 21.1 Sort by lastName, then firstName, then zipCode

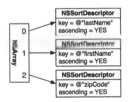

The property you sort on can be any instance variable or the result of any method of the object.

Let's return to the BMITime project to see sorting in practice. In **main()**, just before logging the employees array, sort it by **valueOfAssets**. If two employees are holding assets of the same value, sort them by employeeID. Edit main.m:

```
    }

    NSSortDescriptor *voa = [NSSortDescriptor sortDescriptorWithKey:@"valueOfAssets"
                                                          ascending:YES];
    NSSortDescriptor *ei = [NSSortDescriptor sortDescriptorWithKey:@"employeeID"
                                                        ascending:YES];
    [employees sortUsingDescriptors:[NSArray arrayWithObjects:voa, ei, nil]];

    NSLog(@"Employees: %@", employees);
```

Build and run the program. You should see the employees list ordered correctly:

```
Employees: (
    "<Employee 0: $0 in assets>",
    "<Employee 4: $0 in assets>",
    "<Employee 8: $0 in assets>",
    "<Employee 7: $34 in assets>",
    "<Employee 3: $68 in assets>",
    "<Employee 2: $119 in assets>",
    "<Employee 6: $119 in assets>",
    "<Employee 5: $136 in assets>",
    "<Employee 9: $136 in assets>",
    "<Employee 1: $153 in assets>"
```

Filtering

There is a class called **NSPredicate**. A *predicate* contains a statement that might be true, like "The employeeID is greater than 75." **NSMutableArray** has a handy method for discarding all the objects that don't satisfy the predicate:

```
- (void)filterUsingPredicate:(NSPredicate *)predicate;
```

NSArray has a method that creates a new array that contains all the objects that satisfy the predicate:

```
- (NSArray *)filteredArrayUsingPredicate:(NSPredicate *)predicate;
```

Imagine that you are going to reclaim all the assets given to employees who currently hold assets worth more than $70 total. Add the code near the end of main.m:

```
        [employees removeObjectAtIndex:5];

        NSLog(@"allAssets: %@", allAssets);

        NSPredicate *predicate = [NSPredicate predicateWithFormat:
                                          @"holder.valueOfAssets > 70"];
        NSArray *toBeReclaimed = [allAssets filteredArrayUsingPredicate:predicate];
        NSLog(@"toBeReclaimed: %@", toBeReclaimed);
        toBeReclaimed = nil;

        NSLog(@"Giving up ownership of arrays");

        allAssets = nil;
        employees = nil;
    }
    return 0;
}
```

Build and run the program. You should see a list of assets:

```
toBeReclaimed: (
    "<Laptop 1: $17, assigned to <Employee 6: $119 in assets>>",
    "<Laptop 3: $51, assigned to <Employee 5: $136 in assets>>",
    "<Laptop 5: $85, assigned to <Employee 5: $136 in assets>>",
    "<Laptop 6: $102, assigned to <Employee 6: $119 in assets>>",
    "<Laptop 8: $136, assigned to <Employee 9: $136 in assets>>",
    "<Laptop 9: $153, assigned to <Employee 1: $153 in assets>>"
)
```

The format string used to create the predicate can be very complex. If you do a lot of filtering of collections, be sure to read Apple's *Predicate Programming Guide*.

NSSet/NSMutableSet

A set is a collection that has no sense of order, and a particular object can only appear in a set once. Sets are primarily useful for asking the question "Is it in there?" For example, you might have a set of URLs that are not child-appropriate. Before displaying any web page to a child, you would want to do a quick check to see if the URL is in the set. Sets do this incredibly quickly.

An employee's assets have no inherent order, and an asset should never appear twice in the same employee's assets collection. Change your program to use an **NSMutableSet** instead of an **NSMutableArray** for the assets relationship.

Figure 21.2   Using NSMutableSet for assets

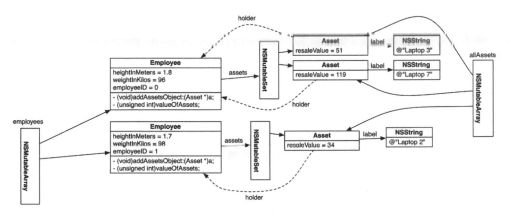

In `Employee.h`, change the variable's declaration:

```
#import "Person.h"
@class Asset;

@interface Employee : Person
{
    int employeeID;
    NSMutableSet *assets;
}
@property int employeeID;
- (void)addAssetsObject:(Asset *)a;
- (unsigned int)valueOfAssets;
@end
```

In `Employee.m`, create an instance of the correct class:

```
- (void)addAssetsObject:(Asset *)a
{
    if (!assets) {
        assets = [[NSMutableSet alloc] init];
    }
    [assets addObject:a];
    [a setHolder:self];
}
```

Build and run the program. It should function the same.

You can't access an object in a set by index because there is no sense of order in a set. Instead, all you can do is ask "Is there one of these in there?" **NSSet** has a method:

```
- (BOOL)containsObject:(id)x;
```

When you send this message to a set, it goes through its collection of objects looking for an object equal to x. If it finds one, it returns YES; otherwise it returns NO.

This brings us to a rather deep question: what does *equal* mean? The class **NSObject** defines a method called **isEqual:**. To check if two objects are equal, you use the **isEqual:** method:

```
if ([myDoctor isEqual:yourTennisPartner]) {
    NSLog(@"my doctor is equal to your tennis partner");
}
```

NSObject has a simple implementation of **isEqual:**. It looks like this:

```
- (BOOL)isEqual:(id)other
{
    return (self == other);
}
```

Thus, if you haven't overridden **isEqual:**, the code snippet is equivalent to:

```
if (myDoctor == yourTennisPartner) {
    NSLog(@"my doctor is equal to your tennis partner");
}
```

Some classes override **isEqual:**. For example, in **NSString**, **isEqual:** is overridden to compare the characters in the string. For these classes, there is a difference between *equal* and *identical*. Let's say I have two pointers to strings:

```
NSString *x = ...
NSString *y = ...
```

x and y are *identical* if they contain the exact same address. x and y are *equal* if the strings they point to contain the same letters in the same order.

Thus, identical objects are always equal. Equal objects are not always identical.

Does this difference matter? Yes. For example, **NSMutableArray** has two methods:

```
- (NSUInteger)indexOfObject:(id)anObject;
```

```
- (NSUInteger)indexOfObjectIdenticalTo:(id)anObject;
```

The first steps through the collection asking each object "isEqual:anObject?" The second steps through the collection asking each object "== anObject"?

NSDictionary/NSMutableDictionary

As you know, arrays are indexed by a number; it is easy to ask "Give me object 10." Dictionaries are indexed by a string; it is easy to ask "Give me the object stored under the key favoriteColor." More precisely, a dictionary is a collection of key-value pairs. The key is typically a string, and the value can be any sort of object. These key-value pairs are not kept in any particular order.

Let's make a dictionary of executives. The key will be an executive title, and the value will be an instance of **Employee**. The first employee will be put in the dictionary under @"CEO"; the second under @"CTO". Change your main.m to create and populate the **NSMutableDictionary**. Then, print out the dictionary of executives. Finally, set the pointer to the dictionary to nil so that you can see the dictionary being deallocated.

```
        // Create an array of Employee objects
        NSMutableArray *employees = [[NSMutableArray alloc] init];

        // Create a dictionary of executives
        NSMutableDictionary *executives = [[NSMutableDictionary alloc] init];

        for (int i = 0; i < 10; i++) {

            // Create an instance of Employee
            Employee *person = [[Employee alloc] init];

            // Give the instance variables interesting values
            [person setWeightInKilos:90 + i];
            [person setHeightInMeters:1.8 - i/10.0];
            [person setEmployeeID:i];

            // Put the employee in the employees array
            [employees addObject:person];

            // Is this the first employee?
            if (i == 0) {
                [executives setObject:person forKey:@"CEO"];
            }

            // Is this the second employee?
            if (i == 1) {
                [executives setObject:person forKey:@"CTO"];
            }

        }

        ...

        NSLog(@"allAssets: %@", allAssets);

        NSLog(@"executives: %@", executives);
        executives = nil;

        NSPredicate *predicate = [NSPredicate predicateWithFormat:
                                          @"holder.valueOfAssets > 70"];
        NSArray *toBeReclaimed = [allAssets filteredArrayUsingPredicate:predicate];
        NSLog(@"toBeReclaimed: %@", toBeReclaimed);
        toBeReclaimed = nil;

        NSLog(@"Giving up ownership of arrays");

        allAssets = nil;
        employees = nil;
    }
    return 0;
}
```

Build and run the program. The executives dictionary should log itself out:

```
executives = {
    CEO = "<Employee 0: $0 in assets>";
    CTO = "<Employee 1: $153 in assets>";
}
```

Figure 21.3   Two instances of Employee in an NSMutableDictionary

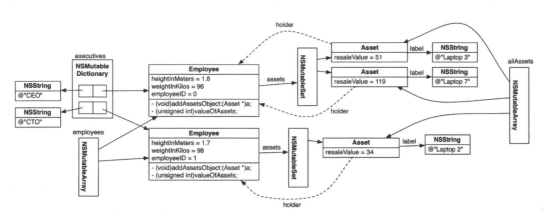

C primitive types

The collections covered in this chapter only hold objects. What if you want a collection of floats or ints or pointers to structures? You can wrap common C primitive types in an object. There are two classes that are designed specifically for this purpose. **NSNumber** holds C number types. **NSValue** can hold a pointer and some types of structs.

For instance, if you wanted to put the numbers 4 and 5.6 into an array, you would use **NSNumber**:

```
NSMutableArray *numList = [[NSMutableArray alloc] init];
[numList addObject:[NSNumber numberWithInt:4]];
[numList addObject:[NSNumber numberWithFloat:5.6]];
```

Collections and nil

You are not allowed to add nil to any of the collection classes we have covered. What if you need to put that idea of nothingness, a "hole," into a collection? There is a class called **NSNull**. There is exactly one instance of **NSNull**, and it is an object that represents nothingness. Here's an example.

```
NSMutableArray *hotel = [[NSMutableArray alloc] init];

// Lobby on the ground floor
[hotel addObject:lobby];

// Pool on the second
[hotel addObject:pool];

// The third floor has not been built out
[hotel addObject:[NSNull null]];

// Bedrooms on fourth floor
[hotel addObject:bedrooms];
```

Challenge

Explore the reference pages for **NSArray**, **NSMutableArray**, **NSDictionary**, and **NSMutableDictionary**. You will use these classes every day.

22

Constants

We have spent a lot of time discussing variables, which as the name indicates, change their values as the program runs. There are, however, pieces of information that *do not* change value. For example, the mathematical constant π never changes. We call these things *constants*, and there are two common ways that Objective-C programmers define constants: #define and global variables.

In Xcode, create a new Foundation Command Line Tool called Constants.

In the standard C libraries, constants are defined using the #define preprocessor directive. The math part of the standard C library is declared in the file math.h. One of the constants defined there is M_PI. Use it in main.m:

```
#import <Foundation/Foundation.h>

int main (int argc, const char * argv[])
{
    @autoreleasepool {

        // In literal NSString, use \u for arbitrary unicode chars
        NSLog(@"\u03c0 is %f", M_PI);

    }
    return 0;
}
```

When you build and run it, you should see:

π is 3.141593

To see the definition, Command-click on M_PI in the editor. It will take you to the following line in math.h:

```
#define M_PI        3.14159265358979323846264338327950288
```

Preprocessor directives

Compiling a file of C, C++, or Objective-C code is done in two passes. First, the *preprocessor* runs through the file. The output from the preprocessor then goes into the real compiler. Preprocessor directives start with #, and the three most popular are #include, #import, and #define.

#include and #import

#include and #import do essentially the same thing: request that the preprocessor read a file and add it to its output. Usually, you are including a file of declarations (a .h file), and those declarations are used by the compiler to understand the code it is compiling.

What is the difference between #include and #import? #import ensures that the preprocessor only includes a file once. #include will allow you to include the same file many times. C programmers tend to use #include. Objective-C programmers tend to use #import.

When specifying the name of the file to be imported, you can wrap the filename in quotes or angle brackets. Quotes indicate that the header is in your project directory. Angle brackets indicate that the header is in one of the standard locations that the preprocessor knows about. (<math.h>, for example, is /Developer/SDKs/MacOSX10.7.sdk/usr/include/math.h.) Here are two examples of #import directives:

```
// Include the headers I wrote for Pet Store operations
#import "PetStore.h"

// Include the headers for the OpenLDAP libraries
#import <ldap.h>
```

In a project, it used to be pretty common to include a collection of headers in *every* file of code. This led to clutter at the beginning of your file and made compiles take longer. To make life easier and compiles faster, most Xcode projects have a file that lists headers to be precompiled and included in every file. In your Constants project, this file is called Constants-Prefix.pch.

So, how did a constant from math.h get included when main.m was compiled? Your main.m file has the following line:

```
#import <Foundation/Foundation.h>
```

The file Foundation.h has this line:

```
#include <CoreFoundation/CoreFoundation.h>
```

The file CoreFoundation.h has this line:

```
#include <math.h>
```

#define

#define tells the preprocessor, "Whenever you encounter A, replace it with B before the compiler sees it." Look at the line from math.h again:

```
#define M_PI        3.14159265358979323846264338327950288
```

In the #define directive, you just separate the two parts (the token and its replacement) with whitespace.

#define can actually be used to make something like a function. In main.m, print the larger of two numbers:

```
#import <Foundation/Foundation.h>

int main (int argc, const char * argv[])
{
    @autoreleasepool {

        NSLog(@"\u03c0 is %f", M_PI);
        NSLog(@"%d is larger", MAX(10, 12));

    }
    return 0;
}
```

MAX is not a function; it is a #define. The most basic C version of MAX is:

```
#define MAX(A,B)     ((A) > (B) ? (A) : (B))
```

So, by the time the compiler saw the line you just added, it looked like this:

```
NSLog(@"%d is larger", ((10) > (12) ? (10) : (12)));
```

When you use #define to do function-like stuff instead of simply substituting a value, you are creating a *macro*.

Global variables

Instead of using #define, Objective-C programmers commonly use global variables to hold constant values.

Let's add to your program to explain. First, there is a class named **NSLocale** that stores information about different geographical locations. You can get an instance of the user's current locale and then ask it questions. For instance, if you wanted to know what the currency is in the user's locale, you could ask for it like this:

```
#import <Foundation/Foundation.h>

int main (int argc, const char * argv[])
{
    @autoreleasepool {

        NSLog(@"\u03c0 is %f", M_PI);
        NSLog(@"%d is larger", MAX(10, 12));

        NSLocale *here = [NSLocale currentLocale];
        NSString *currency = [here objectForKey:@"currency"];
        NSLog(@"Money is %@", currency);

    }
    return 0;
}
```

Build and run it. Depending on where you are, you should see something like

```
Money is USD
```

If, however, you mistype the key as @"Kuruncy", you won't get anything back. To prevent this problem, the Foundation framework defines a global variable called NSLocaleCurrencyCode. It isn't easier to type, but if you do mistype it, the compiler will complain. Also, code completion in Xcode works properly for a global variable, but not for the string @"currency". Change your code to use the constant:

```
#import <Foundation/Foundation.h>

int main (int argc, const char * argv[])
{
    @autoreleasepool {

        NSLog(@"\u03c0 is %f", M_PI);
        NSLog(@"%d is larger", MAX(10, 12));

        NSLocale *here = [NSLocale currentLocale];
        NSString *currency = [here objectForKey:NSLocaleCurrencyCode];
        NSLog(@"Money is %@", currency);

    }
    return 0;
}
```

When the class **NSLocale** was written, this global variable appeared in two places. In NSLocale.h, the variable was declared something like this:

```
extern NSString const *NSLocaleCurrencyCode;
```

The const means that this pointer will not change for the entire life of the program. The extern means "I promise this exists, but it will be defined in some other file." And sure enough, in the file NSLocale.m, there is a line like this:

```
NSString const *NSLocaleCurrencyCode = @"currency";
```

enum

Often you will need to define a set of constants. For example, imagine that you were developing a blender with five speeds: Stir, Chop, Liquefy, Pulse, and Ice Crush. Your class **Blender** would have a method called **setSpeed:**. It would be best if the type indicated that only one of the five speeds was allowed. To do this, you would define an enumeration:

```
enum BlenderSpeed {
    BlenderSpeedStir = 1,
    BlenderSpeedChop = 2,
    BlenderSpeedLiquify = 5,
    BlenderSpeedPulse = 9,
    BlenderSpeedIceCrush = 15
};

@interface Blender : NSObject
{
    // speed must be one of the five speeds
    enum BlenderSpeed speed;
}

// setSpeed: expects one of the five speeds
- (void)setSpeed:(enum BlenderSpeed)x;
@end
```

Developers get tired of typing enum BlenderSpeed, so they often use typedef to create a shorthand for it:

```
typedef enum  {
    BlenderSpeedStir = 1,
    BlenderSpeedChop = 2,
    BlenderSpeedLiquify = 5,
    BlenderSpeedPulse = 9,
    BlenderSpeedIceCrush = 15
} BlenderSpeed;

@interface Blender : NSObject
{
    // speed must be one of the five speeds
    BlenderSpeed speed;
}

// setSpeed: expects one of the five speeds
- (void)setSpeed:(BlenderSpeed)x;
@end
```

Often you won't care what numbers the five speeds represent – only that they are different from each other. You can leave out the values, and the compiler will make up values for you:

```
typedef enum  {
    BlenderSpeedStir,
    BlenderSpeedChop,
    BlenderSpeedLiquify,
    BlenderSpeedPulse,
    BlenderSpeedIceCrush
} BlenderSpeed;
```

#define vs global variables

Given that you can define a constant using #define or a global variable (which includes the use of enum), why do Objective-C programmers tend to use global variables? In some cases, there are performance advantages to using global variables. For example, you can use == instead of **isEqual:** to compare strings if you consistently use the global variable (and an arithmetic operation is faster than a message send). Also, global variables are easier to work with when you are in the debugger.

You should use global variables and enum for constants, not #define.

23

Writing Files with NSString and NSData

The Foundation framework gives the developer a few easy ways to read from and write to files. In this chapter, you'll try a few of them out.

Writing an NSString to a file

First, let's see how you would take the contents of an **NSString** and put it into a file. When you write a string to a file, you need to specify which *string encoding* you are using. A string encoding describes how each character is stored as an array of bytes. ASCII is a string encoding that defines the letter 'A' as being stored as `01000001`. In UTF-16, the letter 'A' is stored as `0000000001000001`.

The Foundation framework supports about 20 different string encodings. UTF can handle an incredible collection of writing systems. It comes in two flavors: UTF-16, which uses two or more bytes for every character, and UTF-8, which uses one byte for the first 128 ASCII characters and two or more for other characters. For most purposes, UTF-8 is a good fit.

Create a new project: a Foundation Command Line Tool called Stringz. In **main()**, use methods from the **NSString** class to create a string and write it to the filesystem:

```
#import <Foundation/Foundation.h>

int main (int argc, const char * argv[])     {
    @autoreleasepool {

        NSMutableString *str = [[NSMutableString alloc] init];
        for (int i = 0; i < 10; i++) {
            [str appendString:@"Aaron is cool!\n"];
        }
        [str writeToFile:@"/tmp/cool.txt"
             atomically:YES
               encoding:NSUTF8StringEncoding
                  error:NULL];
        NSLog(@"done writing /tmp/cool.txt");

    }
    return 0;
}
```

This program will create a text file that you can read and edit in any text editor. The string `/tmp/cool.txt` is known as the file path. File paths can be absolute or relative: absolute paths start with a / that represents the top of the file system, whereas relative paths start at the working directory of the program. Relative paths do not start with a /. In Objective-C programming, you'll find that we nearly always use absolute paths because we typically don't know what the working directory of the program is.

NSError

As you can imagine, all sorts of things can go wrong when you try to write a string to a file. For example, the user may not have write-access to the directory where the file would go. Or the directory may not exist at all. Or the filesystem may be full. For situations like these, where an operation may be impossible to complete, the method needs a way to return a description of what went wrong in addition to the boolean value for success or failure.

Recall from Chapter 9 that when you need a function to return something in addition to its return value, you can use pass-by-reference. You pass the function (or method) a reference to a variable where it can directly store or manipulate a value. The reference is the memory address for that variable.

For error handling, many methods take an **NSError** pointer by reference. Add error handling to the example above:

```
#import <Foundation/Foundation.h>

int main (int argc, const char * argv[])     {
    @autoreleasepool {

        NSMutableString *str = [[NSMutableString alloc] init];
        for (int i = 0; i < 10; i++) {
            [str appendString:@"Aaron is cool!\n"];
        }

        // Declare a pointer to an NSError object, but don't instantiate it.
        // The NSError instance will only be created if there is, in fact, an error.
        NSError *error = nil;

        // Pass the NSError pointer by reference to the NSString method
        BOOL success = [str writeToFile:@"/tmp/cool.txt"
                            atomically:YES
                              encoding:NSUTF8StringEncoding
                                 error:&error];

        // Test the returned BOOL, and query the NSError if the write failed
        if (success) {
            NSLog(@"done writing /tmp/cool.txt");
        } else {
            NSLog(@"writing /tmp/cool.txt failed: %@", [error localizedDescription]);
        }

    }
    return 0;
}
```

Build and run it. Now change the code to pass the write method a file path that doesn't exist, like @"/ too/darned/bad.txt". You should get a friendly error message.

Notice that you declare a pointer to an instance of **NSError** in this code, but you don't create, or *instantiate*, an **NSError** object to assign to that pointer.

Why not? You want to avoid creating an unnecessary error object if there's no error. If there is an error, **writeToFile:atomically:encoding:error:** will be responsible for creating a new **NSError** instance and then modifying the error pointer you declared to point to the new error object. Then you can ask that object what went wrong via your error pointer.

This conditional creation of the **NSError** requires you to pass a reference to error (&error) because there's no object yet to pass. However, unlike the passing by reference you did in Chapter 9 where you passed the reference of a primitive C variable, here you're passing the address of a pointer variable. In essence, you're passing the address of another address (which may become the address of an **NSError** object).

To revisit our international espionage analogy from Chapter 9, you might tell your spy, "If anything goes wrong, make a complete report (much too large to put in the steel pipe) and hide it in a book at the library. I need to know where you hid it, so put the call number of the book in the steel pipe." That is, you are giving the spy a location where she can put the address of an error report she created.

Here's a look inside the **NSString** class where **writeToFile:atomically:encoding:error:** is declared:

```
- (BOOL)writeToFile:(NSString *)path
         atomically:(BOOL)useAuxiliaryFile
           encoding:(NSStringEncoding)enc
              error:(NSError **)error
```

Notice the double asterisk. When you call this method, you are supplying a pointer to a pointer to an instance of **NSError**.

Methods that pass an **NSError** by reference always return a value that indicates whether there was an error or not. This method, for example, returns NO if there is an error. Don't try to access the **NSError** unless the return value indicates that an error occurred; if the **NSError** object doesn't actually exist, trying to access it will crash your program.

Reading files with NSString

Reading a file into a string is very similar:

```
#import <Foundation/Foundation.h>

int main (int argc, const char * argv[])     {
    @autoreleasepool {

        NSError *error = nil;
        NSString *str = [[NSString alloc] initWithContentsOfFile:@"/etc/resolv.conf"
                                                encoding:NSASCIIStringEncoding
                                                   error:&error];

        if (!str) {
            NSLog(@"read failed: %@", [error localizedDescription]);
        } else {
            NSLog(@"resolv.conf looks like this: %@", str);
        }

    }
    return 0;
}
```

Writing an NSData object to a file

An **NSData** object represents a buffer of bytes. For example, if you fetch some data from a URL, you get an instance of **NSData**. And you can ask an **NSData** to write itself to a file. Create a new Foundation Command Line Tool named ImageFetch that fetches an image from the Google website into an instance of **NSData**. Then ask the **NSData** to write its buffer of bytes to a file:

```
#import <Foundation/Foundation.h>

int main (int argc, const char * argv[])
{
    @autoreleasepool {

        NSURL *url = [NSURL URLWithString:
                            @"http://www.google.com/images/logos/ps_logo2.png"];
        NSURLRequest *request = [NSURLRequest requestWithURL:url];
        NSError *error = nil;
        NSData *data = [NSURLConnection sendSynchronousRequest:request
                                            returningResponse:NULL
                                                        error:&error];

        if (!data) {
            NSLog(@"fetch failed: %@", [error localizedDescription]);
            return 1;
        }

        NSLog(@"The file is %lu bytes", [data length]);

        BOOL written = [data writeToFile:@"/tmp/google.png"
                                 options:0
                                   error:&error];

        if (!written) {
            NSLog(@"write failed: %@", [error localizedDescription]);
            return 1;
        }

        NSLog(@"Success!");

    }
    return 0;
}
```

Build and run the program. Open the resulting image file in Preview.

Note that the **writeToFile:options:error:** method takes a number that indicates options to be used in the saving process. The most common option is NSDataWritingAtomic. Let's say that you've already fetched an image, and you're just re-fetching and replacing it with a newer version. While the new image is being written, the power goes off. A half-written file is worthless. In cases where a half-written file is worse than no file at all, you can make the writing atomic. Add this option:

```
NSLog(@"The file is %lu bytes", [data length]);

BOOL written = [data writeToFile:@"/tmp/google.png"
                         options:NSDataWritingAtomic
                           error:&error];
```

```
    if (!written) {
        NSLog(@"write failed: %@", [error localizedDescription]);
        return 1;
    }
```

Now, the data will be written out to a temporary file, and, when the writing is done, the file is renamed the correct name. This way, you either get the whole file or nothing.

Reading an NSData from a file

You can also create an instance of **NSData** from the contents of a file. Add two lines to your program:

```
#import <Foundation/Foundation.h>

int main (int argc, const char * argv[])
{
    @autoreleasepool {

        NSURL *url = [NSURL URLWithString:
                            @"http://www.google.com/images/logos/ps_logo2.png"];
        NSURLRequest *request = [NSURLRequest requestWithURL:url];
        NSError *error;

        // This method will block until all the data has been fetched
        NSData *data = [NSURLConnection sendSynchronousRequest:request
                                            returningResponse:NULL
                                                        error:&error];

        if (!data) {
            NSLog(@"fetch failed: %@", [error localizedDescription]);
            return 1;
        }

        NSLog(@"The file is %lu bytes", [data length]);


        BOOL written = [data writeToFile:@"/tmp/google.png"
                                 options:NSDataWritingAtomic
                                   error:&error];

        if (!written) {
            NSLog(@"write failed: %@", [error localizedDescription]);
            return 1;
        }

        NSLog(@"Success!");

        NSData *readData = [NSData dataWithContentsOfFile:@"/tmp/google.png"];
        NSLog(@"The file read from the disk has %lu bytes", [readData length]);

    }
    return 0;
}
```

Build and run the program.

24

Callbacks

Thus far, your code has been the boss. It has been sending messages to standard Foundation objects, like instances of **NSString** and **NSArray**, and telling them what to do. Thus far, your programs have run and exited in milliseconds.

You have been living a sweet and simple existence. In the real world, applications run for hours and your objects act as slaves to the stream of events pouring in from the user, the clock, the network, etc.

In a real-world application, there needs to be an object that waits for events like mouse movements, touch events, timers, and network activity. On Mac OS X and iOS, this object is an instance of **NSRunLoop**. The run loop sits and waits, and when something happens, it sends a message to another object.

We say that when something happens, the run loop causes a *callback* to occur. For Objective-C programmers, there are three forms that a callback can take. (Because these are very general ideas, I am going to use *x* for "a specific something" that happens. I'll fill in the details in the sections that follow.)

- *Target-action:* Before the wait begins, you say "When *x* happens, send this particular message to that particular object." The object receiving the message is the *target*. The selector for the message is the *action*.

- *Helper objects:* Before the wait begins, you say "Here is a helper object that conforms to your protocol. Send it messages when things happen." (More on protocols in Chapter 25.) Helper objects are often known as *delegates* or *data sources*.

- *Notifications:* There is an object called the notification center. Before the wait begins, you say to the notification center "This object is waiting for these sorts of notifications. When one of those notifications arrives, send the object this message." When *x* happens, an object posts a notification to the notification center, and the center forwards it on to your object.

In this chapter, you will implement all three types of callbacks and learn which to employ in which circumstances.

Target-action

Timers use a target-action mechanism. You create a timer with a delay, a target, and an action. After that delay, the timer sends the action message to its target.

You are going to create a program with a run loop and timer. Every two seconds, the timer will send the action message to its target. You will create a class, and an instance of that class will be the target.

Figure 24.1   Logger is the target of the NSTimer

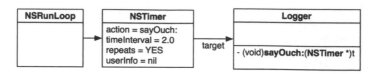

In Xcode, create a new project: a Foundation Command Line Tool named Callbacks. As a goof, first you are just going to get a run loop and start it running. Edit main.m:

```
#import <Foundation/Foundation.h>

int main (int argc, const char * argv[])
{
    @autoreleasepool {

        [[NSRunLoop currentRunLoop] run];

    }
    return 0;
}
```

Build and run the program. Notice that the method run never returns. The run loop is in an infinite loop waiting for something to happen. You'll need to terminate the program. (Choose Product → Stop.)

Now you are going to create a custom class to act as the target of the timer. Create a new file: an Objective-C class called **Logger** that is a subclass of **NSObject**. (Remember, to get to the class template, choose File → New → New File....) In Logger.h, declare the action method:

```
#import <Foundation/Foundation.h>

@interface Logger : NSObject
- (void)sayOuch:(NSTimer *)t;
@end
```

Notice that the action method takes one argument – the object that is sending the action message. In this case, it is the timer object.

Implement a simple **sayOuch:** method in Logger.m:

```
#import "Logger.h"

@implementation Logger

- (void)sayOuch:(NSTimer *)t
{
    NSLog(@"Ouch!");
}

@end
```

At this point, we need to take a short detour and discuss *selectors*. Remember that when you send a message to an object, the object's class is asked if it has a method with that name. The search goes up the inheritance hierarchy until a class responds with "Yeah, I've got a method with that name."

Figure 24.2   The search for a method with the right name

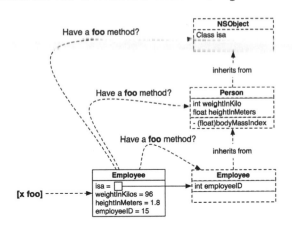

As you can imagine, this search has to happen very, very quickly. If we used the actual name of the method (which could be very long), method lookup would be really slow. To speed things up, the compiler assigns a unique number to each method name it encounters. At runtime, we use that number instead of the method name.

Figure 24.3   How it really works

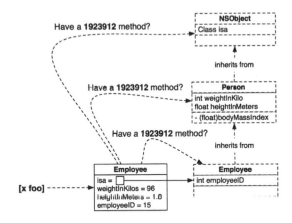

That unique number that represents a particular method name is known as a *selector*. To create a timer that sends the message **sayOuch:** to our **Logger**, you must ask the compiler to look up its selector. This is done with the @selector compiler directive.

In main.m, create an instance of **Logger** and make it the target of an instance of **NSTimer**. Set the action to be the selector for **sayOuch:**.

```
#import <Foundation/Foundation.h>
#import "Logger.h"

int main (int argc, const char * argv[])
{
    @autoreleasepool {

        Logger *logger = [[Logger alloc] init];

        NSTimer *timer = [NSTimer scheduledTimerWithTimeInterval:2.0
                                                target:logger
                                              selector:@selector(sayOuch:)
                                              userInfo:nil
                                               repeats:YES];


        [[NSRunLoop currentRunLoop] run];

    }
    return 0;
}
```

Build and run the program. (You will get an unused variable warning. Ignore it for now.) You should see Ouch! appear in the console every 2 seconds.

Note that the colon is part of the selector. @selector(sayOuch) is *not* equal to @selector(sayOuch:).

Take a second look at the warning from the compiler. It is saying, "Hey, you created the variable timer, but didn't use it." In some settings, like this one, you need to flag a variable as purposefully unused to silence the warnings. This is done with the __unused modifier. Add that now.

```
__unused NSTimer *timer = [NSTimer scheduledTimerWithTimeInterval:2.0
                                                target:logger
                                              selector:@selector(sayOuch:)
                                              userInfo:nil
                                               repeats:YES];
```

Build it again, and the warning should be gone.

Helper objects

Timers are simple. They only do one thing: fire. Thus, target-action is a good fit. A lot of simple user interface controls, like buttons and sliders, also use the target-action mechanism. What about something more complex?

In Chapter 23, you used an **NSURLConnection** method to fetch data from a web server. It worked fine, but there are two problems with the method:

- It blocks the main thread while waiting for all the data to arrive. If you used this method in a real application, the user interface would become unresponsive while the data was fetched.

- It has no way to callback if, for example, the webserver demands a username and password.

For these reasons, we typically use an **NSURLConnection** asynchronously. That is, we start it fetching and then await callbacks as the data arrives or the web server demands credentials or the fetch fails.

How do you get these callbacks? You supply the **NSURLConnection** with a helper object. When things happen, the connection sends messages to the helper object. What messages? The guy who wrote

NSURLConnection made up a *protocol* – a list of method declarations – that the helper object can implement. Here are some of the methods in that protocol:

```
- (NSURLRequest *)connection:(NSURLConnection *)c
            willSendRequest:(NSURLRequest *)req
          redirectResponse:(NSURLResponse *)res;

- (void)connection:(NSURLConnection *)sender
        didReceiveAuthenticationChallenge:(NSURLAuthenticationChallenge *)ch;

- (void)connection:(NSURLConnection *)sender
    didReceiveData:(NSData *)data;

- (void)connectionDidFinishLoading:(NSURLConnection *)sender;

- (void)connection:(NSURLConnection *)sender didFailWithError:(NSError *)error;

- (NSCachedURLResponse *)connection:(NSURLConnection *)sender
                willCacheResponse:(NSCachedURLResponse *)cachedResponse;
```

As you can see, an **NSURLConnection** lives a much richer life than an **NSTimer**. Now you are going to create an object that implements some or all of these methods and then introduce that object to the **NSURLConnection** as its helper object. In particular, the **NSURLConnection** has a pointer called delegate.

Figure 24.4   Logger is the delegate of the NSURLConnection

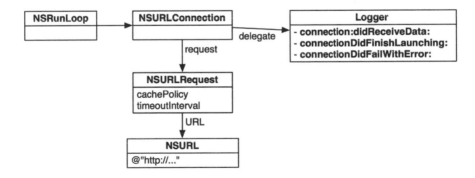

In **main()**, create an **NSURLConnection** and set the instance of **Logger** to be its delegate:

```
#import <Foundation/Foundation.h>
#import "Logger.h"

int main (int argc, const char * argv[])
{
    @autoreleasepool {

        Logger *logger = [[Logger alloc] init];

        NSURL *url = [NSURL URLWithString:
                    @"http://www.gutenberg.org/cache/epub/205/pg205.txt"];
```

```
        NSURLRequest *request = [NSURLRequest requestWithURL:url];

        __unused NSURLConnection *fetchConn
                            = [[NSURLConnection alloc] initWithRequest:request
                                                             delegate:logger
                                                      startImmediately:YES];

        __unused NSTimer *timer
                    = [NSTimer scheduledTimerWithTimeInterval:2.0
                                                       target:logger
                                                     selector:@selector(sayOuch:)
                                                     userInfo:nil
                                                      repeats:YES];

        [[NSRunLoop currentRunLoop] run];

    }
    return 0;
}
```

The instance of **Logger** will need an instance of **NSMutableData** to hold onto the bytes as they arrive. Add an instance variable to Logger.h:

```
#import <Foundation/Foundation.h>

@interface Logger : NSObject {
    NSMutableData *incomingData;
}
- (void)sayOuch:(NSTimer *)t;
@end
```

Now implement some of the delegate methods in Logger.m:

```
#import "Logger.h"

@implementation Logger

- (void)sayOuch:(NSTimer *)t
{
    NSLog(@"Ouch!");
}

// Called each time a chunk of data arrives
- (void)connection:(NSURLConnection *)connection
    didReceiveData:(NSData *)data
{
    NSLog(@"received %lu bytes", [data length]);

    // Create a mutable data if it doesn't already exist
    if (!incomingData) {
        incomingData = [[NSMutableData alloc] init];
    }

    [incomingData appendData:data];
}

// Called when the last chunk has been processed
- (void)connectionDidFinishLoading:(NSURLConnection *)connection
{
    NSLog(@"Got it all!");
```

```
    NSString *string = [[NSString alloc] initWithData:incomingData
                                      encoding:NSUTF8StringEncoding];
    incomingData = nil;
    NSLog(@"string has %lu characters", [string length]);

    // Uncomment the next line to see the entire fetched file
    // NSLog(@"The whole string is %@", string);

}

// Called if the fetch fails
- (void)connection:(NSURLConnection *)connection
  didFailWithError:(NSError *)error
{
    NSLog(@"connection failed: %@", [error localizedDescription]);
    incomingData = nil;
}
```

```
@end
```

Notice that you didn't implement all the methods in the protocol – just the ones that you cared about.

Build and run the program. You should see that the data comes from the web server in reasonable sized chunks. Eventually, the delegate gets informed that the fetch is complete.

Here are the rules, so far, for callbacks: When sending one callback to one object, Apple uses target-action. When sending an assortment of callbacks to one object, Apple uses a helper object with a protocol. (We'll talk more about protocols in the next chapter.) These helper objects are typically called delegate or data source.

What if the callback needs to go to multiple objects?

Notifications

When the user changes the time zone on a Mac, many objects in your program might want to know that the change has occurred. Each one of them can register as an observer with the notification center. When the time zone is changed, the notification NSSystemTimeZoneDidChangeNotification will be posted to the center, and the center will forward it to all the relevant observers.

In main.m, register the instance of **Logger** to receive a notification when the time zone changes:

```
#import <Foundation/Foundation.h>
#import "Logger.h"

int main (int argc, const char * argv[])
{
    @autoreleasepool {

        Logger *logger = [[Logger alloc] init];

        [[NSNotificationCenter defaultCenter]
                            addObserver:logger
                               selector:@selector(zoneChange:)
                                   name:NSSystemTimeZoneDidChangeNotification
                                 object:nil];
```

```
        NSURL *url = [NSURL URLWithString:
                            @"http://www.gutenberg.org/cache/epub/205/pg205.txt"];
        NSURLRequest *request = [NSURLRequest requestWithURL:url];

        __unused NSURLConnection *fetchConn
                            = [[NSURLConnection alloc] initWithRequest:request
                                                        delegate:logger
                                                   startImmediately:YES];

        __unused NSTimer *timer
                    = [NSTimer scheduledTimerWithTimeInterval:2.0
                                                 target:logger
                                               selector:@selector(sayOuch:)
                                               userInfo:nil
                                                repeats:YES];

        [[NSRunLoop currentRunLoop] run];

    }
    return 0;
}
```

Now implement the method that will get called in Logger.m:

```
- (void)zoneChange:(NSNotification *)note
{
    NSLog(@"The system time zone has changed!");
}
```

Build and run the program. While it is running, open System Preferences and change the time zone for your system. You should see that your **zoneChange:** method gets called. (On some systems, it seems to get called twice. This is not cause for concern.)

Which to use?

In this chapter, you have seen three kinds of callbacks. How does Apple decide which one to use in any particular situation?

- Objects that do just one thing (like **NSTimer**) use target-action.

- Objects that have more complicated lives (like an **NSURLConnection**) use helper objects, and the most common type of helper object is the delegate.

- Objects that might need to trigger callbacks in several other objects (like **NSTimeZone**) use notifications.

Callbacks and object ownership

With all of these callbacks, there is a danger that objects waiting for the callbacks might not get deallocated correctly. Thus, it was decided that:

- *Notification centers do not own their observers.* If an object is an observer, it will typically remove itself from the notification center in its **dealloc** method:

```
- (void)dealloc
{
    [[NSNotificationCenter defaultCenter] removeObserver:self];
}
```

- *Objects do not own their delegates or data sources.* If you create an object that is a delegate or data source, your object should "excuse" itself in its **dealloc** method:

```
- (void)dealloc
{
    [windowThatBossesMeAround setDelegate:nil];
    [tableViewThatBegsForData setDataSource:nil];
}
```

- *Objects do not own their targets.* If you create an object that is a target, your object should zero the target pointer in its **dealloc** method:

```
- (void)dealloc
{
    [buttonThatKeepsSendingMeMessages setTarget:nil];
}
```

None of these issues exist in this program because your **Logger** object will not be deallocated before the program terminates. (Also, in a bit of a fluke, in this exercise I used two well-documented exceptions to the rules: an **NSURLConnection** owns its delegate and an **NSTimer** owns its target.)

25

Protocols

At this point, I need to talk about a slightly abstract concept. Someone once said, "It is important to remember that who you are is different from what you do." The same is true of objects: the class of an object is different from its *role* in a working system. For example, an object may be an instance of **NSMutableArray**, but its role in an application may be as a queue of print jobs to be run.

Like the array-as-print-queue example, really great classes are more general than the role they may play in any particular application. Thus, instances of that class can be used in several different ways.

We've talked about how to specify a class. Is it possible to specify a role? To some degree, we can specify a role using the @protocol construct.

For example, in an iOS application, you frequently display data in an instance of the class **UITableView**. However, the **UITableView** object does not contain the data it displays; it has to get data from another source. You have to tell it "Here is the object that will fulfill the role of your data source."

Figure 25.1   UITableView datasource

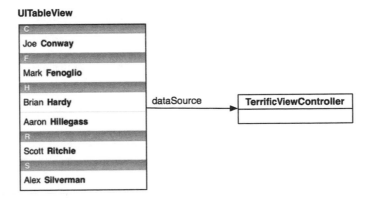

How did the developer who created the **UITableView** class specify the role of **UITableView**'s data source? He created a *protocol*. A protocol is a list of method declarations. Some methods are required, and some are optional. If your object is to fulfill the role, it must implement the required methods and may choose to implement the optional methods.

The data source protocol for **UITableView** is named UITableViewDataSource, and here it is (comments are mine):

```
// Just like classes, protocols can inherit from other protocols.
// This protocol inherits from the NSObject protocol
@protocol UITableViewDataSource <NSObject>

// The following methods must be implemented by any table view data source
@required

// A table view has sections, each section can have several rows
- (NSInteger)tableView:(UITableView *)tv numberOfRowsInSection:(NSInteger)section;

// This index path is two integers (a section and a row)
// The table view cell is what the user sees in that section/row
- (UITableViewCell *)tableView:(UITableView *)tv
        cellForRowAtIndexPath:(NSIndexPath *)ip;


// These methods may (or may not) be implemented by a table view data source
@optional

// If data source doesn't implement this method, table view has only one section
- (NSInteger)numberOfSectionsInTableView:(UITableView *)tv;

// Rows can be deleted and moved
- (BOOL)tableView:(UITableView *)tv canEditRowAtIndexPath:(NSIndexPath *)ip;

- (BOOL)tableView:(UITableView *)tv canMoveRowAtIndexPath:(NSIndexPath *)ip;

- (void)tableView:(UITableView *)tv
commitEditingStyle:(UITableViewCellEditingStyle)editingStyle
 forRowAtIndexPath:(NSIndexPath *)ip;

- (void)tableView:(UITableView *)tv
moveRowAtIndexPath:(NSIndexPath *)sourceIndexPath
        toIndexPath:(NSIndexPath *)destinationIndexPath;
```

// To save ink and paper, I'm leaving out a few optional method declarations.

@end

(Like classes, protocols have reference pages in Apple's developer documentation, which you can search for and browse to see the methods a protocol contains.)

When you create a class to fulfill the role of **UITableView**'s data source, you explicitly say, "This class conforms to the UITableViewDataSource protocol" in the header file. It looks like this:

```
@interface TerrificViewController : UIViewController <UITableViewDataSource>
...
@end
```

That is, "**TerrificViewController** is a subclass of **UIViewController** and conforms to the UITableViewDataSource protocol."

If your class conforms to several protocols, list them within the angle brackets:

```
@interface TerrificViewController : UIViewController
      <UITableViewDataSource, UITableViewDelegate, UITextFieldDelegate>
```

Then, in the TerrificController.m file, you need to implement the required methods in each protocol. If you forget to implement one of the required methods, you will get a stern warning from the compiler.

You will also browse through the optional methods and pick out the ones that you wish to implement. If you implement them, they will be called automatically at the appropriate time.

Final note: In the Callbacks program in Chapter 24, you made an instance of **Logger** the delegate of an **NSURLConnection** object. But you didn't declare in Logger.h that **Logger** conforms to a protocol. As this is being written, there is no formal protocol for **NSURLConnection** delegates. I would not be surprised if this changes. (If when building Callbacks you received a warning along the lines of "This object doesn't conform to the NSURLConnectionDelegate protocol," this change has occurred.)

26

Property Lists

Sometimes you need a file format that can be read by both computers and people. For example, let's say that you want to keep a description of your stock portfolio in a file. As you add new stocks, it would be nice to be able to edit that file easily by hand. But, it might also be handy for one of your programs to be able to read it. When facing this problem, most Objective-C programmers use a *property list*.

A property list is a combination of any of the following things:

- **NSArray**

- **NSDictionary**

- **NSString**

- **NSData**

- **NSDate**

- **NSNumber** (integer, float or Boolean)

For example, an array of dictionaries with string keys and date objects is a property list (or just a "P-list").

Reading and writing a property list to a file is really easy. In Xcode, create a new project: a Foundation Command Line Tool named stockz and add the following code:

```
#import <Foundation/Foundation.h>

int main(int argc, const char * argv[])
{
    @autoreleasepool {

        NSMutableArray *stocks = [[NSMutableArray alloc] init];

        NSMutableDictionary *stock;

        stock = [NSMutableDictionary dictionary];
        [stock setObject:@"AAPL"
                forKey:@"symbol"];
        [stock setObject:[NSNumber numberWithInt:200]
                forKey:@"shares"];
        [stocks addObject:stock];
```

```
        stock = [NSMutableDictionary dictionary];
        [stock setObject:@"GOOG"
                forKey:@"symbol"];
        [stock setObject:[NSNumber numberWithInt:160]
                forKey:@"shares"];
        [stocks addObject:stock];

        [stocks writeToFile:@"/tmp/stocks.plist"
                atomically:YES];

    }
    return 0;
}
```

(Notice that I reused the stock pointer. I used it to point to the first dictionary and then to the second.)

Figure 26.1   An array of dictionaries

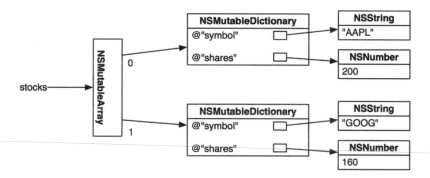

When you run the program, you'll get a file stocks.plist. If you open it in a text editor, it looks like this:

```
<?xml version="1.0" encoding="UTF-8"?>
<!DOCTYPE plist PUBLIC
  "-//Apple//DTD PLIST 1.0//EN" "http://www.apple.com/DTDs/PropertyList-1.0.dtd">
<plist version="1.0">
<array>
    <dict>
        <key>shares</key>
        <integer>200</integer>
        <key>symbol</key>
        <string>AAPL</string>
    </dict>
    <dict>
        <key>shares</key>
        <integer>160</integer>
        <key>symbol</key>
        <string>GOOG</string>
    </dict>
</array>
</plist>
```

Nice, eh? Human-readable. XML. One line of code.

If you find yourself creating property lists by hand, you should know that Xcode has a built-in editor specifically for property lists.

Now add the code that reads the file in:

```
int main(int argc, const char * argv[])
{
    @autoreleasepool {

        NSMutableArray *stocks = [[NSMutableArray alloc] init];

        NSMutableDictionary *stock;

        stock = [NSMutableDictionary dictionary];
        [stock setObject:@"AAPL"
                forKey:@"symbol"];
        [stock setObject:[NSNumber numberWithInt:200]
                forKey:@"shares"];
        [stocks addObject:stock];

        stock = [NSMutableDictionary dictionary];
        [stock setObject:@"GOOG"
                forKey:@"symbol"];
        [stock setObject:[NSNumber numberWithInt:160]
                forKey:@"shares"];
        [stocks addObject:stock];

        [stocks writeToFile:@"/tmp/stocks.plist"
                atomically:YES];

        NSArray *stockList = [NSArray arrayWithContentsOfFile:@"/tmp/stocks.plist"];

        for (NSDictionary *d in stockList) {
            NSLog(@"I have %@ shares of %@",
                    [d objectForKey:@"shares"], [d objectForKey:@"symbol"]);
        }

    }
    return 0;
}
```

Build and run the program.

Challenge

Write a tool that creates a property list that has all 8 types in it: array, dictionary, string, data, date, integer, float, boolean.

Part IV
Event-Driven Applications

Here's where we've been heading and why you've been reading this book – writing iOS and Cocoa apps. In the next two chapters, you'll get a taste of application development. Your applications will have a GUI (graphical user interface), and they will be event-driven.

In a command-line program, you execute the program, and then it does its own thing until it's all finished. An *event-driven application* is different. It launches and then starts a run loop which waits for events. When an event happens, the application leaps into action, executing methods, sending messages, etc.

First, you'll write an iOS application and then a similar Cocoa application. Cocoa is the collection of frameworks written by Apple that you use to write applications on the Mac. You're already familiar with one of these frameworks – Foundation.

To write iOS apps, you use another set of frameworks called Cocoa Touch. Cocoa and Cocoa Touch have some frameworks in common, like Foundation. Others are specific to one platform or the other.

27

Your First iOS Application

In this chapter, you are going to create an iOS application: a simple to-do list application called iTahDoodle that stores its data as a property list. Here's what iTahDoodle will look like when you're done.

Figure 27.1   Complete iTahDoodle application

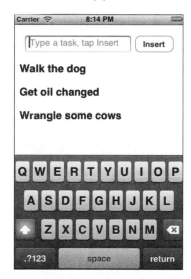

All iOS applications are event-driven applications. The run loop waits for events. The waiting application then responds to events generated by the user (like a button tap) or the system (like a low-memory warning).

Getting started with iTahDoodle

In Xcode, choose File → New → New Project.... Under the iOS section (not the Mac OS X section), click on Application. From the template choices that appear, select Empty Application.

Figure 27.2   Creating a new iOS Application

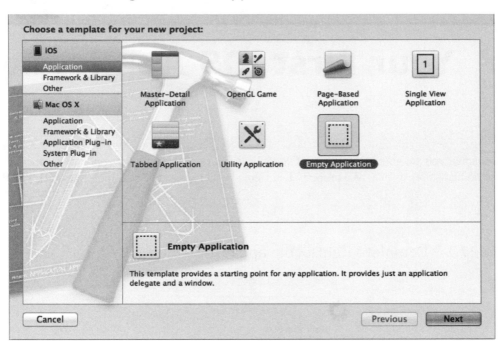

Xcode's project templates exist to make your job easier. They contain boilerplate code that can speed up development. However, here we intentionally choose the Empty Application template, which is as close to a blank template as you can get. Allowing Xcode to generate too much boilerplate code at this point gets in the way of your learning how things work.

In addition, the names of these templates often change with new Xcode releases, so don't worry if the templates you see don't exactly match Figure 27.2. Look for the simplest-sounding template and then make changes to align your code with the book's code. If you have trouble reconciling your code or project templates, visit the Big Nerd Ranch forum for this book at forums.bignerdranch.com for help.

After choosing the Empty Application template, click Next and name this project iTahDoodle. The Company Identifier and Bundle Identifier are related to keeping each app on the App Store unique. Both are strings in reverse-domain notation. Big Nerd Ranch uses com.bignerdranch as its Company Identifier.

Figure 27.3   Configuring the iTahDoodle project

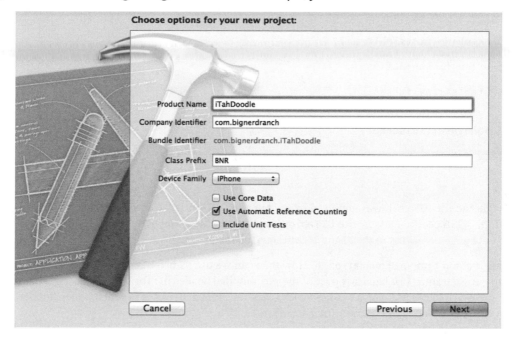

Whatever you enter as the Class Prefix will be prepended to the name of the initial class that the template creates for you. This two- or three-letter prefix will keep your class names distinct from Apple's or anyone else's. (Use BNR for now to keep our code in sync.)

Notice that Apple's code includes prefixes. All of Apple's classes that you've seen so far begin with the prefix **NS**, which stands for NeXTSTEP, the platform for which the Foundation framework was originally designed. In this chapter, you'll also use classes from the UIKit framework, and they will begin with **UI**.

Finally, make iTahDoodle an iPhone (as opposed to iPad or Universal) application. iTahDoodle will use Automatic Reference Counting but not use Core Data or unit tests.

BNRAppDelegate

When Xcode created your project via the Empty Application template, it created one class for you: **BNRAppDelegate**. Your "app delegate" is the starting point of your application, and every iOS application has one. The single instance of **BNRAppDelegate** is responsible for processing events and coordinating the work of other objects in the application.

Open BNRAppDelegate.h. Add four instance variables and an instance method. The first three instance variables are pointers to objects that the user can see and interact with – a table view that will display all the tasks to be done, a text field where you can enter a new task, and a button that will add the new task to the table. The fourth object is a mutable array. This is where you will store the tasks as strings.

```
#import <UIKit/UIKit.h>

@interface BNRAppDelegate : UIResponder
<UIApplicationDelegate>
{
    UITableView *taskTable;
    UITextField *taskField;
    UIButton *insertButton;

    NSMutableArray *tasks;
}

- (void)addTask:(id)sender;

@property (strong, nonatomic) UIWindow *window;

@end
```

Notice that the file UIKit.h was imported by the template. UIKit is the framework that contains most of the iOS-specific classes, like **UITableView**, **UITextField**, and **UIButton**. In addition, **BNRAppDelegate** conforms to the UIApplicationDelegate protocol.

Note that we don't import Foundation.h. How then can we use **NSMutableArray**? In this template, the Foundation framework header is part of the precompiled header file for this project, so Foundation classes are available to use. (Don't believe me? Click on iTahDoodle-Prefix.pch under Supporting Files in the project navigator and see for yourself.)

Adding a C helper function

We can tell from the instance variable declarations that the iTahDoodle application will include at least four additional objects. However, before we get to these objects, you're going to write a C function. In Objective-C, we usually get things done with methods rather than functions. So when we do use a C function in an Objective-C application, we often refer to them as "helper" functions.

iTahDoodle will store the user's tasks as a property list – an XML file. Therefore, you will need a way to get this file's location while your application is running. You're going to write a C function that returns that file path as an **NSString**.

To add a helper function to your application, you first need to declare it in BNRAppDelegate.h.

```
#import <UIKit/UIKit.h>

// Declare a helper function that we will use to get a path
// to the location on disk where we can save the to-do list
NSString *docPath(void);

@interface BNRAppDelegate : UIResponder
<UIApplicationDelegate>
{
    UITableView *taskTable;
    UITextField *taskField;
    UIButton *insertButton;

    NSMutableArray *tasks;
}
```

```
- (void)addTask:(id)sender;

@property (strong, nonatomic) UIWindow *window;

@end
```

Notice that you declare **docPath()** above the class declaration. That's because even though **docPath()** is declared in the file BNRAppDelegate.h, it is not part of the **BNRAppDelegate** class. In fact, this function could have its own pair of files in the iTahDoodle project. However, because there is just one of these helper functions in iTahDoodle, we're putting it the app delegate's class files to keep things simple.

Now open BNRAppDelegate.m and implement your helper function. Again, because **docPath()** is not part of the class, implement it after the #import but before the @implementation line (which is where the implementation of the class begins).

```
#import "BNRAppDelegate.h"


// Helper function to fetch the path to our to-do data stored on disk
NSString *docPath()
{
    NSArray *pathList = NSSearchPathForDirectoriesInDomains(NSDocumentDirectory,
                                                  NSUserDomainMask, YES);
    return [[pathList objectAtIndex:0] stringByAppendingPathComponent:@"data.td"];
}


@implementation
```

The **docPath()** function calls another C function, **NSSearchPathForDirectoriesInDomains()**. This function searches for directories that match specific criteria and returns an array of them. Don't worry about what the arguments are; in nearly all iOS applications you will ever write, you'll pass in the exact same three arguments and get back an array with exactly one item. (If you're curious about how it works, you'll find **NSSearchPathForDirectoriesInDomains()** in the *Foundation Functions Reference* in the developer documentation.)

Objects in iTahDoodle

Now we can get back to our objects. You already know about the five objects that make up the iTahDoodle application. There's the instance of **BNRAppDelegate**, and this object has pointers to four others: instances of **UITableView**, **UITextField**, **UIButton**, and **NSMutableArray**.

Figure 27.4   Object diagram for iTahDoodle

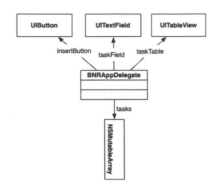

Before we continue configuring and connecting these objects, let's look at some theory about objects and their relationships.

Model-View-Controller

Model-View-Controller, or MVC, is a design pattern that centers on the idea that any class that you create should fall into one of three job categories: model, view, or controller. Here's a breakdown of the division of labor:

- *Models* are responsible for storing data and making it available to other objects. Models have no knowledge of the user interface or how to draw themselves on the screen; their sole purpose is holding and managing data. **NSString**, **NSDate**, and **NSArray** are traditional model objects. In iTahDoodle, your one model object so far is the **NSMutableArray** where tasks are stored. However, each individual task will be described an instance of **NSString**, and these will also be model objects.

- *Views* are the visual elements of an application. Views know how to draw themselves on the screen and how to respond to user input. Views have no knowledge of the actual data that they display or how it is structured and stored. **UIView** and its various subclasses, including **UIWindow**, are common examples of view objects. In iTahDoodle, your view objects are the instances of **UITableView**, **UITextView**, and **UIButton**. A simple rule of thumb is that if you can see it, it's a view.

- *Controllers* perform the logic necessary to connect and drive the different parts of your application. They process events and coordinate the other objects in your application. Controllers are the real workhorses of any application. While **BNRAppDelegate** is the only controller in iTahDoodle, a complex application will have many different controllers that coordinate model and view objects as well as other controllers.

Figure 27.5 shows the flow of control between objects in response to a user event, like a button tap. Notice that models and views do not talk to each other directly; controllers sit squarely in the middle of everything, receiving messages from some objects and dispatching instructions to others.

Figure 27.5 MVC flow with user input

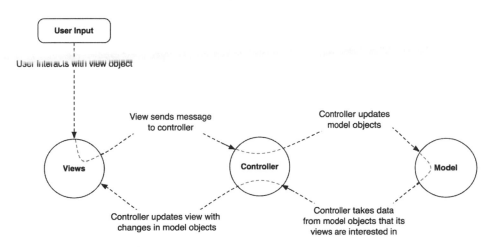

It's critical not to underestimate the division of responsibilities denoted by the MVC pattern. Most of the Cocoa and Cocoa Touch APIs are written with MVC in mind, and your own code should be, too. Now let's return to our controller, the instance of **BNRAppDelegate**.

The application delegate

When an iOS application first launches, there is a lot of behind-the-scenes setting up. During this phase, an instance of **UIApplication** is created to control your application's state and act as liaison to the operating system. An instance of **BNRAppDelegate** is also created and set as the delegate of the **UIApplication** instance (which explains the name "app delegate").

While the application is being launched, it is not ready for work or input.
When this changes, the **UIApplication** instance sends its delegate the message **application:didFinishLaunchingWithOptions:**. This method is very important. It's where you put everything that needs to happen or needs to be in place before the user interacts with the application.

In iTahDoodle, one of the things we need to do in this method is find the property list and load it into an array. In BNRAppDelegate.m, notice that there is already a *stub* for the **application:didFinishLaunchingWithOptions:** method. Find it and replace the code between its braces with the following:

```
#pragma mark - Application delegate callbacks

- (BOOL)application:(UIApplication *)application
didFinishLaunchingWithOptions:(NSDictionary *)launchOptions
{
  // Attempt to load an existing to-do dataset from an array stored to disk.
    NSArray *plist = [NSArray arrayWithContentsOfFile:docPath()];
    if (plist) {
        // If there was a dataset available, copy it into our instance variable.
        tasks = [plist mutableCopy];
    } else {
```

```
        // Otherwise, just create an empty one to get us started.
        tasks = [[NSMutableArray alloc] init];
    }
}
```

Wondering about the `#pragma mark` at the start of this code? Objective-C programmers often use this construct to group their methods within a class. Xcode knows about it, too. On the navigation bar at the top of the editor, find the item to the right of BNRAppDelegate.m. (Right now, this item probably reads @implementation AppDelegate, but it depends on where your cursor is in the code.) Click on this item, and Xcode will show you a list of locations in this file. You can click on any of these to be taken to that location in the code. Notice that your new pragma mark shows up on this list. This is very handy when you have many methods in a class.

Setting up views

Another thing we need to do before the application is ready for action is set up our view objects. This includes creating them, configuring them, and putting them on the screen. Makes sense, right? The user can't tap a button that doesn't exist or is not on the screen.

In iTahDoodle, you're going to set up your views programmatically in `application:didFinishLaunchingWithOptions:`. There is also a visual "drag-and-drop" tool for setting up views that we'll use in the next chapter.

I should warn you that here's where the code starts getting dense. The detailed syntax of creating and showing views on the screen is a topic for a book specifically about iOS application programming. Try to follow the gist of what's going on as you type in the code. You create each object and then configure it by setting some of its properties. Next, the configured view objects are added as *subviews* of the window object, and, finally, the window is placed on the screen.

```
#pragma mark - Application delegate callbacks

- (BOOL)application:(UIApplication *)application
didFinishLaunchingWithOptions:(NSDictionary *)launchOptions
{
    // Attempt to load an existing to-do dataset from an array stored to disk.
    NSArray *plist = [NSArray arrayWithContentsOfFile:docPath()];
    if (plist) {
        // If there was a dataset available, copy it into our instance variable.
        tasks = [plist mutableCopy];
    } else {
        // Otherwise, just create an empty one to get us started.
        tasks = [[NSMutableArray alloc] init];
    }

    // Create and configure the UIWindow instance
    // A CGRect is a struct with an origin (x,y) and size (width,height)
    CGRect windowFrame = [[UIScreen mainScreen] bounds];
    UIWindow *theWindow = [[UIWindow alloc] initWithFrame:windowFrame];
    [self setWindow:theWindow];

    // Define the frame rectangles of the three UI elements
    // CGRectMake() creates a CGRect from (x, y, width, height)
    CGRect tableFrame = CGRectMake(0, 80, 320, 380);
    CGRect fieldFrame = CGRectMake(20, 40, 200, 31);
    CGRect buttonFrame = CGRectMake(228, 40, 72, 31);
```

```
    // Create and configure the table view
    taskTable = [[UITableView alloc] initWithFrame:tableFrame
                                        style:UITableViewStylePlain];
    [taskTable setSeparatorStyle:UITableViewCellSeparatorStyleNone];

    // Create and configure the text field where new tasks will be typed
    taskField = [[UITextField alloc] initWithFrame:fieldFrame];
    [taskField setBorderStyle:UITextBorderStyleRoundedRect];
    [taskField setPlaceholder:@"Type a task, tap Insert"];

    // Create and configure a rounded rect Insert button
    insertButton = [UIButton buttonWithType:UIButtonTypeRoundedRect];
    [insertButton setFrame:buttonFrame];

    // Buttons behave using a target/action callback
    // Configure the Insert button's action to call this object's -addTask: method
    [insertButton addTarget:self
                    action:@selector(addTask:)
            forControlEvents:UIControlEventTouchUpInside];

    // Give the button a title
    [insertButton setTitle:@"Insert"
                forState:UIControlStateNormal];

    // Add our three UI elements to the window
    [[self window] addSubview:taskTable];
    [[self window] addSubview:taskField];
    [[self window] addSubview:insertButton];

    // Finalize the window and put it on the screen
    [[self window] setBackgroundColor:[UIColor whiteColor]];
    [[self window] makeKeyAndVisible];

    return YES;
}
```

Running on the iOS simulator

Now that you've set up your views, we can build the application to see how they look. In Xcode, find the Scheme dropdown menu near the Run button. Select iPhone 5.X Simulator for the latest version of the iOS simulator:

Figure 27.6   Scheme selector

Build and run the application. You'll get a warning from the compiler that you that you haven't implemented **addTask:**. Ignore that for now; you'll implement **addTask:** shortly.

The simulator lets you run Cocoa Touch applications on your desktop. This is a quick and easy way to see what your program should look and act like when it runs on an iOS device.

You can see the views that you set up and laid out in
application:didFinishLaunchingWithOptions:, but they can't do anything yet. In fact, tapping
the Insert button will crash the application because the button's action method, **addTask:**, isn't
implemented yet. (That's one of the reasons the compiler warned you about it.)

Figure 27.7   iTahDoodle object diagram

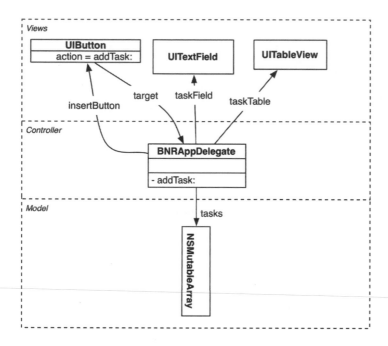

Wiring up the table view

You've got a table view on the screen, but it has no clue about what it should display. As a view object,
the table view does not contain anything about actual data. It needs an object to act as its data source.
In iTahDoodle, your table view's data source will be the instance of **BNRAppDelegate**.

In BNRAppDelegate.m, update **application:didFinishLaunchingWithOptions:** to send a message to
the table view that makes the **BNRAppDelegate** instance its data source:

```
...
// Create and configure the table view
taskTable = [[UITableView alloc] initWithFrame:tableFrame
                                    style:UITableViewStylePlain];
[taskTable setSeparatorStyle:UITableViewCellSeparatorStyleNone];

// Make this object the table view's dataSource
[taskTable setDataSource:self];

// Create and configure the text field where new tasks will be typed
taskField = [[UITextField alloc] initWithFrame:fieldFrame];
...
```

In order for the table view's data source to do its job, it must implement methods in the UITableViewDataSource protocol. First, update BNRAppDelegate.h to declare that **BNRAppDelegate** conforms to this protocol:

```
@interface BNRAppDelegate : UIResponder
<UIApplicationDelegate, UITableViewDataSource>
{
    UITableView *taskTable;
    UITextField *taskField;
    UIButton *insertButton;

    NSMutableArray *tasks;
}
- (void)addTask:(id)sender;
```

The UITableViewDataSource protocol has two required methods that **BNRAppDelegate** must now implement. At a minimum, a table view's data source must be prepared to tell the table view how many rows are in a given section of the table, and what the cell in a given row should be.

Implement the callbacks accordingly:

```
#pragma mark - Table View management

- (NSInteger)tableView:(UITableView *)tableView
 numberOfRowsInSection:(NSInteger)section
{
    // Because this table view only has one section,
    // the number of rows in it is equal to the number
    // of items in our tasks array
    return [tasks count];
}

- (UITableViewCell *)tableView:(UITableView *)tableView
        cellForRowAtIndexPath:(NSIndexPath *)indexPath
{
    // To improve performance, we reconfigure cells in memory
    // that have scrolled off the screen and hand them back
    // with new contents instead of always creating new cells.
    // First, we check to see if there's a cell available for reuse.
    UITableViewCell *c = [taskTable dequeueReusableCellWithIdentifier:@"Cell"];

    if (!c) {
        // ...and only allocate a new cell if none are available
        c = [[UITableViewCell alloc] initWithStyle:UITableViewCellStyleDefault
                                    reuseIdentifier:@"Cell"];
    }

    // Then we (re)configure the cell based on the model object,
    // in this case our todoItems array
    NSString *item = [tasks objectAtIndex:[indexPath row]];
    [[c textLabel] setText:item];

    // and hand back to the table view the properly configured cell
    return c;
}
```

To test the application, add some data directly to the array at the top of
application:didFinishLaunchingWithOptions:.

```
- (BOOL)application:(UIApplication *)application
didFinishLaunchingWithOptions:(NSDictionary *)launchOptions
{
    // Attempt to load an existing to-do dataset from an array stored to disk.
    NSArray *plist = [NSArray arrayWithContentsOfFile:docPath()];
    if (plist) {
        // If there was a dataset available, copy it into our instance variable.
        tasks = [plist mutableCopy];
    } else {
        // Otherwise, just create an empty one to get us started.
        tasks = [[NSMutableArray alloc] init];
    }

    // Is tasks empty?
    if ([tasks count] == 0) {
        // Put some strings in it
        [tasks addObject:@"Walk the dogs"];
        [tasks addObject:@"Feed the hogs"];
        [tasks addObject:@"Chop the logs"];
    }

    // Create and configure the UIWindow instance
    CGRect windowFrame = [[UIScreen mainScreen] bounds];
    UIWindow *theWindow = [[UIWindow alloc] initWithFrame:windowFrame];
    [self setWindow:theWindow];

    ...
}
```

Figure 27.8   Complete object diagram for iTahDoodle

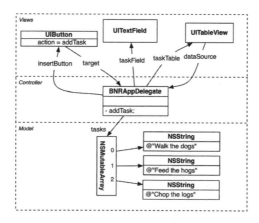

Build and run the application. The table view should display your test data. You still can't add new tasks, though. Once more into the breach!

Adding new tasks

When you created the **UIButton** instance in **application:didFinishLaunchingWithOptions:**, you gave it a target/action pair:

```
[insertButton addTarget:self
                  action:@selector(addTask:)
        forControlEvents:UIControlEventTouchUpInside];
```

The target is self, and the action is **addTask:**. So the Insert button sends the **BNRAppDelegate** the **addTask:** message. Thus, we need to implement the **addTask:** method in BNRAppDelegate.m.

```
- (void)addTask:(id)sender
{
    // Get the to-do item
    NSString *t = [taskField text];

    // Quit here if taskField is empty
    if ([t isEqualToString:@""]) {
        return;
    }

    // Add it to our working array
    [tasks addObject:t];
    // Refresh the table so that the new item shows up
    [taskTable reloadData];
    // And clear out the text field
    [taskField setText:@""];
    // Dismiss the keyboard
    [taskField resignFirstResponder];
}
```

What's this **resignFirstResponder** business? Here's the short version:

Some view objects are also *controls* – views that the user can interact with. Buttons, sliders, and text fields are examples of controls. When there are controls on the screen, one of them can be the *first responder*. Having first responder status means that the control gets dibs on handling any text input from the keyboard or any shake events (such as "Shake to Undo").

When the user taps a control that can accept first responder status, that control is sent the **becomeFirstResponder** message. Until another control becomes the first responder or the current control is sent the **resignFirstResponder** message, that control will keep this status and receive keyboard and shake input.

When a text input control (like a text field) becomes the first responder, the keyboard materializes on the screen. As long as the current first responder is a control that accepts text input, the keyboard will remain on the screen. At the end of **addTask:**, we tell the text field to resign its status, which causes the keyboard to dematerialize.

Build and run the application. Now you can add tasks!

Saving task data

There is one final feature that you'll add to iTahDoodle. Naturally, when users quit the app, they'd like their to-do lists to stick around for later.

When a Cocoa Touch application quits or is sent to the background, it sends its delegate a message from the UIApplicationDelegate protocol so that the delegate can take care of business and respond to these events gracefully. In BNRAppDelegate.m, fill in the stubs of these two application delegate callbacks to save the to-do list:

```
- (void)applicationDidEnterBackground:(UIApplication *)application
{
    // This method is only called in iOS 4.0+

    // Save our tasks array to disk
    [tasks writeToFile:docPath() atomically:YES];
}
- (void)applicationWillTerminate:(UIApplication *)application
{
    // This method is only called in iOS versions prior to 4.0

    // Save our tasks array to disk
    [tasks writeToFile:docPath() atomically:YES];
}
```

Now build and run your completed application. This exercise was intended to give you a taste of iOS development. There's much, much more out there to do and learn.

For the More Curious: What about main()?

When you began learning C and Objective-C, you learned that the entry point into your program's code is the main() function. It's absolutely true in Cocoa / Cocoa Touch development as well, although it's extremely rare to edit this function in Cocoa and Cocoa Touch applications. Open main.m, and you'll see why:

```
return UIApplicationMain(argc, argv, nil, NSStringFromClass([BNRAppDelegate class]));
```

Well, that was anti-climactic. Only one line of actual code.

The UIApplicationMain() function creates the necessary objects for your application to run. First, it creates a single instance of the UIApplication class. Then, it creates an instance of whatever class is denoted by the fourth and final argument and sets it to be the application's delegate, so that it can send its delegate messages when memory gets low, when the application is quit or backgrounded, or when it finishes launching.

And that's the trail from main() to application:didFinishLaunchingWithOptions: and your custom code.

28

Your First Cocoa Application

In this chapter, you are going to create TahDoodle, a desktop Cocoa application. Like iTahDoodle, TahDoodle is a simple to-do list application that stores its data as a property list; however, there are some differences. In the iOS application, you used instances of **UITableView**, **UITextField**, and **UIButton**. In this desktop application, you will place the task list in an **NSTableView** where it can be edited directly. You will also have an **NSButton** that will insert a new row in the table view where you can add a new task.

Figure 28.1 Complete TahDoodle application

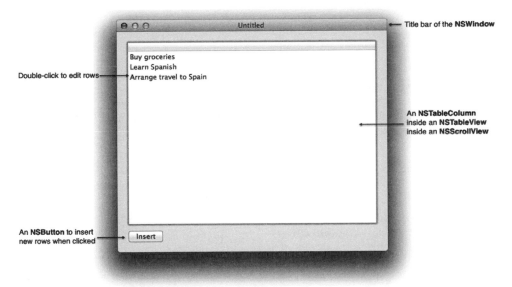

In addition, in the last chapter, you built your user interface programmatically. In this chapter, you will use a tool included in Xcode called Interface Builder to create, configure, and connect the elements of your user interface.

In Xcode, choose File → New → New Project.... Under the Mac OS X section, click on Application. From the template choices that appear, select Cocoa Application and name the project TahDoodle. TahDoodle is *document-based*, which means the user can have multiple to-do lists open simultaneously.

Document Extension refers to the filename extension to be used when saving your documents (to-do lists) to disk. Set the extension for your data files to be tdl. TahDoodle will not use Core Data or need unit tests.

Figure 28.2   Creating a new Cocoa Application

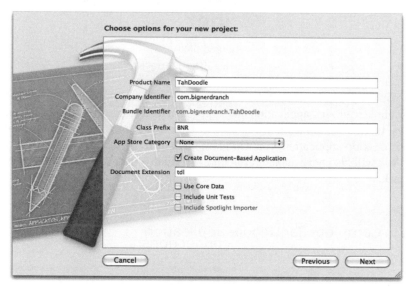

Edit BNRDocument.h

Open BNRDocument.h and add a method and two instance variables: todoItems will be a mutable array of strings and itemTableView will be a pointer to the **NSTableView** object that will display the strings in todoItems. Also, declare that **BNRDocument** conforms to the NSTableViewDataSource protocol.

```
#import <Cocoa/Cocoa.h>

@interface BNRDocument : NSDocument <NSTableViewDataSource>
{
    NSMutableArray *todoItems;
    IBOutlet NSTableView *itemTableView;
}
- (IBAction)createNewItem:(id)sender;

@end
```

Note that there is no instance variable for the Insert button. (You'll see why later.) There is, however, an action for the button – the **createNewItem:** method.

In the last chapter, the target of the button's action was the instance of the application delegate class, **BNRAppDelegate**. A document-based application doesn't have an application delegate object and instead is built around a subclass of **NSDocument**. For TahDoodle, that class is **BNRDocument**.

In a document-based application, the user can have multiple instances of document objects open at the same time. So when TahDoodle is running, you can have multiple instances of **BNRDocument** (multiple to-do lists). Each instance will have its own table view, button, tasks array, and window. Each instance will respond to messages independently of the others, and each instance will be its own button's target.

In the declarations you entered, there are also two new terms: IBOutlet and IBAction. These tell Xcode "This is a pointer (IBOutlet) or an action method (IBAction) that the developer will use Interface Builder to connect rather than doing so programmatically."

A look at Interface Builder

In the project navigator, find and select a file named BNRDocument.xib. When you select a file in the project navigator that ends in .xib (XML Interface Builder document), Interface Builder appears in the editor pane, displaying a layout grid.

Right now, there is only one view object on the layout grid – a window object. That's an instance of **NSWindow**, to which you'll add other view objects shortly.

Now, in the upper-right corner of the Xcode window, click on the righthand View button to reveal the Utilities. At the top of Utilities, click the ▤ button to reveal the *inspector*.

The inspector is subdivided into separate inspectors. In this chapter, you'll use the attributes, size, and connections inspectors.

Figure 28.3   Attributes, size, and connections inspectors

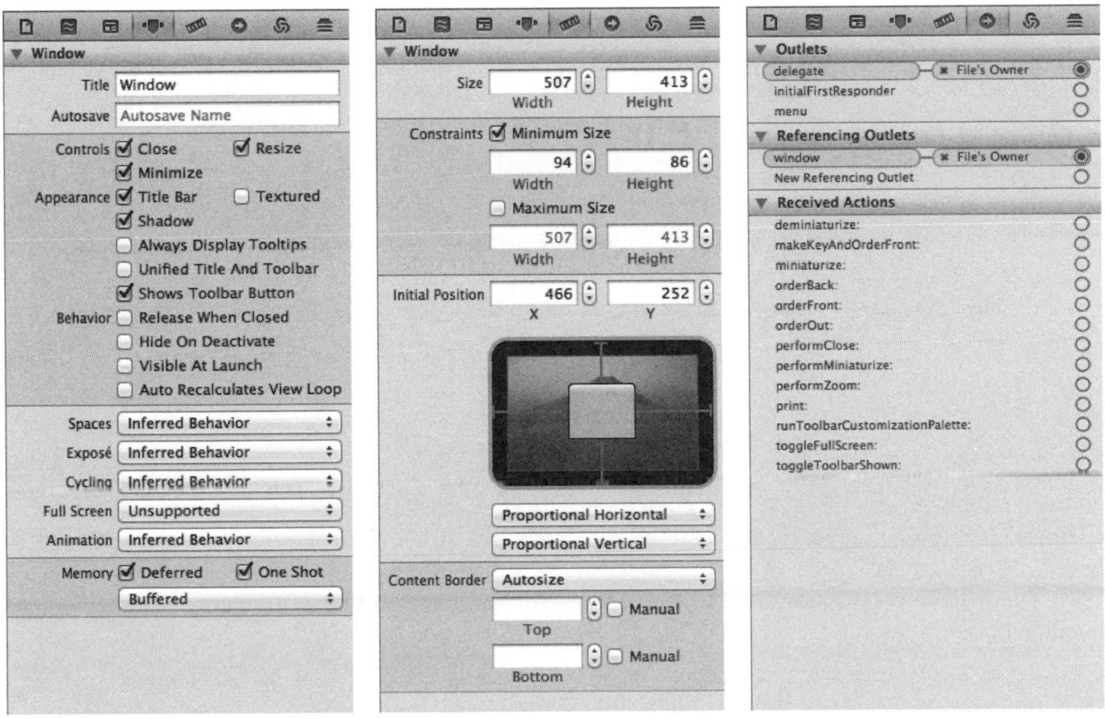

At the bottom of the Utilities pane, below the inspector, is the *library*, which is also divided into tabs. Select the ⬢ button to reveal the *object library*. This library presents a list of all of the different object types that Interface Builder knows about, and it's where you get the interface elements to drag and drop on the window object.

At the bottom of the library is a search field. Type table to filter the list of objects. The first item, Table View, represents an instance of the **NSTableView** class. You can click on it to see its details.

Edit BNRDocument.xib

Drag an instance of **NSTableView** from the object library onto the window object. Resize the table to fill most of the window but leave room on the bottom for a button.

Figure 28.4   Adding an NSTableView

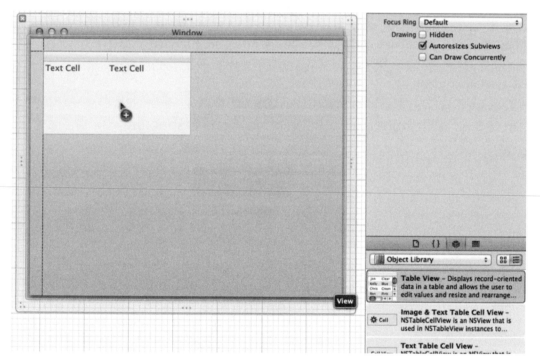

Notice that the object's edges snap to guides when they approach the edges of the window or other objects. These guides align view objects in accordance with Apple's *Human Interface Guidelines*, or *HIG*. These are the rules that any developer should follow when designing user interfaces for the Mac. There are also HIGs for the iPhone and iPad. You can find all of the HIGs in the developer documentation.

Now you're going to set some of the table view's attributes in the *attributes inspector*. Normally, you click on an object on the layout grid, and the inspector changes context to show you the attributes of that object. Getting to the attributes of an instance of **NSTableView** is trickier. The table view object that you dragged onto the window is actually a collection of nested objects: an **NSScrollView**, an **NSTableView**, and one or more **NSTableColumn** instances. To get to a particular object in this collection, hold down the Control and Shift keys while clicking on the table view. You will see a list of the objects under the cursor, and from there, you can select the object you're really interested in. Select the **NSTableView**.

Figure 28.5   Selecting a view from a stack

In the attributes inspector, set the table view to have one column. Then, back in the editor, select the table view's header and resize the lone column to be the full width of the table view.

Figure 28.6   Resizing columns

You've sized your views nicely, but what will happen when the user resizes the windows in your application? You can make the table view resize with the window. Actually, you are going to make the *scroll view* that contains the table view resize with the window. Control-Shift-click on the table view, and select the **NSScrollView** from the list. At the top of the inspector pane, click the ⬤ button to reveal the *size inspector*. Then find the section called Autosizing.

The autosizing section contains the autosizing mask – a control that lets you configure how the selected view object will react when its superview is resized. Views exist in a hierarchy much like classes do. So views can have superviews and subviews. The **NSScrollView**'s superview is the instance of **NSWindow**.

The autosizing mask contains four *struts* that look like I-beams and two *springs* shown as double-headed arrows. Enabling one of the springs allows the selected view object to expand in the indicated direction as its superview expands. Enabling a strut anchors the selected view object to the indicated edge of its superview. Fortunately, there is a handy animation right next to the autosizing mask that lets you preview the effect a combination of springs and struts will have on the selected view object.

Set all four struts and both springs in the autosizing mask. This will anchor all four sides of the scroll view to their respective edges of the window and allow the scroll view (and the table view within it) to expand horizontally and vertically as the window is resized.

Figure 28.7   Setting the autosizing mask

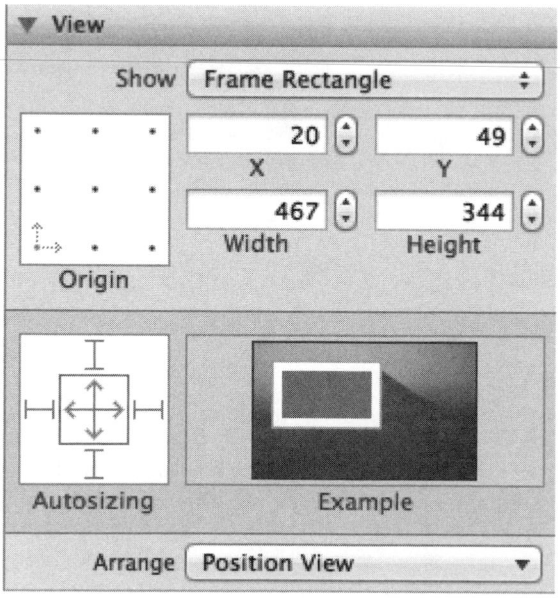

Now let's move from the table view and turn to the button. Head back to the object library. Find and drag an instance of **NSButton** onto the window object. You can choose any of the button styles listed in the library; Rounded Rect Button is a classic. Once you've dragged the button onto the window, you can change its label by double-clicking on the button's text and typing. Make it an Insert button.

Finally, in the size inspector, use the autosizing mask to make the button stick to the lower left corner of the window and maintain its present size.

Figure 28.8   Autosize mask for Insert button

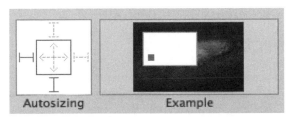

So what you've done is create the two view objects you need for TahDoodle: an **NSTableView** and an **NSButton**. You also configured these objects. You set the number of columns in the table view and set the button's title. You also made sure they will resize and position themselves appropriately when the window is resized.

Figure 28.9   BNRDocument.xib with views configured

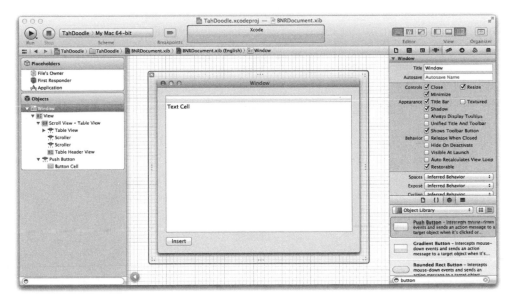

When you double-clicked on the **NSButton** and typed in a title, you were doing the same thing as in the last chapter when you added this line of code:

```
[insertButton setTitle:@"Insert"
            forState:UIControlStateNormal];
```

So when do you use Interface Builder and when do you set up views programmatically? Under simple circumstances, either will work. We could have built iTahDoodle's interface with a XIB. In general, however, the more complex your user interface, the more sense it makes to use Interface Builder.

(Now that you've seen more of Xcode, take a look at the tear-out card at the back of this book. This card contains keyboard shortcuts for navigating around Xcode. There are a bunch of them! As you continue with Xcode, use this card to find shortcuts that will save you time and clicks.)

Making connections

Creating and configuring views is not all that you can do in Interface Builder. You can also connect, or "wire," these view objects to your application's code. In particular, you can set target-action pairs and assign pointers.

To the left of the layout grid is a list of "placeholders" and objects. This is called the *document outline*. (If you just see a stack of icons without labels, click the ● button to reveal the expanded list.)

Figure 28.10   Minimized and expanded document outline

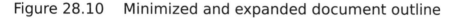

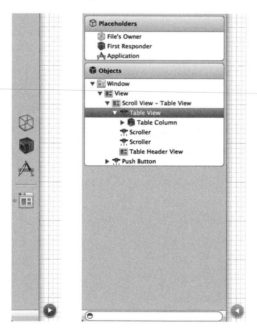

Find File's Owner under the Placeholders section of the document outline. A placeholder stands in for a particular object that cannot be specified until runtime. File's Owner stands in for whichever object will load this XIB as its user interface. In your case, File's Owner represents an instance of **BNRDocument**.

Now select the Insert button in the editor and Control-drag to File's Owner.

Figure 28.11 Making connections

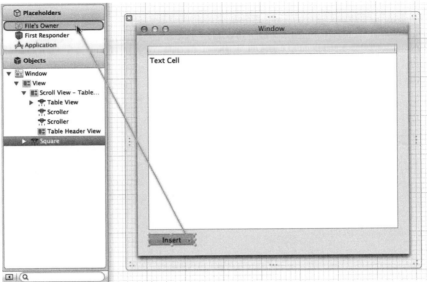

When you release the mouse button, a small pop-up will appear showing the available connections that you can make. Choose `createNewItem:` as the action to be triggered by the button.

Figure 28.12 Selecting an action

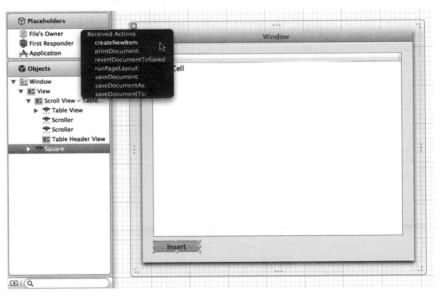

You've now configured the target-action pair. This is equivalent to the following code in iTahDoodle.

```
[insertButton addTarget:self
              action:@selector(addTask:)
        forControlEvents:UIControlEventTouchUpInside];
```

Next, connect **BNRDocument**'s itemTableView outlet. Control-drag from File's Owner (standing in for the **BNRDocument**) to the **NSTableView** and release. Choose the only option that appears for this outlet: itemTableView.

Figure 28.13   Making more connections

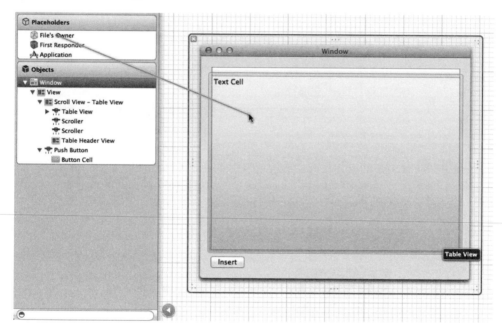

Finally, Control-Shift-click on the table view and select the **NSTableView** from the list. Then Control-drag from the table view to File's Owner and select dataSource from the connection pop-up.

Figure 28.14   Connecting the table view's data source

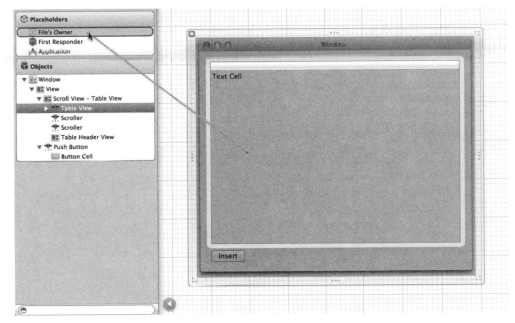

So what, exactly, did you just do? You assigned pointers. Your **BNRDocument** class declares a pointer to an **NSTableView**. You instructed Interface Builder that you want this pointer to point to the specific **NSTableView** instance that you dragged onto the window. Similarly, the table view has a few pointers of its own, like dataSource. You instructed Interface Builder to point the table view's dataSource pointer at your **BNRDocument**. This is equivalent to when you set the table view's data source programmatically in iTahDoodle.

```
[taskTable setDataSource:self];
```

When you entered the IBOutlet and IBAction keywords, you were flagging those outlets and actions for Interface Builder, saying "Hey! When I try to connect a pointer in IB, make sure and put this item in the list of available connections!" As you write your code, Interface Builder scans for IBOutlet and IBAction keywords so that it knows what connections you might want to make.

Here are the actual definitions:

```
#define IBAction void
#define IBOutlet
```

From what we learned about #define, we know that IBAction is replaced with void before the compiler sees it and that IBOutlet disappears altogether. Thus, at compile time, all IBOutlet keywords are removed entirely (leaving behind the outlets themselves). IBAction keywords are replaced by void because actions invoked by user interface controls are not expected to have a return value.

Note that you don't allocate XIB-based user interface elements as you do when creating your interface programmatically. They are automatically allocated when the XIB is loaded at runtime.

Finally, recall that there is no pointer to the button. This is because an object only needs instance variables for objects it needs to send messages to. The button needs to send messages to the

BNRDocument instance, which is why we wired its action. The **BNRDocument**, however, does not need to send messages to the button, and so it does not need a pointer to it.

Revisiting MVC

Now that you've laid out your user interface, let's have a look at the object diagram for this project:

Figure 28.15   Object diagram for TahDoodle

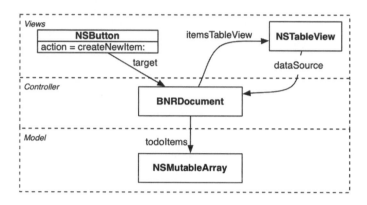

NSDocument, the superclass from which your **BNRDocument** class inherits, is an interesting beast. At first glance, it appears to be a model object. If you look up the class reference for **NSDocument**, though, you'll discover that it's more of a controller than anything else. **NSDocument** coordinates various disk-related activities and connects directly to the views responsible for issuing user input. When you create the **NSDocument** subclass **BNRDocument**, you added pointers to the real model objects (an **NSMutableArray** of **NSString** objects).

Edit BNRDocument.m

Now that you've got the user interface of your application created, configured, and connected, it's time to get back to writing code. Click on BNRDocument.m in the project navigator to reopen it in the editor, and implement **createNewItem:**.

```
#import "BNRDocument.h"

@implementation BNRDocument

#pragma mark - NSDocument Overrides

- (NSString *)windowNibName
{
    return @"BNRDocument";
}
```

```
#pragma mark - Actions

- (IBAction)createNewItem:(id)sender
{
    // If there's no array yet, go ahead and create one to store our new task
    if (!todoItems) {
        todoItems = [NSMutableArray array];
    }

    [todoItems addObject:@"New Item"];

    // -reloadData tells the table view to refresh and ask its dataSource
    // (which happens to be this BNRDocument object in this case)
    // for new data to display
    [itemTableView reloadData];

    // -updateChangeCount: tells the application whether or not the document
    // has unsaved changes. NSChangeDone flags the document as unsaved.
    [self updateChangeCount:NSChangeDone];
}
```

Now implement the required table view data source methods (as defined by the
NSTableViewDataSource protocol):

```
#pragma mark Data Source Methods

- (NSInteger)numberOfRowsInTableView:(NSTableView *)tv
{
    // This table view is meant to display the todoItems,
    // so the number of entries in the table view will be the same
    // as the number of objects in the array.
    return [todoItems count];
}

- (id)tableView:(NSTableView *)tableView
    objectValueForTableColumn:(NSTableColumn *)tableColumn
                          row:(NSInteger)row
{
    // Return the item from todoItems that corresponds to the cell
    // that the table view wants to display
    return [todoItems objectAtIndex:row];
}

- (void)tableView:(NSTableView *)tableView
        setObjectValue:(id)object
        forTableColumn:(NSTableColumn *)tableColumn
                   row:(NSInteger)row
{
    // When the user changes a to-do item on the table view,
    // update the todoItems array
    [todoItems replaceObjectAtIndex:row withObject:object];
    // And then flag the document as having unsaved changes.
    [self updateChangeCount:NSChangeDone];
}
```

Build and run the program. TahDoodle will appear on the screen, and you can add and change to-
do items. The big missing feature, however, is the ability to save and reopen a to-do list. To make
this happen, you need to override the following methods inherited from **BNRDocument**'s superclass,
NSDocument:

```
- (NSData *)dataOfType:(NSString *)typeName
                  error:(NSError **)outError
{
    // This method is called when our document is being saved
    // We are expected to hand the caller an NSData object wrapping our data
    // so that it can be written to disk

    // If there's no array, we'll write out an empty array for now
    if (!todoItems) {
        todoItems = [NSMutableArray array];
    }

    // Pack our todoItems array into an NSData object
    NSData *data = [NSPropertyListSerialization
                             dataWithPropertyList:todoItems
                                           format:NSPropertyListXMLFormat_v1_0
                                          options:NSPropertyListMutableContainers
                                            error:outError];

    // return our newly-packed NSData object
    return data;
}

- (BOOL)readFromData:(NSData *)data
              ofType:(NSString *)typeName
               error:(NSError **)outError
{
    // This method is called when a document is being loaded
    // We are handed an NSData object and expected to pull our data out of it

    // Extract our todoItems
    todoItems = [NSPropertyListSerialization propertyListWithData:data
                                                  options:0
                                                  format:NULL
                                                   error:outError];

    // return success or failure depending on success of the above call
    return (todoItems != nil);
}
```

Notice that for the first time, you're implementing a method that takes in an
NSError**. In this case, we are merely handing back the **NSError** generated by
propertyListWithData:options:format:error:, but you could also create and hand back a new
NSError as well, depending on the nature of the failure.

Build and run the application again. Now you can save and load task lists.

Challenges

Add a Delete Selected Item button.

Look up the **NSError** class reference in the developer documentation and create new **NSError** instances
to hand back when saving and loading fails, as mentioned at the end of the chapter.

Part V
Advanced Objective-C

You now know enough Objective-C to get started with iOS or Cocoa programming. But don't rush off just yet. These next chapters provide a gentle discussion of techniques and concepts that will be useful in your first year as an Objective-C programmer.

29

init

In the class **NSObject**, there is a method named **init**. After an object has been allocated, you send the **init** message to the new instance so that it can initialize its instance variables to usable values. So **alloc** creates the space for an object, and **init** makes the object ready to work. Using **init** looks like this:

```
NSMutableArray *things = [[NSMutableArray alloc] init];
```

Notice that **init** is an instance method that returns the address of the initialized object. It is the *initializer* for **NSObject**. This chapter is about how to write initializers.

Writing init methods

Create a new project: a Foundation Command Line Tool called Appliances. In this program, you are going to create two classes: **Appliance** and **OwnedAppliance** (a subclass of **Appliance**). An instance of **Appliance** will have a productName and a voltage. An instance of **OwnedAppliance** will also have a set containing the names of its owners.

Figure 29.1   Appliance and its subclass, OwnedAppliance

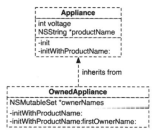

Create a new file: an **NSObject** subclass named **Appliance**. In Appliance.h, create instance variables and property declarations for productName and voltage:

```
#import <Foundation/Foundation.h>

@interface Appliance : NSObject {
    NSString *productName;
    int voltage;
}
@property (copy) NSString *productName;
@property int voltage;

@end
```

(We'll talk about the copy property attribute in Chapter 30.)

In Appliance.m, synthesize the properties to create the accessor methods for the instance variables:

```
#import "Appliance.h"

@implementation Appliance

@synthesize productName, voltage;

...
```

You would create an instance of **Appliance** like this:

```
Appliance *a = [[Appliance alloc] init];
```

Note that because **Appliance** doesn't implement an **init** method, it will execute the **init** method defined in **NSObject**. When this happens, all the instance variables specific to **Appliance** are zero-ed out. Thus, the productName of a new instance of **Appliance** will be nil, and voltage will be zero.

A basic init method

In some cases, an initial value of zero for your instance variables may work fine. In others, however, you'll need instances of your class to come into the world with their instance variables initialized to non-zero values.

Let's say that every instance of **Appliance** should start its life with a voltage of 120. In Appliance.m, override **NSObject**'s **init** method by adding a new implementation of **init**.

```
- (id)init
{
    // Call the NSObject's init method
    self = [super init];

    // Give voltage a starting value
    voltage = 120;

    // Return a pointer to the new object
    return self;
}
```

Now when you create a new instance of **Appliance**, it will have a voltage of 120 by default. (Note that this doesn't change anything about the accessor methods. After the instance is initialized, it can be changed just as before using **setVoltage:**.)

Notice that you called the superclass's **init** method, which initializes the instance variables declared in the superclass and returns a pointer to the initialized object. Most of the time, this works flawlessly. However, a few classes have deviant **init** methods. Here are the two possible forms of deviance:

- The **init** method figures out a clever optimization that it can do, deallocates the original object, allocates a different object, and returns the new object.

- The **init** method fails, deallocates the object, and returns nil.

To deal with the first case, Apple requires that you set self to point to the object returned from the superclass's **init** method. You did this in the first line of your **init** method.

To deal with the second case, Apple recommends that you check that your superclass's initializer returns a valid object and not nil. After all, there's no point in performing custom set-up on an object that doesn't exist. Change your **init** method to match Apple's recommendation:

```
- (id)init
{
    // Call NSObject's init method
    self = [super init];

    // Did it return something non-nil?
    if (self) {

        // Give voltage a starting value
        voltage = 120;
    }
    return self;
}
```

Truthfully, these sorts of checks are only necessary in a couple of very specific cases. Thus, in practice, many Objective-C programmers often skip the extra checks. In this book, however, we will always do the checks because it is the Apple-approved way to implement **init** methods.

Using accessors

So far you have a perfectly good **init** method for **Appliance**, but I want to show you a variation that you will see in other people's code. I typically do a plain assignment in an **init** method, but many programmers will use the accessor method. Change your **init** method to do this:

```
- (id)init
{
    // Call NSObject's init method
    self = [super init];

    // Did it return something non-nil?
    if (self) {

        // Give voltage a starting value
        [self setVoltage:120];
    }
    return self;
}
```

In most cases, there is little reason to do one over the other, but it makes for a great argument. The argument goes like this: The assign guy says, "You can't use an accessor method in an **init** method! The accessor assumes that the object is ready for work, and it isn't ready for work until *after* the **init** method is complete." Then the accessor method guy says, "Oh, come on. In the real world that is almost never an issue. My accessor method might be taking care of other stuff for me. I use my accessor anytime I set that variable." In reality, either approach will work in the vast majority of cases.

init methods that take arguments

Sometimes an object can't be initialized properly without some information from the method that is calling it. For example, imagine that an appliance can't function without a name. (nil doesn't count.) In this case, you need to be able to pass the initializer a name to use.

You can't do this with **init** because, for now and always, **init** has no arguments. So you have to create a new initializer instead. Then, when another method creates an instance of **Appliance**, it would look like this:

```
Appliance *a = [[Appliance alloc] initWithProductName:@"Toaster"];
```

The new initializer for **Appliance** is **initWithProductName:**, and it accepts an **NSString** as an argument. Declare this new method in Appliance.h:

```
#import <Foundation/Foundation.h>

@interface Appliance : NSObject {
    NSString *productName;
    int voltage;
}
@property (copy) NSString *productName;
@property int voltage;
- (id)initWithProductName:(NSString *)pn;

@end
```

In Appliance.m, find the implementation of **init**. Change the name of the method to **initWithProductName:** and set productName using the passed-in value.

```
- (id)initWithProductName:(NSString *)pn
{
    // Call NSObject's init method
    self = [super init];

    // Did it return something non-nil?
    if (self) {

        // Set the product name
        [self setProductName:pn];

        // Give voltage a starting value
        [self setVoltage:120];
    }
    return self;
}
```

Before you continue, build the project to make sure the syntax is right.

Now you can create an instance of **Appliance** with a given name. However, if you give Appliance.h and Appliance.m to another programmer, she may not realize she needs to call **initWithProductName:**. What if she creates an instance of **Appliance** in the most common way?

```
Appliance *a = [[Appliance alloc] init];
```

This is not an unreasonable action. As a subclass of **NSObject**, an instance **Appliance** is expected to do anything an instance of **NSObject** can do. And instances of **NSObject** respond to **init** messages. However, it causes a problem here because the above line of code creates an instance of **Appliance** that has nil for a product name and zero for voltage. And we decided earlier that every instance of **Appliance** needs a voltage of 120 and an actual name to function correctly. How can you prevent this from happening?

The solution is simple. In Appliance.m, add an **init** method to call **initWithProductName:** with a default value for the name.

```
- (id)init
{
    return [self initWithProductName:@"Unknown"];
}
```

Notice that this new overridden **init** doesn't do much work – it just calls the **initWithProductName:** method, which does the heavy lifting.

To test out your two initializers, you'll need a **description** method. Implement **description** in Appliance.m:

```
- (NSString *)description
{
    return [NSString stringWithFormat:@"<%@: %d volts>", productName, voltage];
}
```

Now, in main.m, exercise the class a bit:

```
#import <Foundation/Foundation.h>
#import "Appliance.h"

int main (int argc, const char * argv[])
{

    @autoreleasepool {

        Appliance *a = [[Appliance alloc] init];
        NSLog(@"a is %@", a);
        [a setProductName:@"Washing Machine"];
        [a setVoltage:240];
        NSLog(@"a is %@", a);

    }
    return 0;
}
```

Build and run the program.

Let's take our exploration of initializers further. Create a new file: a subclass of **Appliance** named **OwnedAppliance**.

Figure 29.2   Creating a subclass of Appliance

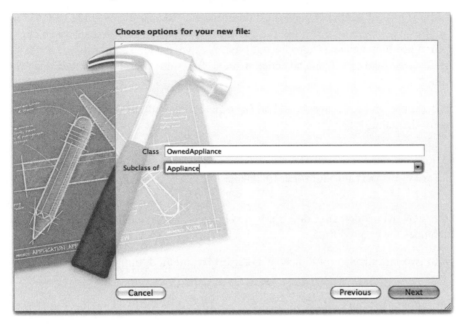

In OwnedAppliance.h, add a mutable set of owner names and three methods.

```
#import "Appliance.h"

@interface OwnedAppliance : Appliance {
    NSMutableSet *ownerNames;
}
- (id)initWithProductName:(NSString *)pn
         firstOwnerName:(NSString *)n;
- (void)addOwnerNamesObject:(NSString *)n;
- (void)removeOwnerNamesObject:(NSString *)n;

@end
```

Notice that one of the methods you've declared is an initializer that takes two arguments.

Implement the methods in OwnedAppliance.m:

```
#import "OwnedAppliance.h"

@implementation OwnedAppliance

- (id)initWithProductName:(NSString *)pn
         firstOwnerName:(NSString *)n
{
    // Call the superclass's initializer
    self = [super initWithProductName:pn];

    if (self) {
        // Make a set to hold owner names
```

```
        ownerNames = [[NSMutableSet alloc] init];

        // Is the first owner name non-nil?
        if (n) {
            [ownerNames addObject:n];
        }
    }
    // Return a pointer to the new object
    return self;
}

- (void)addOwnerNamesObject:(NSString *)n
{
    [ownerNames addObject:n];
}

- (void)removeOwnerNamesObject:(NSString *)n
{
    [ownerNames removeObject:n];
}
```

@end

Note that this class doesn't initialize voltage or productName. The **initWithProductName:** in **Appliance** takes care of those. When you create a subclass, you typically only need to initialize the instance variables that *you* introduced; let the superclass take care of the instance variables that it introduced.

Now, however, you face the same situation as you did with **Appliance** and its superclass's initializer, **init**. At the moment, one of your co-workers might create a terrible bug with this line of code:

```
OwnedAppliance *a = [[OwnedAppliance alloc] initWithProductName:@"Toaster"];
```

This code will cause the **initWithProductName:** method in **Appliance** to run. This method knows nothing about the ownerNames set, which means ownerNames will not get properly initialized for this **OwnedAppliance** instance.

The fix here is the same as before. In OwnedAppliance.m, add an implementation of the superclass's initializer **initWithProductName:** that calls **initWithProductName:firstOwnerName:** and passes a default value for firstOwnerName.

```
- (id)initWithProductName:(NSString *)pn
{
    return [self initWithProductName:pn firstOwnerName:nil];
}
```

Quiz time: Do you also need to implement **init** in **OwnedAppliance**? No. At this point, the following code will work fine:

```
OwnedAppliance *a = [[OwnedAppliance alloc] init];
```

Why? Because there is no implementation of **init** in **OwnedAppliance**, this line will trigger the **init** method implemented in **Appliance**, which calls [self initWithProductName:@"Unknown"]. self is an instance of **OwnedAppliance**, so it calls **initWithProductName:** in **OwnedAppliance**, which calls [self initWithProductName:pn firstOwnerName:nil].

What you wind up with is a chain of initializers that call other initializers.

Figure 29.3   Initializer chain

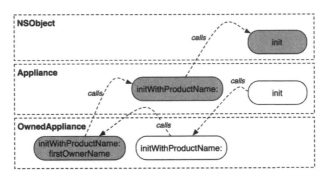

Notice that Figure 29.3 shows one shaded initializer for each class. This initializer is the *designated initializer* for that class. **init** is the designated initializer for **NSObject**, **initWithProductName:** is the designated initializer for **Appliance**, and **initWithProductName:firstOwnerName:** is the designated initializer for **OwnedAppliance**. A class has only one designated initializer method. If the class has other initializers, then the implementation of those initializers must call (directly or indirectly) the designated initializer. Thus, the designated initializer acts as a funnel-point.

When you create a class whose designated initializer has a different name than its superclass's designated initializer (as you did in **Appliance** and **OwnedAppliance**), you have a responsibility to document that in the header file. Add the appropriate comment in Appliance.h:

```
#import <Foundation/Foundation.h>

@interface Appliance : NSObject {
    NSString *productName;
    int voltage;
}
@property (copy) NSString *productName;
@property int voltage;

// The designated initializer
- (id)initWithProductName:(NSString *)pn;

@end
```

and in OwnedAppliance.h:

```
#import "Appliance.h"

@interface OwnedAppliance : Appliance {
    NSMutableSet *ownerNames;
}
// The designated initializer
- (id)initWithProductName:(NSString *)pn
          firstOwnerName:(NSString *)n;
- (void)addOwnerNamesObject:(NSString *)n;
- (void)removeOwnerNamesObject:(NSString *)n;

@end
```

Thus, we arrive at the rules that all stylish Objective-C programmers follow when writing initializers:

- If a class has several initializers, only one should do the real work. That method is known as the designated initializer. All other initializers should call, either directly or indirectly, the designated initializer.

- The designated initializer will call the superclass's designated initializer before initializing its instance variables.

- If the designated initializer of your class has a different name than the designated initializer of its superclass, you must override the superclass's designated initializer so that it calls the new designated initializer.

- If you have several initializers, clearly document which is the designated initializer in the header.

Deadly init methods

Every once in a while, however, you can't safely override the superclass's designated initializer. Let's say that you are creating a subclass of **NSObject** called **WallSafe**, and its designated initializer is **initWithSecretCode:**. However, having a default value for secretCode is not secure enough for your application. This means that the pattern we have been using – overriding **init** to call the new class's designated initializer with default values – is not acceptable.

So what do you do? An instance of **WallSafe** will still respond to an **init** message. Someone could easily do this:

```
WallSafe *ws = [[WallSafe alloc] init];
```

The best thing to do is to override the superclass's designated initializer in a way that lets developers know that they have made a mistake and tells them how to fix it:

```
- (id)init
{
    @throw [NSException exceptionWithName:@"WallSafeInitialization"
                                  reason:@"Use initWithSecretCode:, not init"
                                userInfo:nil];
}
```

30
Properties

In the last chapter, you created a class called **Appliance** that had two properties: productName and voltage. Let's review how those properties work.

In Appliance.h, you declared two instance variables to hold the data:

```
{
    NSString *productName;
    int voltage;
}
```

You also declared accessor methods for them. You *could* have declared the accessors like this:

```
- (void)setProductName:(NSString *)s;
- (NSString *)productName;
- (void)setVoltage:(int)x;
- (int)voltage;
```

However, you used the @property construct instead:

```
@property (copy) NSString *productName;
@property int voltage;
```

In Appliance.m, you *could* have implemented the accessor methods explicitly like this:

```
- (void)setProductName:(NSString *)s
{
    productName = [s copy];
}

- (NSString *)productName
{
    return productName;
}

- (void)setVoltage:(int)x
{
    voltage = x;
}

- (int)voltage
{
    return voltage;
}
```

However, you used the @synthesize construct to implement them:

```
@synthesize productName, voltage;
```

Objective-C compiler trivia: When compiling for iOS or a 64-bit Mac OS X program, you don't need to declare the instance variables. The @property/@synthesize calls are sufficient to make the space for the data.

Open up Appliances and comment out the instance variables in Appliance.h:

```
{
    // NSString *productName;
    // int voltage;
}
```

Rebuild and run the program.

In this book, we always declare the instance variables. It is a nice form of documentation and makes your code usable within 32-bit Mac OS X programs. Uncomment the instance variables.

Property attributes

Now let's take a closer look at the different attributes you can use to control how the accessors for a property will be created.

Mutability

A property can be declared readwrite or readonly. The default is readwrite, which means that both a setter and a getter method are created. If you don't want a setter method to be created, you mark the property as readonly:

```
@property (readonly) int voltage;
```

Lifetime specifiers

A property can also be declared unsafe_unretained, strong, weak, or copy. This option determines how the setter handles its memory management.

unsafe_unretained is the default and the simplest: it just assigns the passed-in value to the property. Imagine this declaration and definition:

```
@property (unsafe_unretained) int averageScore;
// "@property int averageScore" would also work here
...
@synthesize averageScore;
```

This would result in a setter method that's pretty much equivalent to:

```
- (void)setAverageScore:(int)d
{
    averageScore = d;
}
```

In **Appliance**, voltage is an unsafe, unretained property. You will always use unsafe_unretained for properties that hold non-objects.

strong, as you learned in Chapter 20, will ensure that a strong reference is kept to the passed-in object. It will also let go of ownership of the old object (which will then deallocate itself if it has no other owners). For properties that hold objects, you will usually use strong.

weak does not imply ownership of the object pointed to. It will synthesize a setter that sets the property to the passed-in object. If this object is deallocated, the property will be set to nil. (Note that if the pointer is unsafe_unretained and the object it points to is deallocated, you will have a "dangling pointer." Sending a message to a dangling pointer usually crashes your program.)

copy forms a strong reference to a copy of the object passed in. But, there is a detail in this that most people misunderstand...

copy

The copy option makes a copy of an object and then changes the pointer to refer to this copy. Imagine you had a property declaration and definition like this:

```
@property (copy) NSString *lastName;
@synthesize lastName;
```

The generated setter method would look somewhat like this:

```
- (void)setLastName:(NSString *)d
{
    lastName = [d copy];
}
```

Use of the copy attribute is most common with object types that have mutable subclasses. For example, **NSString** has a subclass called **NSMutableString**. You can imagine that your **setLastName:** method might be passed a mutable string:

```
// Create a mutable string
NSMutableString *x = [[NSMutableString alloc] initWithString:@"Ono"];

// Pass it to setLastName:
[myObj setLastName:x];

// 'copy' prevents this from changing the lastName
[x appendString:@" Lennon"];
```

What if the object passed in is *not* mutable? It seems wasteful to make a copy of an immutable object. The **copy** method just calls **copyWithZone:** and passes nil as the argument. For example, in **NSString**, the **copyWithZone:** method is overridden to look like this:

```
- (id)copyWithZone:(NSZone *)z
{
    return self;
}
```

That is, it doesn't make a copy at all. (Note that **NSZone** and memory zoning in general are all but deprecated, vestigial features of Cocoa programming, so we won't go further into them here. **copyWithZone:** still has some use, however, and has not been entirely phased out.)

For objects that come in mutable and immutable versions, the **copy** method returns an immutable copy. For example, **NSMutableString** has a **copy** method that returns an instance of **NSString**. If you want the copy to be a mutable object, use the **mutableCopy** method.

There is no property lifetime specifier called `mutableCopy`. If you wish for your setter to set the property to be a mutable copy of an object, you must implement the setter yourself so that it calls the **mutableCopy** method on the incoming object. For example, in **OwnedAppliance**, you might create a **setOwnerNames:** method:

```
- (void)setOwnerNames:(NSSet *)newNames
{
    ownerNames = [newNames mutableCopy];
}
```

More about copying

Most Objective-C classes have no **copyWithZone:** method at all. Objective-C programmers make fewer copies than you might think.

Curiously, the **copy** and **mutableCopy** methods are defined in **NSObject** like this:

```
- (id)copy
{
    return [self copyWithZone:NULL];
}

- (id)mutableCopy
{
    return [self mutableCopyWithZone:NULL];
}
```

Thus, if you have some code like this:

```
Appliance *b = [[Appliance alloc] init];
Appliance *c = [b copy];
```

You will get an error like this:

```
-[Appliance copyWithZone:]: unrecognized selector sent to instance 0x100110130
```

Advice on atomic vs. nonatomic

This is an introductory book on programming, and the `atomic/nonatomic` option relates to a relatively advanced topic known as multithreading. Here is what you need to know: the `nonatomic` option will make your setter method run a tiny bit faster. If you look at the headers for Apple's UIKit, every property is marked as `nonatomic`. You should make your properties `nonatomic`, too.

(I give this advice to everyone. In every group, however, there is someone who knows just enough to be a pain. That person says, "But when I make my app multithreaded, I'll need the protection that atomic setter methods get me." And I *should* say, "I don't think you will write multithreaded code anytime soon. And when you do, I don't think atomic setter methods are going to help." But what I really say is "OK, then you should leave your setters atomic." Because you can't tell someone something they aren't ready to hear.)

In `Appliance.h`, make your accessors non-atomic:

```
@property (copy, nonatomic) NSString *productName;
@property (nonatomic) int voltage;
```

Sadly, at this time, the default for properties is `atomic`, so you do have to make this change.

Key-value coding

Key-value coding is the ability to read and set a property using its name. The key-value coding methods are defined in **NSObject**, and thus every object has this capability.

Open main.m and find the line:

```
[a setProductName:@"Washing Machine"];
```

Rewrite the same line to use key-value coding:

```
[a setValue:@"Washing Machine" forKey:@"productName"];
```

In this case, the **setValue:forKey:** method, as defined in **NSObject**, will go looking for a setter method named **setProductName:**. If the object doesn't have a **setProductName:** method, it will access the instance variable directly.

You can also read the value of a variable using key-value coding. Add a line to main.m that prints out the product name:

```
int main (int argc, const char * argv[])
{
    @autorelease {

        Appliance *a = [[Appliance alloc] init];
        NSLog(@"a is %@", a);
        [a setValue:@"Washing Machine" forKey:@"productName"];
        [a setVoltage:240];
        NSLog(@"a is %@", a);

        NSLog(@"the product name is %@", [a valueForKey:@"productName"]);

    }
    return 0;
}
```

In this case, the **valueForKey:** method, as defined in **NSObject**, goes looking for an accessor named **productName**. If there is no **productName** method, the instance variable is accessed directly.

If you type the name of the property wrong, you won't get warning from the compiler, but there will be a runtime error. Make this mistake in main.m:

```
NSLog(@"the product name is %@", [a valueForKey:@"productNammmme"]);
```

When you build and run it, you will see an error:

```
*** Terminating app due to uncaught exception 'NSUnknownKeyException',
reason: '[<Appliance 0x100108dd0> valueForUndefinedKey:]:
this class is not key value coding-compliant for the key productNammmme.'
```

Fix the error before you go on.

Why is key-value coding interesting? Anytime a standard framework wants to push data into your objects, it will use **setValue:forKey:**. Anytime a standard framework wants to read data from your objects, it will use **valueForKey:**. For example, Core Data is a framework that makes it easy to save your objects to a SQLite database and then bring them back to life. It manipulates your custom data-bearing objects using key-value coding.

To prove that key-value coding will manipulate your variables even if you have no accessors, comment out the @property declaration for productName in Appliance.h:

```
#import <Foundation/Foundation.h>

@interface Appliance : NSObject {
    NSString *productName;
    int voltage;
}
// @property (copy) NSString *productName;
@property (nonatomic) int voltage;

// The designated initializer
- (id)initWithProductName:(NSString *)pn;

@end
```

Also, remove all use of the methods **setProductName:** and **productName** from Appliance.m:

```
@implementation Appliance

@synthesize voltage;

- (id)initWithProductName:(NSString *)pn
{
    self = [super init];
    if (self) {
        productName = [pn copy];
        [self setVoltage:120];
    }
    return self;
}

- (id)init
{
    return [self initWithProductName:@"Unknown"];
}

- (NSString *)description
{
    return [NSString stringWithFormat:@"<%@: %d volts>", productName, voltage];
}

@end
```

Build and run the program. Note that even though you have no accessor methods for productName, the variable can still be set and read from other methods. This is an obvious violation of the idea of *object encapsulation* – methods of an object are public, but the instance variables are delicate and should be kept private. If key-value coding weren't astonishingly useful, no one would tolerate it.

Non-object types

The key-value coding methods are designed to work with objects, but some properties hold a non-object type, like an int or a float. For example, voltage is an int. How do you set voltage using key-value coding? You use an **NSNumber**.

In main.m, change the line for setting the voltage from this:

```
[a setVoltage:240];
```

to this:

```
[a setValue:[NSNumber numberWithInt:240] forKey:@"voltage"];
```

Add an explicit accessor to Appliance.m so that you can see it getting called:

```
- (void)setVoltage:(int)x
{
    NSLog(@"setting voltage to %d", x);
    voltage = x;
}
```

Build and run the program.

Similarly, if you ask for the valueForKey:@"voltage", you will get back an **NSNumber** containing the value of voltage.

31

Categories

Categories let a programmer add methods to any existing class. For example, Apple gave us the class **NSString**. We don't get the source code to that class, but categories give us the ability to add new methods to **NSString**.

Create a new Foundation Command Line Tool called VowelCounter. Then create a new file that is an Objective-C category. Name the category VowelCounting and make it a category on NSString.

Now open NSString+VowelCounting.h and declare a method that you want to add to the **NSString** class:

```objc
#import <Foundation/Foundation.h>

@interface NSString (VowelCounting)
- (int)vowelCount;

@end
```

Now implement the method in NSString+VowelCount.m:

```objc
#import "NSString+VowelCounting.h"

@implementation NSString (VowelCounting)

- (int)vowelCount
{
    NSCharacterSet *charSet =
            [NSCharacterSet characterSetWithCharactersInString:@"aeiouyAEIOUY"];

    NSUInteger count = [self length];
    int sum = 0;
    for (int i = 0; i < count; i++) {
        unichar c = [self characterAtIndex:i];
        if ([charSet characterIsMember:c]) {
            sum++;
        }
    }
    return sum;
}

@end
```

Now use the new method in main.m:

```
#import <Foundation/Foundation.h>
#import "NSString+VowelCounting.h"

int main (int argc, const char * argv[])
{
    @autorelease {

        NSString *string = @"Hello, World!";
        NSLog(@"%@ has %d vowels", string, [string vowelCount]);

    }
    return 0;
}
```

Build and run the program. Nifty, eh? Categories turn out to be very useful.

It is important to note that only this program has the category. If you want the method available in another program, you must add the file to your project and compile the category in when you build that program.

32

Blocks

In Chapter 24, you learned about the callback mechanisms delegation and notifications. Callbacks allow other objects to call methods in your object in response to events. While perfectly functional, these approaches break up your code. Pieces of your program that you'd like to be close together for clarity's sake usually aren't.

For example, in your Callbacks program from Chapter 24, you added code to register your object for a notification when the user's time zone changes and to set **zoneChange:** to be triggered when this notification is received. But now I'm reading your code and curious about what this **zoneChange:** method does when it is triggered, so I go looking for the implementation of this method. In the Callbacks example, the code that registers the object for a notification and the implementation of the method that is triggered are right next to each other, but you can imagine that in a larger, more complex application, these two pieces of code could be hundreds of lines away from each other.

Mac OS X 10.6 and iOS 4 introduced a new feature called *blocks*. An Objective-C block is just a chunk of code like a C function, but it can be passed around as data. We'll see shortly how this keeps relevant code together.

Blocks and block syntax are definitely an advanced Objective-C topic and can be confusing at first. However, Apple's APIs are using blocks more and more. In this chapter, we'll step through a couple of simple examples so that you'll be ready when you encounter blocks in the wild.

If you have a background in another programming language, you might know blocks as *anonymous functions*, *closures*, or *lambdas*. If you're familiar with *function pointers*, blocks may appear to be similar, but you'll soon see that proper use of blocks allows for more elegant code than can be written with function pointers.

Defining blocks

This is a block:

```
^{
    NSLog(@"I'm a log statement within a block!");
}
```

This looks like a function, but it has a caret (^) instead of a function name. The caret identifies this bit of code as a block. Also, like a function, a block can take arguments:

```
^(double dividend, double divisor) {
    double quotient = dividend / divisor;
    return quotient;
}
```

This block takes two doubles as arguments. A block can have a return value as well, but we'll come back to that.

Do these blocks have names? Not yet. These blocks are values, like the number 5 is a value. To be able to access a block by a name, we have to assign it to a *block variable*.

Using blocks

To see how this works, we're going to dive right into some code. In this exercise, you're going to use a block to remove all of the vowels from each of the strings in an array.

Create a new Foundation Command Line Tool and call it VowelMovement. In this program, you will use a block to iterate over an array of strings, transforming each one. First, you're going to create three arrays: one to store the original strings, one to store the "devowelized" strings, and a third to store the characters to strip from the strings. In main.m, replace the code inside of the @autoreleasepool's curly braces:

```
int main (int argc, const char * argv[])
{
    @autoreleasepool {

        // Create the array of strings to devowelize and a container for new ones
        NSArray *oldStrings = [NSArray arrayWithObjects:
                    @"Sauerkraut", @"Raygun", @"Big Nerd Ranch", @"Mississippi", nil];
        NSLog(@"old strings: %@", oldStrings);
        NSMutableArray *newStrings = [NSMutableArray array];

        // Create a list of characters that we'll remove from the string
        NSArray *vowels = [NSArray arrayWithObjects:
                        @"a", @"e", @"i", @"o", @"u", nil];

    }
    return 0;
}
```

Nothing new here; you're just setting up arrays. Build and run your program. You can ignore the warnings about unused variables for now.

Declaring a block variable

Now comes the code for the block. Although blocks look like functions, they can be stored in variables. Like other variables, block variables are declared and then assigned values. Add the following code to main.m to declare your block variable.

```
int main (int argc, const char * argv[])
{
    @autoreleasepool {
        // Create the array of strings to devowelize and a container for new ones
        NSArray *oldStrings = [NSArray arrayWithObjects:
                    @"Sauerkraut", @"Raygun", @"Big Nerd Ranch", @"Mississippi", nil];
        NSLog(@"old strings: %@", oldStrings);
        NSMutableArray *newStrings = [NSMutableArray array];
```

```
        // Create a list of characters that we'll remove from the string
        NSArray *vowels = [NSArray arrayWithObjects:
                            @"a", @"e", @"i", @"o", @"u", nil];

        // Declare the block variable
        void (^devowelizer)(id, NSUInteger, BOOL *);

    }
    return 0;
}
```

Let's break down this declaration to see what's going on.

Figure 32.1   Block variable declaration

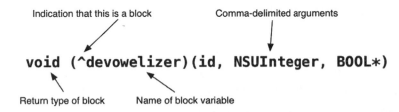

When declaring a primitive variable, you give its type and then its name, like int i. For a block variable, however, the name is in the middle of the declaration right after the caret. The type of the block variable is dependent on how the block is constructed. In this case, devowelizer's type is "a block that takes an object, an integer, and a BOOL pointer, and returns nothing."

Assigning a block

Now let's assign a value to our new variable. For a block variable, the value is always a set of instructions inside curly braces. In main.m, add the following assignment:

```
int main (int argc, const char * argv[])
{
    @autoreleasepool {
        // Create the array of strings to devowelize and a container for new ones
        NSArray *oldStrings = [NSArray arrayWithObjects:
                @"Sauerkraut", @"Raygun", @"Big Nerd Ranch", @"Mississippi", nil];
        NSLog(@"old strings: %@", oldStrings);
        NSMutableArray *newStrings = [NSMutableArray array];

        // Create a list of characters that we'll remove from the string
        NSArray *vowels = [NSArray arrayWithObjects:
                            @"a", @"e", @"i", @"o", @"u", nil];

        // Declare the block variable
        void (^devowelizer)(id, NSUInteger, BOOL *);
```

```
        // Assign a block to the variable
        devowelizer = ^(id string, NSUInteger i, BOOL *stop) {

            NSMutableString *newString = [NSMutableString stringWithString:string];

            // Iterate over the array of vowels, replacing occurrences of each
            // with an empty string.
            for (NSString *s in vowels) {
                NSRange fullRange = NSMakeRange(0, [newString length]);
                [newString replaceOccurrencesOfString:s
                                           withString:@""
                                              options:NSCaseInsensitiveSearch
                                                range:fullRange];
            }

            [newStrings addObject:newString];

        }; // End of block assignment

    }
    return 0;
}
```

Build your program again to check your typing. The warnings about unused variables should disappear.

Now you've composed a block – a set of instructions – and assigned the block to the block variable devowelizer. Notice that the block assignment ends with a semi-colon just like any variable assignment would.

As with any variable, you can perform the declaration and assignment of devowelizer together:

```
void (^devowelizer)(id, NSUInteger, BOOL *) = ^(id string, NSUInteger i, BOOL *stop) {

    NSMutableString *newString = [NSMutableString stringWithString:string];

    // Iterate over the array of vowels, replacing occurrences of each
    // with an empty string.
    for (NSString *s in vowels) {
        NSRange fullRange = NSMakeRange(0, [newString length]);
        [newString replaceOccurrencesOfString:s
                                   withString:@""
                                      options:NSCaseInsensitiveSearch
                                        range:fullRange];
    }

    [newStrings addObject:newString];
};
```

Just like before, here we declare a block variable that takes three arguments, returns nothing, and is called devowelizer. Then we compose an actual block and store it in devowelizer.

Passing in a block

Because devowelizer is a variable, you can pass it as an argument. **NSArray** has a method called **enumerateObjectsUsingBlock:**. This method expects a block as its sole argument. It will execute that block once for each object in the array.

In main.m, add the following code to call **enumerateObjectsUsingBlock:** with devowelizer and then print out the devowelized strings.

```
int main (int argc, const char * argv[])
{
    @autoreleasepool {
        // Create the array of strings to devowelize and a container for new ones
        NSArray *oldStrings = [NSArray arrayWithObjects:
                @"Sauerkraut", @"Raygun", @"Big Nerd Ranch", @"Mississippi", nil];
        NSLog(@"old strings: %@", oldStrings);
        NSMutableArray *newStrings = [NSMutableArray array];

        // Create a list of characters that we'll remove from the string
        NSArray *vowels = [NSArray arrayWithObjects:
                            @"a", @"e", @"i", @"o", @"u", nil];

        // Declare the block variable
        void (^devowelizer)(id, NSUInteger, BOOL *);

        // Assign a block to the variable
        devowelizer = ^(id string, NSUInteger i, BOOL *stop) {

            NSMutableString *newString = [NSMutableString stringWithString:string];

            // Iterate over the array of vowels, replacing occurrences of each
            // with an empty string.
            for (NSString *s in vowels) {
                NSRange fullRange = NSMakeRange(0, [newString length]);
                [newString replaceOccurrencesOfString:s
                                           withString:@""
                                              options:NSCaseInsensitiveSearch
                                                range:fullRange];
            }

            [newStrings addObject:newString];

        }; // End of block assignment

        // Iterate over the array with our block
        [oldStrings enumerateObjectsUsingBlock:devowelizer];
        NSLog(@"new strings: %@", newStrings);


    }
    return 0;
}
```

Build and run your program. You'll see two arrays logged to the console. The second array should match the first array – without all those pesky vowels.

```
2011-09-03 10:27:02.617 VowelMovement[787:707] old strings: (
    Sauerkraut,
    Raygun,
    "Big Nerd Ranch",
    Mississippi
)
```

```
2011-09-03 10:27:02.618 VowelMovement[787:707] new strings: (
    Srkrt,
    Rygn,
    "Bg Nrd Rnch",
    Mssssppp
)
```

It's important to note that **enumerateObjectsUsingBlock:** won't accept just any block as its argument. This method requires "a block that takes an object, an integer, and a BOOL pointer and returns nothing." That's why we constructed the block that we assigned to devowelizer as we did. Its three arguments are specifically designed for going through an array.

The first argument is a pointer to the current object. Notice that this pointer's type is id so that it will work no matter what kind of objects the array contains. The second argument is an **NSUInteger** that is the index of the current object. The third object is a pointer to a **BOOL**, which defaults to NO. We can change it to YES if we want the array to stop after the current iteration.

Add a check at the beginning of the block assignment:

```
devowelizer = ^(id string, NSUInteger i, BOOL *stop){

    NSRange yRange = [string rangeOfString:@"y"
                                   options:NSCaseInsensitiveSearch];

    // Did I find a y?
    if (yRange.location != NSNotFound) {
        *stop = YES; // Prevent further iterations
        return;      // Stop this iteration
    }

    NSMutableString *newString = [NSMutableString stringWithString:string];

    // Iterate over the array of vowels, replacing occurrences of each
    // with an empty string.
    for (NSString *s in vowels) {
        NSRange fullRange = NSMakeRange(0, [newString length]);
        [newString replaceOccurrencesOfString:s
                                   withString:@""
                                      options:NSCaseInsensitiveSearch
                                        range:fullRange];
    }

    [newStrings addObject:newString];

}; // End of block assignment
```

This will check to see if the string for the current iteration contains an uppercase or lowercase 'y' character. If it does, the pointer is set to YES (which will prevent the block from performing any more iterations) and then the current iteration is halted.

Build and run the program. Again, two arrays are logged to the debugger output, but this time, the array enumeration was cancelled during the second iteration when the block encountered a word with the letter 'y' in it. All you get is Srkrt.

Now that you've had some practice with blocks, let's return to how blocks help solve the problem of far-flung code bits in your programs. When you use a callback, such as in Chapter 24 where you had this line of code:

```
[[NSNotificationCenter defaultCenter]
                    addObserver:logger
                       selector:@selector(zoneChange:)
                           name:NSSystemTimeZoneDidChangeNotification
                         object:nil];
```

you identify a method (typically using @selector()), and then you implement that method somewhere else in the file:

```
- (void)zoneChange:(NSNotification *)note
{
    NSLog(@"The system time zone has changed!");
}
```

You could use the **NSNotificationCenter** method **addObserverForName:object:queue:usingBlock:** and pass a block instead. With this method, you hand the **NSNotificationCenter** the instructions right then, so you don't have to put the code for the callback somewhere else. Anyone reading your code will see the instructions and the message send to the **NSNotificationCenter** in the same chunk of code. (You'll get to make exactly this change to your Callbacks program in a challenge at the end of the chapter.)

typedef

Block syntax can be confusing, but you can make it friendlier using the typedef keyword that you learned about in Chapter 10. Remember that typedefs belong at the top of the file or in a header, outside of any method implementations. In main.m, add the following line of code:

```
#import <Foundation/Foundation.h>

typedef void (^ArrayEnumerationBlock)(id, NSUInteger, BOOL *);

int main (int argc, const char * argv[])
{
```

Notice that this looks identical to a block variable declaration. However, here we are defining a type rather than a variable, so we put an appropriate type name next to the caret. This allows us to simplify declarations of similar blocks. Instead of declaring devowelizer this way

```
void (^devowelizer)(id, NSUInteger, BOOL *);
```

you can replace that line with the following declaration:

```
ArrayEnumerationBlock devowelizer;
```

This makes your block variable declaration a bit more familiar. Note that the block type itself only defines the block's arguments and return types; it has no bearing on the set of instructions within a block of that type.

Return values

Finally, when a block returns a value, you can call its block variable like a function.

```
double (^divBlock)(double,double) = ^(double k, double j) {
    return k/j;
}
```

In this code, you've declared divBlock as a block variable that returns a double and expects two doubles as arguments. Then you assigned it a value which includes the instruction to return the result of dividing the two arguments.

You can use this block like so:

```
double quotient = divBlock(42.0, 12.5);
```

Memory management

Like primitive variables, blocks are created and stored on the stack. That is, the block will be destroyed along with the stack frame when the function or method that created the block returns. Sometimes, however, your block needs to live longer than that. For example, it could become an instance variable of an object. In this case, you must copy your block from the stack to the heap.

To copy a block from the stack to the heap, you send it the **copy** message:

```
ArrayEnumerationBlock iVarDevowelizer = [devowelizer copy];
```

Now a copy of your block exists on the heap. It is now a *heap-based block* instead of a *stack-based* block, and the new block variable is a pointer to the block.

Methods that take blocks as arguments, such as **NSArray**'s **enumerateObjectsUsingBlock:** or **NSNotificationCenter**'s **addObserverForName:object:queue:usingBlock:**, are expected to copy blocks passed to them to keep them around. In doing so, they create pointers – and strong references – to those blocks.

So we've seen blocks be declared, assigned values, and passed like variables. We've also seen that they look like functions. Now we're sending a block a message as if it were an object.

A heap-based block behaving like an object comes with some memory management issues:

What about variables that are used with the block?

A block typically uses other variables (both primitive and pointers to objects) within its code that were created outside of it. To make sure these *external variables* will be available for as long as the block needs them, the variables are *captured* by the block when the copy is made.

For primitive variables, this means the values are copied and stored as local variables within the block. For pointers, the block itself will keep a strong reference to any objects it references. That means that any objects referred to by the block are guaranteed to live at least as long as the block itself. (If you've been wondering about the difference between blocks and function pointers, it's right here. Let's see a function pointer do that!)

As an example, take a look at our VowelMovement program. The devowelizer block mentions two objects that were created outside of the block: newStrings (an array for storing the modified versions of strings) and string (the current string to be copied for modification). devowelizer will keep strong references to both of these objects, keeping them alive as long as the block itself exists.

Can these strong references lead to retain cycles/circular references?

You bet. The fix is the same: one of the references needs to become a weak reference. To do this, declare a __weak pointer outside the block and then reference this pointer within the block instead.

Can I change the variables that the block has copied?

By default, the variables captured by a block are constant within the block, and you cannot change their values. Object pointer variables, for example, are constant within the scope of the block. (Although you can still send the object messages that can change its contents, you cannot modify the pointer itself.)

Sometimes, however, you want to be able to modify an external variable within a block. To do this, you must declare the external variable using the __block keyword. For instance, in the following code, you increment the external variable counter.

```
__block int counter = 0;
void (^counterBlock)() = ^{ counter++; };
...
counterBlock(); // Increments counter to 1
counterBlock(); // Increments counter to 2
```

Without the __block keyword, you would get a compilation error in the block definition, indicating that the value of counter cannot be changed.

The block-based future

Blocks can be difficult to understand and to use. However, they are extremely useful and powerful in heavily event-driven applications common in Mac and iOS programming. Apple's APIs are using blocks more and more. For instance, the **ALAssetLibrary** and **GameKit** frameworks use many block-based methods. It's a good idea to use Apple's block-based methods whenever they are available to become more comfortable with blocks.

Challenges

Anonymous block

The example in this chapter puts the block declaration, assignment, and usage on three separate lines of code for readability.

When you need to pass an integer into a method, such as **NSNumber**'s **numberWithInt:**, you can pass the int anonymously:

```
// Option 1: Totally break it down
int i;
i = 5;
NSNumber *num = [NSNumber numberWithInt:i];

// Option 2: Skip the variable declaration
NSNumber *num = [NSNumber numberWithInt:5];
```

Because blocks are variables, you can do this with blocks as well. In fact, this is the most common way to use blocks. You will rarely declare a block variable so that you can pass the block into methods; you'll usually use them anonymously.

Modify the exercise in this chapter to pass the block anonymously as an argument to **enumerateObjectsUsingBlock:**. That is, keep the block, but get rid of the block variable.

NSNotificationCenter

In Chapter 24, you used **NSNotificationCenter**'s **addObserver:selector:name:object:** method to register to receive callbacks via your **zoneChange:** method. Update that exercise to use the **addObserverForName:object:queue:usingBlock:** method instead. Look up its details in the developer documentation.

This method takes a block as an argument and then executes the block instead of calling back to your object when the specified notification is posted. This means that your **zoneChange:** method will never be called. The code inside this method will instead be in the block.

The passed-in block should take a single argument (an **NSNotification** *) and return nothing, just as the **zoneChange:** method does.

You can pass nil as the argument for queue:; this argument is used for concurrency, a topic we won't cover in this book.

Part VI
Advanced C

To be a competent Objective-C programmer, you must also be a competent C programmer. There are a few more things that you should really know about C. These topics are not ideas that you will use everyday, but you will encounter them occasionally, so I wanted to introduce you to them here.

33

Bitwise Operations

In the first part of this book, I described the memory of a computer as a vast meadow of switches (billions of switches) that could be turned on or off. Each switch represents one bit, and we usually use 1 to mean "on" and 0 to mean "off."

However, you never address a single bit. Instead, you deal with byte-sized chunks of bits. If you think of a byte as an unsigned 8-bit integer, each bit represents another power of two:

Figure 33.1 One byte representing the decimal number 60

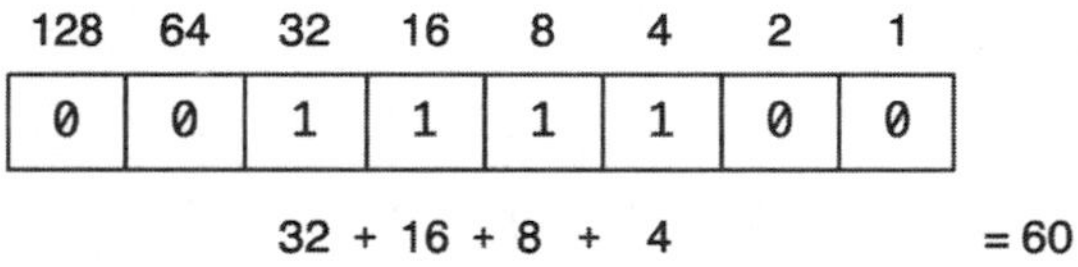

128	64	32	16	8	4	2	1
0	0	1	1	1	1	0	0

32 + 16 + 8 + 4   = 60

As a side-effect of living with 10 fingers, people like to work with decimal numbers (base-10). Computers, however, like powers of 2. Programmers often use a base-16 number system ($16 = 2^4$) known as *hexadecimal* or just "hex." This is especially true when we are dealing with individual bits of an integer.

We use the letters a, b, c, d, e, and f for the extra digits. Thus, counting in hex goes like this: 0, 1, 2, 3, 4, 5, 6, 7, 8, 9, a, b, c, d, e, f, 10, 11, ...

To make it clear when we are writing in hex, we prefix the number with 0x. Here is the same number and byte expressed using hex:

Figure 33.2 One byte representing the hex number 0x3c

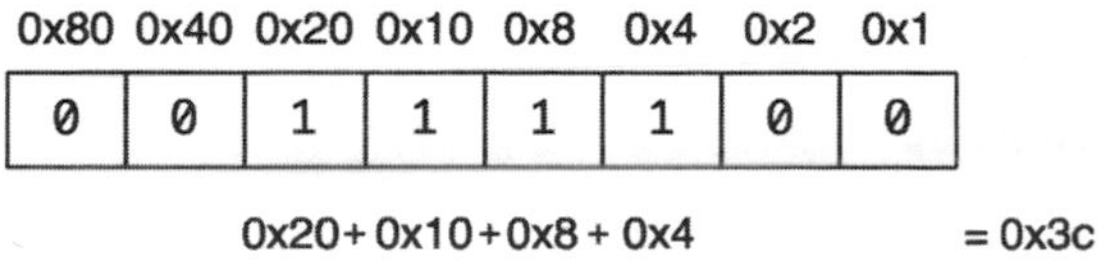

0x80	0x40	0x20	0x10	0x8	0x4	0x2	0x1
0	0	1	1	1	1	0	0

0x20+0x10+0x8+0x4   = 0x3c

Note that one byte can always be described as a two-digit hex number (like 3c). This makes hex a reasonable way to look at binary data. A tough-guy programmer thing to say is "I reversed engineered the file format by studying the document files in a hex editor." Want to see a file as a list of hex-encoded bytes? In Terminal, run hexdump on the file:

```
$ hexdump myfile.txt
0000000 3c 3f 78 6d 6c 20 76 65 72 73 69 6f 6e 3d 22 31
0000010 2e 30 22 3f 3e 0a 3c 62 6f 6f 6b 20 78 6d 6c 6e
0000020 73 3d 22 68 74 74 70 3a 2f 2f 64 6f 63 62 6f 6f
0000030 6b 2e 6f 72 67 2f 6e 73 2f 64 6f 63 62 6f 6f 6b
0000040 22
0000041
```

The first column is the offset (in hex) from the beginning of the file of the byte listed in the second column. Each two digit number represents one byte.

Bitwise-OR

If you have two bytes, you can bitwise-OR them together to create a third byte. A bit on the third byte will be 1 if at least one of the corresponding bits in the first two bytes is 1.

Figure 33.3   Two bytes bitwise-ORed together

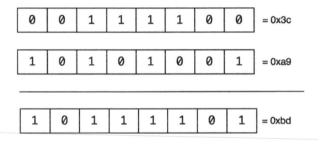

This is done with the | operator. To try your hand at manipulating bits, create a new project: a C Command Line Tool (not Foundation) named bitwize.

Edit main.c:

```c
#include <stdio.h>

int main (int argc, const char * argv[])
{
    unsigned char a = 0x3c;
    unsigned char b = 0xa9;
    unsigned char c = a | b;

    printf("Hex: %x | %x = %x\n", a, b, c);
    printf("Decimal: %d | %d = %d\n", a, b, c);

    return 0;
}
```

When you run this program, you will see the two bytes bitwise-ORed together:

```
Hex: 3c | a9 = bd
Decimal: 60 | 169 = 189
```

What's this good for? In Objective-C, we often use an integer to specify a certain setting. An integer is always a sequence of bits, and each bit is used to represent one aspect of the setting that can be turned on or off. We create this integer (also known as a *bit mask*) by picking and choosing from a set of constants. These constants are integers, too, and each constant specifies a single aspect of the setting by having only one of its bits turned on. You can bitwise-OR together the constants that represent the particular aspects you want. The result is the exact setting you're looking for.

Let's look at an example. iOS comes with a class called **NSDataDetector**. Instances of **NSDataDetector** go through text and look for common patterns like dates or URLs. The patterns an instance will look for is determined by the bitwise-OR result of a set of integer constants.

NSDataDetector.h defines these constants: NSTextCheckingTypeDate, NSTextCheckingTypeAddress, NSTextCheckingTypeLink, NSTextCheckingTypePhoneNumber, and NSTextCheckingTypeTransitInformation. When you create an instance of **NSDataDetector**, you tell it what to search for. For example, if you wanted it to search for phone numbers and dates, you would do this:

```
NSError *e;
NSDataDetector *d = [NSDataDetector dataDetectorWithTypes:
                    NSTextCheckingTypePhoneNumber|NSTextCheckingTypeDate
                                        error:&e];
```

Notice the bitwise-OR operator. You'll see this pattern a lot in Cocoa and iOS programming, and now you'll know what's going on behind the scenes.

Bitwise-AND

You can also bitwise-AND two bytes together to create a third. In this case, a bit on the third byte is 1 if the corresponding bits in the first two bytes are *both* 1.

Figure 33.4   Two bytes bitwise-ANDed together

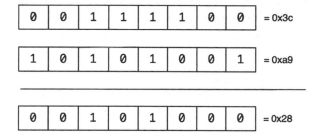

This is done with the & operator. Add the following lines to main.c:

```
#include <stdio.h>

int main (int argc, const char * argv[])
{
    unsigned char a = 0x3c;
    unsigned char b = 0xa9;
    unsigned char c = a | b;

    printf("Hex: %x | %x = %x\n", a, b, c);
    printf("Decimal: %d | %d = %d\n", a, b, c);
```

```
    unsigned char d = a & b;

    printf("Hex: %x & %x = %x\n", a, b, d);
    printf("Decimal: %d & %d = %d\n", a, b, d);

    return 0;
}
```

When you run it, you will see the two bytes bitwise-ANDed together:

```
Hex: 3c & a9 = 28
Decimal: 60 & 169 = 40
```

In Objective-C, we use bitwise-AND to see if a certain bit, or *flag*, is on. For example, if you were handed an instance of **NSDataDetector**, you could check if it was set to look for phone numbers like this:

```
if ([currentDetector checkingTypes] & NSTextCheckingTypePhoneNumber) {
    NSLog(@"This one is looking for phone numbers");
}
```

The **checkingTypes** method returns an integer that is the bitwise-OR result of all the flags this instance of **NSDataDetector** has on. You bitwise-AND this integer with a particular NSTextCheckingType constant and check the result. If the bit that is on in NSTextCheckingTypePhoneNumber is not on in the data detector's setting, then the result of bitwise-ANDing them will be all zeroes. Otherwise, you'll get a non-zero result, and you'll know that this data detector does look for phone numbers.

Note that when we use bits this way, we don't care what the integers in these cases equate to numerically. We use the bit placement within the integer to represent something other than a certain power of 2.

Other bitwise operators

For completeness, here are the other bitwise operators. These are less commonly used in Objective-C but good to know.

Exclusive OR

You can exclusive-or (XOR) two bytes together to create a third. A bit in the third byte is 1 if exactly one of the corresponding bits in the input bytes is 1.

Figure 33.5   Two bytes bitwise-XORed together

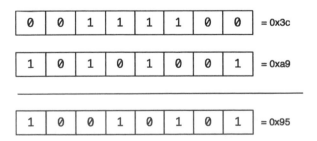

This is done with the ^ operator. Add to main.c:

```
unsigned char e = a ^ b;

printf("Hex: %x ^ %x = %x\n", a, b, e);
printf("Decimal: %d ^ %d = %d\n", a, b, e);

return 0;
}
```

When you run it you will see:

```
Hex: 3c ^ a9 = 95
Decimal: 60 ^ 169 = 149
```

This operator sometimes causes beginners some confusion. In most spreadsheet programs, the ^ operator is exponentiation: 2^3 means 2^3. In C, we use the **pow()** function for exponentiation:

```
double r = pow(2.0, 3.0); // Calculate 2 raised to the third power
```

Complement

If you have a byte, the complement is the byte that is the exact opposite: each 0 becomes a 1 and each 0 becomes a 1.

Figure 33.6   The complement

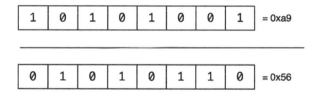

This is done with the ~ operator. Add a few lines to main.c:

```
unsigned char f = ~b;
printf("Hex: The complement of %x is %x\n", b, f);
printf("Decimal: The complement of %d is %d\n", b, f);

return 0;
}
```

You should see:

```
Hex: The complement of a9 is 56
Decimal: The complement of 169 is 86
```

Left-shift

If you left-shift the bits, you take each bit and move it toward the most significant bit. The ones that are on the left side of the number are forgotten, and the holes created on the right are filled with zeros.

Figure 33.7   Left-shifting by 2

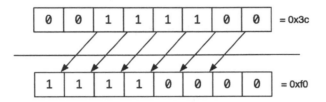

Left-shift is done with the << operator. Add a shift of two places to main.c:

```
unsigned char g = a << 2;
printf("Hex: %x shifted left two places is %x\n", a, g);
printf("Decimal: %d shifted left two places is %d\n", a, g);

return 0;
}
```

When this code runs, you will see:

```
Hex: 3c shifted left two places is f0
Decimal: 60 shifted left two places is 240
```

Every time you left-shift a number one place, you double its value.

Right-shift

The right-shift operator should not be much of a surprise. Add code to main.m:

```
unsigned char h = a >> 1;
printf("Hex: %x shifted right one place is %x\n", a, h);
printf("Decimal: %d shifted right one place is %d\n", a, h);

return 0;
}
```

When run:

```
Hex: 3c shifted right one places is 1e
Decimal: 60 shifted right two places is 30
```

Figure 33.8   Right-shifting by 1

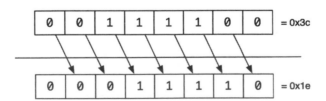

Every time you right-shift a number one place, you half its value. (If it is odd, round down.)

Using enum to define bit masks

Often you will want to define a list of constants, each representing an integer with one bit turned on. Then, these integers can be bitwise-ORed together and tested for using bitwise-AND, as described above.

The elegant way to do this is to define an enum that uses the left-shift operator to define the values. Here is how the constants for the **UIDataDetector** are defined:

```
enum {
    UIDataDetectorTypePhoneNumber   = 1 << 0,
    UIDataDetectorTypeLink          = 1 << 1,
    UIDataDetectorTypeAddress       = 1 << 2,
    UIDataDetectorTypeCalendarEvent = 1 << 3,
    UIDataDetectorTypeNone          = 0,
    UIDataDetectorTypeAll           = NSUIntegerMax
};
```

More bytes

In this chapter, we worked with unsigned char, which is one 8-bit byte. Any unsigned integer type will work the same way. For example, NSTextCheckingTypePhoneNumber is actually declared uint64_t, a 64-bit unsigned number.

Challenge

Write a program that creates an unsigned 64-bit integer such that every other bit is turned on. (There are actually two possible resulting numbers: one is even, the other is odd. Create the odd one.) Display the number.

34
C Strings

Given the choice, an Objective-C programmer will always choose to work with **NSString** objects rather than C strings. However, sometimes we don't have a choice. The most common reason we end up using C strings? When we access a C library from within our Objective-C code. For example, there is a library of C functions that lets your program talk to a PostgreSQL database server. The functions in that library use C strings, not instances of **NSString**.

char

In the last section, we talked about how a byte could be treated as a number. We can also treat a byte as a character. As mentioned earlier, there are many different string encodings. The oldest and most famous is ASCII. ASCII (American Standard Code for Information Interchange) defines a different character for each byte. For example, 0x4b is the character 'K'.

Create a new C Command Line Tool and name it yostring. In this program, you are going to list some of the characters in the ASCII standard. Edit main.c:

```c
#include <stdio.h>

int main (int argc, const char * argv[])
{
    char x = 0x21; // The character '!'

    while (x <= 0x7e) { // The character '~'
        printf("%x is %c\n", x, x);
        x++;
    }

    return 0;
}
```

You may be wondering "Hey, a byte can hold any one of 256 numbers. You just printed out 94 characters. What happened to the to the rest?" It is important to realize that ASCII was written to drive old teletype-style terminals that printed to paper instead of to a screen. For example, the number 7 in ASCII makes the terminal bell ring. In fact, the characters 0 - 31 in ASCII are unprintable control codes. Number 32 is the space character. Number 127 is the delete – it causes the previous character to disappear. What about characters 128 – 255? ASCII only uses 7 bits. There is no ASCII character for the number 128.

You can use ASCII characters as literals in code. Just put them inside single quotes. Change your code to use these:

```
int main (int argc, const char * argv[])
{
    char x = '!'; // The character '!'

    while (x <= '~') { // The character '~'
        printf("%x is %c\n", x, x);
        x++;
    }

    return 0;
}
```

Build it and run it.

The non-printable characters can be expressed using escape sequences that start with \. You've already used \n for the newline character. Here are some common ones:

Table 34.1   Common escape sequences

\n	new line
\t	tab
\'	single-quote
\"	double-quote
\0	null byte (0x00)
\\	backslash

char *

A C string is just a bunch of characters right next to each other in memory. The string ends when the character 0x00 is encountered.

Figure 34.1   The word "Love" as a C string

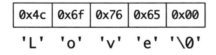

Functions that take C strings expect the address of the string's first character. **strlen()**, for example, will count the number of characters in a string. Try building a string and using **strlen()** to count the letters:

```
#include <stdio.h>  // For printf
#include <stdlib.h> // For malloc/free
#include <string.h> // For strlen


int main (int argc, const char * argv[])
{
    char x = '!'; // The character '!'

    while (x <= '~') { // The character '~'
        printf("%x is %c\n", x, x);
        x++;
    }

    // Get a pointer to 5 bytes of memory on the heap
    char *start = malloc(5);

    // Put 'L' in the first byte
    *start = 'L';

    // Put 'o' in the second byte
    *(start + 1) = 'o';

    // Put 'v' in the third byte
    *(start + 2) = 'v';

    // Put 'e' in the fourth byte
    *(start + 3) = 'e';

    // Put zero in the fifth byte
    *(start + 4) = '\0';

    // Print out the string and its length
    printf("%s has %zu characters\n", start, strlen(start));

    // Print out the third letter
    printf("The third letter is %c\n", *(start + 2));

    // Free the memory so that it can be reused
    free(start);
    start = NULL;

    return 0;
}
```

Build and run it.

Notice the places where you added a pointer and a number together. start is declared to be a char *. A char is one byte. So start + 1 is a pointer one byte further in memory than start. start + 2 is two bytes further in memory than start.

Figure 34.2   The address of each character

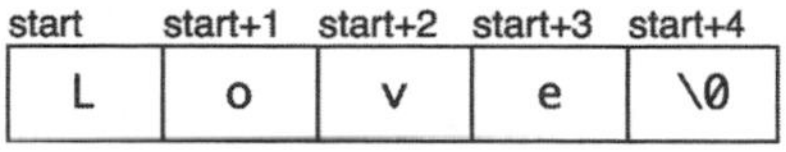

start	start+1	start+2	start+3	start+4
L	o	v	e	\0

This adding to a pointer and dereferencing the result is so common that there is a shorthand for it: start[2] is equivalent to *(start + 2). Change your code to use it:

```
char *start = malloc(5);
start[0] = 'L';
start[1] = 'o';
start[2] = 'v';
start[3] = 'e';
start[4] = '\0';

printf("%s has %zu characters\n", start, strlen(start));
printf("The third letter is %c\n", start[2]);

free(start);
start = NULL;

return 0;
}
```

Build and run it.

It should be mentioned that this works with any data type. Here, for example, I can make a list of my favorite 3 floating point numbers and print them out:

```
int main (int argc, const char * argv[])
{
    // Claim a chunk of memory big enough to hold three floats
    float *favorites = malloc(3 * sizeof(float));

    // Push values into the locations in that buffer
    favorites[0] = 3.14158;
    favorites[1] = 2.71828;
    favorites[2] = 1.41421;

    // Print out each number on the list
    for (int i = 0; i < 3; i++) {
        printf("%.4f is favorite %d\n", favorites[i], i);
    }

    // Free the memory so that it can be reused
    free(favorites);
    favorites = NULL;

    return 0;
}
```

The only interesting difference here is that favorites is typed as a float *. A float is 4 bytes. Thus favorites + 1 is 4 bytes further in memory than favorites.

String literals

If you were dealing with C strings a lot, malloc'ing the memory and stuffing the characters in one-by-one would be a real pain. Instead, you can create a pointer to a string of characters (terminated with the zero character) by putting the string in quotes. Change your code to use a string literal:

```
int main (int argc, const char * argv[])
{
    char x = '!'; // The character '!'

    while (x <= '~') { // The character '~'
        printf("%x is %c\n", x, x);
        x++;
    }

    char *start = "Love";
    printf("%s has %zu characters\n", start, strlen(start));
    printf("The third letter is %c\n", start[2]);

    return 0;
}
```

Build it and run it.

Notice that you don't need to malloc and free memory for a string literal. It is a constant and appears in memory only once, so the compiler takes care of its memory use. As a side-effect of its constant-ness, bad things happen if you try to change the characters in the string. Add a line that should crash your program:

```
char *start = "Love";
start[2] = 'z';
printf("%s has %zu characters\n", start, strlen(start));
```

When you build and run it, you should get a EXC_BAD_ACCESS signal. You tried to write into memory that you are not allowed to write in.

To enable the compiler to warn you about writing to constant parts of memory, you can use the const modifier to specify that a pointer is referring to data that must not be changed. Try it:

```
const char *start = "Love";
start[2] = 'z';
printf("%s has %zu characters\n", start, strlen(start));
```

Now when you build, you should get an error from the compiler.

Delete the problematic line (start[2] = 'z';) before continuing.

You can use the escape sequences mentioned above in your string literals. Use a few:

```
const char *start = "A backslash after two newlines and a tab:\n\n\t\\";
printf("%s has %zu characters\n", start, strlen(start));
printf("The third letter is \'%c\'\n", start[2]);

    return 0;
}
```

Build and run it.

Converting to and from NSString

If you are using C strings in an Objective-C program, you will need to know how to make an **NSString** from a C string. The **NSString** class has a method for this:

```
char *greeting = "Hello!";
NSString *x = [NSString stringWithCString:greeting encoding:NSUTF8StringEncoding];
```

You can also get a C string from an **NSString**. This is a little trickier because **NSString** can handle some characters that certain encodings cannot. It is a good idea to check that the conversion can occur:

```
NSString *greeting = "Hello!";
const char *x = NULL;
if ([greeting canBeConvertedToEncoding:NSUTF8StringEncoding]) {
    x = [greeting cStringUsingEncoding:NSUTF8StringEncoding];
}
```

You do not own the resulting C string; the system will eventually free it for you. You are guaranteed that it will live at least as long as the current autorelease pool, but if you are going to need the C string to live for a long time, you should copy it into a buffer you've created with **malloc()**.

Challenge

Write a function called **spaceCount()** that counts the space characters (ASCII 0x20) in a C string. Test it like this:

```
#include <stdio.h>

int main (int argc, const char * argv[])
{

    const char *sentence = "He was not in the cab at the time.";
    printf("\"%s\" has %d spaces\", sentence, spaceCount(sentence));

    return 0;
}
```

Remember: when you run into '\0', you have reached the end of the string!

35

C Arrays

In the last chapter, we worked with C strings, and a C string turned out to be a list of characters packed one next to the other in memory. C arrays are lists of other data types packed one next to the other in memory. Just as with strings, you deal with the list by holding onto the address of the first one.

Imagine that you wanted to write a program that would calculate the average of 3 grades. Create a new C Command Line Tool project and name it gradeInTheShade.

Edit main.c:

```c
#include <stdio.h>
#include <stdlib.h> // malloc(), free()

float averageFloats(float *data, int dataCount)
{
    float sum = 0.0;
    for (int i = 0; i < dataCount; i++) {
        sum = sum + data[i];
    }
    return sum / dataCount;
}

int main (int argc, const char * argv[])
{

    // Create an array of floats
    float *gradeBook = malloc(3 * sizeof(float));
    gradeBook[0] = 60.2;
    gradeBook[1] = 94.5;
    gradeBook[2] = 81.1;

    // Calculate the average
    float average = averageFloats(gradeBook, 3);

    // Free the array
    free(gradeBook);
    gradeBook = NULL;

    printf("Average = %.2f\n", average);

    return 0;
}
```

Build and run it.

Figure 35.1   Pointers on the stack to a buffer of floats

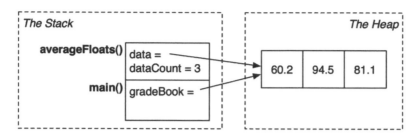

`malloc()` allocates a buffer on the heap, so you need to make sure that you free it when you are done. Wouldn't it be great if you could declare that buffer as part of the frame (on the stack) so that it would be deallocated automatically when the function is done executing? You can. Change `main.c`:

```
import <stdio.h>

float averageFloats(float *data, int dataCount)
{
    float sum = 0.0;
    for (int i = 0; i < dataCount; i++) {
        sum = sum + data[i];
    }
    return sum / dataCount;
}

int main (int argc, const char * argv[])
{

    // Declares the array as part of the frame
    float gradeBook[3];

    gradeBook[0] = 60.2;
    gradeBook[1] = 94.5;
    gradeBook[2] = 81.1;

    // Calculate the average
    float average = averageFloats(gradeBook, 3);

    // No need to free the array!
    // Cleanup happens automatically when the function returns

    printf("Average = %.2f\n", average);

    return 0;
}
```

Build and run it.

The string literal made it easy to pack an array with characters. There are also array literals. Use one to initialize `gradeBook`:

```
int main (int argc, const char *argv[])
{
    float gradeBook[] = {60.2, 94.5, 81.1};

    float average = averageFloats(gradeBook, 3);

    printf("Average = %.2f", average);

    return 0;
}
```

Build and run the program.

Notice that you didn't need to specify the length of gradeBook as 3; the compiler figures that out from the array literal. You can use this type in many places where you might use *. For example, change the declaration of **averageFloats()** to do this:

```
float averageFloats(float data[], int dataCount)
{
    float sum = 0.0;
    for (int i = 0; i < dataCount; i++) {
        sum = sum + data[i];
    }
    return sum / dataCount;
}
```

Build and run the program.

36

Command-Line Arguments

You know the arguments to **main()** that I've been carefully avoiding discussing?

```
int main (int argc, const char * argv[])
{
...
```

Now you are ready to learn about them. argv is an array of C strings. argc tells you how many strings are in the array. What do these string represent? Command-line arguments.

The command-line tools that you've been creating can be run from Terminal. The Terminal app is just a pretty interface to what is called a *shell*. There are a few different shells with catchy names like csh, sh, zsh, and ksh, but nearly all Mac users use bash. When you run a program from bash, after you type in the program name, you can supply any number of arguments separated by whitespace. Those arguments are packed into argv before **main()** is called.

Truthfully, Cocoa and iOS programmers seldom use argv and argc. However, if you ever write a handy command-line tool, you will almost certainly need to know how to utilize them.

In Xcode, create a new C Command Line Tool project called Affirmation. Affirmation will take two arguments, a person's name and a number *n*. When you run it, that person will be declared cool *n* times.

```
$ Affirmation Mikey 3
Mikey is cool.
Mikey is cool.
Mikey is cool.
```

Before we do that, change **main()** to just print out each of the arguments in argv:

```
#include <stdio.h>

int main (int argc, const char * argv[])
{
    for (int i = 0; i < argc; i++) {
        printf("arg %d = %s\n", i, argv[i]);
    }

    return 0;
}
```

If you are running this from bash, you could just type in the arguments on the command line.

```
$ Affirmation Aaron 4
```

However, to run a program with arguments in Xcode, you must first edit the scheme. Under the Product menu, choose Edit Scheme.... When the sheet appears, select Run Affirmation in the table view on the left. Then select the Arguments tab from the choices at the top of the sheet. Find the list entitled Arguments Passed On Launch and use the + button to add two items: a name and a number.

Figure 36.1   Adding arguments

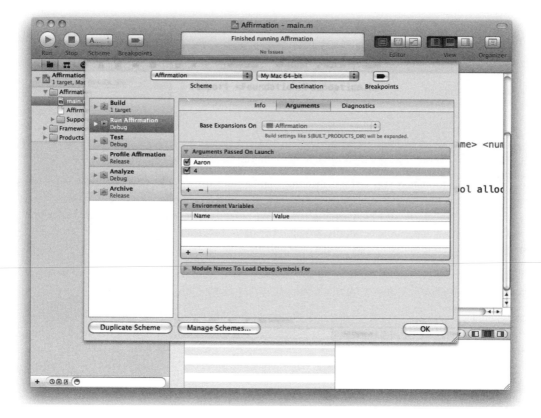

Click OK to dismiss the sheet.

When you run the program, you'll get a list of the strings in argv. The one that surprises most people is argv[0]:

```
arg 0 = /Users/aaron/Library/Developer/Xcode/DerivedData/
    Affirmation-enkfqsgavfsproeggoxwbrmcowvn/Build/Products/Debug/Affirmation
arg 1 = Aaron
arg 2 = 4
```

argv[0] is the path to the executable file.

Figure 36.2 argv and argc in Affirmation

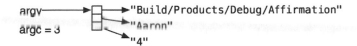

If your program takes arguments, the first thing you should do is make sure that the number of arguments is correct. Edit main.m:

```
#include <stdio.h>
#include <stdio.h> // atoi()


int main (int argc, const char * argv[])
{
    if (argc != 3) {
        fprintf(stderr, "Usage: Affirmation <name> <number>\n");
        return 1;
    }

    int count = atoi(argv[2]);
    for (int j = 0; j < count; j++) {
        printf("%s is cool.\n", argv[1]);
    }

    return 0;
}
```

atoi() is a standard C function that reads a C string and tries to make an int out of it.

Build and run the program.

37
Switch Statements

It is not uncommon to check a variable for a set of values. Using `if-else` statements, it would look like this:

```
int yeastType = ...;

if (yeastType == 1) {
    makeBread();
} else if (yeastType == 2) {
    makeBeer();
} else if (yeastType == 3) {
    makeWine();
} else {
    makeFuel();
}
```

To make this sort of thing easier, C has the `switch` statement. The code above could be changed to this:

```
int yeastType = ...;

switch (yeastType) {
    case 1:
        makeBread();
        break;
    case 2:
        makeBeer();
        break;
    case 3:
        makeWine();
        break;
    default:
        makeFuel();
        break;
}
```

Notice the `break` statements. Without the `break`, after executing appropriate `case` clause, the system would execute all the subsequent `case` clauses. For example, if I had this:

```
int yeastType = 2;

switch (yeastType) {
    case 1:
        makeBread();
    case 2:
        makeBeer();
```

```
    case 3:
        makeWine();
    default:
        makeFuel();
}
```

The program would run **makeBeer()**, **makeWine()**, and **makeFuel()**. This is primarily so that you can have multiple possible values trigger the same code:

```
int yeastType = ...;

switch (yeastType) {
    case 1:
    case 4:
        makeBread();
        break;
    case 2:
    case 5:
        makeBeer();
        break;
    case 3:
        makeWine();
        break;
    default:
        makeFuel();
        break;
}
```

As you can imagine, forgetting to put the break at the end of the case clause is a common programmer error, and it is only discovered when your program starts acting strangely.

In C, switch statements are for a very specific situation: the case can only be a constant integer. As such, you don't see a lot of switch statements in most Objective-C programs. Which is why I snuck it in here just before the book ends.

Next Steps

Well, that's everything you will ever need to know to write brilliant applications for iOS and Mac OS X.

That's what I wish I could tell you. I know you have worked hard to get to this point.

The truth is that you have completed the first leg of a fun and rewarding journey. It is, however, a very long journey. It is now time for you to spend some time studying the standard frameworks that Apple makes available to Objective-C developers like you.

Let me repeat that last phrase so you can relish it: "Objective-C developers like you." Congratulations.

If you are learning to develop applications for iOS, I recommend that you work through *iOS Programming: The Big Nerd Ranch Guide,* but there are several other books on iOS, and you are ready for any of them.

If you are learning to develop applications for Mac OS X, I recommend that you work through *Cocoa Programming for Mac OS X*, but, here again, there are several other books on Cocoa, and you are ready for any of them.

There are groups of developers who meet every month to discuss the craft. In most major cities, there are iOS Developers Meetups and CocoaHeads chapters. The talks are often surprisingly good. There are also discussion groups online. Take some time to find and use these resources.

Shameless plugs

You can find me on Twitter, where I post news about Big Nerd Ranch: @AaronHillegass

Keep an eye out for future guides from Big Nerd Ranch. We also offer week-long courses for developers. And if you just need some code written, we do contract programming. For more information, visit our website at www.bignerdranch.com.

It is you, dear reader, who makes my life of writing, coding, and teaching possible. So thank you for buying my book.

Index

Symbols

! (logical NOT) operator, 24
!= (not equal) operator, 23
\" escape sequence, 248
#define, 145-147
   vs. global variables, 149
#import, 146
#include, 146
% (modulus operator), 44
   (see also tokens)
%= operator, 46
%@, 119
%d, 41
%e, 46
%p, 56
%s, 41
%u, 43
%zu, 58
& operator, retrieving addresses, 55
&& (logical AND) operator, 24
( ) (parentheses)
   cast operators, using, 45
   functions and, 28, 31
* (asterisk)
   arithmetic operator, 44
   pointer operator, 57
*= operator, 46
+ (plus sign), 44
++ (increment operator), 45
+= operator, 46
- (minus sign), 44
-- (decrement operator), 45
-= operator, 46
-> (dereference) operator, 71
.pch (pre-compiled header), 146
/ (division operator), 44
/* ... */ (comments), 12
// (comments), 12
/= operator, 46
8-bit unsigned numbers, 42
; (semicolon), 12
   blocks and, 230
   do-while loop and, 54
< (less than) operator, 23

< > (angle brackets), importing header files, 146
<< operator, 244
<= operator, 23
= operator, 22, 24
== operator, 23, 24
> (greater than) operator, 23
>= operator, 23
>> operator, 244
? (ternary operator), 26
@property, 105
@selector(), 159
@synthesize, 105
\ (backslash), 248
\n, 41
\\ escape sequence, 248
^ (caret)
   exclusive-or operator, 243
   identifying blocks, 227
{ } (curly braces), 12
|| (logical OR) operator, 24
~ (tilde), 243

A

abs(), 46
accessor methods, 103-105
   properties and, 217
actions (target), 157
addObject:, 135
addresses, 55-59
   pointers and, 20
alloc, 81, 207
ampersand (&), retrieving addresses, 55
AND (&&) logical operator, 24
AND (bitwise), 241
angle brackets (< >), importing header files, 146
anonymous
   blocks, 235
   functions, 227
Apple Developer Tools, installing, 7
application:didFinishLaunchingWithOptions:,
183-190
applications
   (see also programs, Xcode)
   Cocoa, 191-204
   Cocoa Touch, 177-190
   desktop, 191-204
   document-based, 192

in blocks, 233
right-shifting bits, 244

S

T

U

V

THE BIG NERD STORY

Big Nerd Ranch exists to broaden the minds of our students and the businesses of our clients. Whether we are training talented individuals or developing a company's mobile strategy, our core philosophy is integral to everything we do.

The brainchild of CEO Aaron Hillegass, Big Nerd Ranch has hosted more than 2,000 students at the Ranch since its inception in 2001. Over the past ten years, we have had the opportunity to work with some of the biggest companies in the world such as Apple, Samsung, Nokia, Google, AOL, Los Alamos National Laboratory and Adobe, helping them realize their programming goals. Our team of software engineers are among the brightest in the business and it shows in our work. We have developed dozens of innovative and flexible solutions for our clients.

The Story Behind the Hat

Back in 2001, Big Nerd Ranch founder, Aaron Hillegass, showed up at WWDC (World Wide Developers Conference) to promote the Big Nerd Ranch brand. Without the money to buy an expensive booth, Aaron donned a ten-gallon cowboy hat to draw attention while passing out Big Nerd literature to prospective students and clients. A week later, we landed our first big client and the cowboy hat has been synonymous with the Big Nerd brand ever since. Already easily recognizable at 6'5, Aaron can be spotted wearing his cowboy hat at speaking engagements and conferences all over the world.

The New Ranch – Opening 2012

In the continuing effort to perfect the student experience, Big Nerd Ranch is building its own facility. Located just 20 minutes from the Atlanta airport, the new Ranch will be a monastic learning center that encompasses Aaron Hillegass' vision for technical education featuring a state-of-the-art classroom, fine dining and exercise facilities.

TRANSPARENT

BiG
nerd
ranch

ACHIEVE NERDVANA

Since 2001, Big Nerd Ranch has offered intensive computer programming courses taught by our expert instructors in a retreat environment. It is at our Ranch where we think our students flourish. Classes, accommodations and dining all take place within the same building, freeing you to learn, code and discuss with your programming peers and instructors. At Big Nerd Ranch, we take care of the details; your only job is to learn.

Our Teachers

Our teachers are leaders in their respective fields. They offer deep understanding of the technologies they teach, as well as a broad spectrum of development experience, allowing them to address the concerns you encounter as a developer. Big Nerd Ranch instructors provide the necessary combination of knowledge and outstanding teaching experience, enabling our students to leave the Ranch with a vastly improved set of skills.

The Big Nerd Way

We have developed "The Big Nerd Ranch Way". This methodology guides the development and presentation of our classes. The style is casual but focused, with brief lectures followed by hands-on exercises designed to give you immediate, relevant understanding of each piece of the technology you are learning.

Your Stay At The Ranch

One fee covers tuition, meals, lodging and transportation to and from the airport. At the Big Nerd Ranch, we remove the distractions inherent in standard corporate training by offering classes in quiet, comfortable settings in Atlanta, Georgia and Frankfurt, Germany.

Available Classes

Advanced Mac OS X
Android
Beginning Cocoa
Beginning iOS (iPhone/iPad)
Beginning Ruby on Rails
Cocoa Commuter Class in Spanish
Cocoa I
Cocoa II
Commuter iOS Class
Django
iOS (iPhone/iPad)
OpenGL
Python Mastery
Ruby on Rails I
Ruby on Rails II

Interested in a class?

Register online at www.bignerdranch.com or call 404.478.9005 for more information.
Full class schedule, pricing and availability also online.

OUR NERDS, YOUR LOCATION

Through our on-site training program you can affordably and conveniently have our renowned classes come to you. Our expert instructors will help your team advance through nerd-based instructional support that is fresh, engaging and allows for unencumbered hands-on learning.

Clients around the globe have praised our on-site instruction for some of the following reasons:

Flexibility

- *Classes can be booked when the timing is right for your team.*
- *We can tailor our existing syllabi to ensure our training meets your organization's unique needs.*
- *Post-class mentorship is available to support your team as they work on especially challenging projects.*

Affordability

- *No need for planes, trains and automobiles for all of your staff; our Nerds come to you.*
- *Train up to 22 students at a significant discount over open-enrollment training.*

Nerd Know-how

- *Our instructors are highly practiced in both teaching and programming. They move beyond theory by bringing their real-life experiences to your team.*
- *On-site training includes post-class access to our Nerds, our extensive Alumni Network, and our Big Nerd Ranch Forums. Learning support doesn't end just because your class does.*

For your on-site training, we provide an instructor, all Big Nerd Ranch copyrighted class materials, gifts, certificates of completion and access to our extensive Alumni Network. You'll provide the classroom set up, computers and related devices for all students, a projector and a screen.

CONSULTING

ACHIEVE NERDVANA IN-HOUSE & ON-SITE

When you contract with Big Nerd Ranch, we'll work directly with you to turn your needs into a full-fledged desktop and/or mobile solution. Our developers and designers have consistently created some of the iPhone App Store's most intriguing applications.

Management Philosophy

Big Nerd Ranch holistically manages every client relationship. Our goal is to communicate and educate our clients from project initiation to completion, while ultimately helping them gain a competitive advantage in their niche marketplace.

Project Strategy

We take a detail-oriented approach to all of our project estimations. We'll work with you to define a strategy, specify product offerings and then build them into software that stands alone.

Our Process

Our consulting process is broken down into three distinct phases: Requirements, Execution and Monitoring/Controlling. Bring your business case to us and we'll develop a plan for a user interface and database design. From there, we'll develop a quote and begin the design and implementation process. Our Nerds will perform many tests, including debugging and performance tuning, ensuring the app does what you want it to do. Finally, we'll beta test your app and get it ready for submission and deployment in the iTunes store and/or the Android Market. Once your app is finished, the Nerds will work with you on subsequent version updates and can even help with the marketing of your app.

Testimonials

"tops has worked closely with Big Nerd Ranch for over eight years. Consistently they have delivered high-quality code for our projects; clean and poetic. Thanks to their contributions, we have become a leader in our field."

Dr. Mark Sanchez
President/Founder
tops Software
topsortho.com

"From the simplest GUI design gig to jobs that plumb the darkest corners of the OS, Big Nerd Ranch should be the first contact in your virtual Rolodex under Mac/iPhone consulting. It's no exaggeration to say that Aaron Hillegass literally wrote the book on Cocoa programming, and you couldn't possibly do better than to bring his and his team's expertise to bear on your application. I've yet to work with a consulting firm that is as competent and communicative as Big Nerd Ranch. Simply put, these guys deliver."

Glenn Zelniker
CEO
Z-Systems Audio Engineering
www.z-sys.com

"We turned to Big Nerd Ranch to develop the Teavana concept into an iPhone app. More than just a developer, they partnered with us to make the app better than we could have imagined alone. The final app was bug-free and functioned exactly as expected. I would definitely recommend Big Nerd Ranch and can't speak highly enough about their work."

Jay Allen
VP of Ecommerce
Teavana Corporation
www.teavana.com

We'd love to talk to you about your project.

Contact our consulting team today for a free consultation at consult@bignerdranch.com or visit www.bignerdranch.com/consulting for more information.

SOFTWARE

FINELY-CRAFTED APPLICATIONS

Big Nerd Ranch is a leading developer of downloadable mobile and desktop Mac applications. Several of our most intriguing iPhone and desktop apps are available for purchase in the iTunes store.

Mobile Applications

Smartphones have started to take over the mobile phone market. Since the inception of the iPhone, we have created dozens of apps for our clients and now have a roster of our own applications including games, utilities, music and educational apps. As an ever-evolving frontier of technology, Big Nerd Ranch is committed to staying ahead of the curve.

Mobile Apps

The world has gone mobile. If your company doesn't have a mobile application, you are behind the curve. As of early 2011, the iTunes app store has grown to nearly 400,000 apps and the Android market has climbed to more than 250,000 applications. Google has unveiled its Android platform with an app store of its own and dozens of smartphone manufacturers have announced Android-powered devices. RIM has launched App World, Palm has its Palm Store, Nokia launched Ovi (its online store) and Microsoft has unveiled Windows Marketplace.

While still leading the way, the iOS market has put up some staggering statistics:

- *Total iOS app store downloads: 10.3 billion*
- *iPhone apps are being downloaded at a rate of 30 million per day.*
- *As of early 2011, when the app store hit 10 billion downloads, it did so in half the time (31 months versus 67 months) that it took for songs in the iTunes store to hit the same mark.*
- *The average number of apps downloaded for iPhone/iPad/iPod touch is currently at more than 60.*

Need an App?
Visit us online at www.bignerdranch.com/software to see all our latest apps. Many Big Nerd apps are also available for sale at the iTunes store.